THE EVENTFUL LIFE OF
PHILIP HANKIN

Caitlin Press Inc.
3375 Ponderosa Way
Qualicum Beach, BC V9K 2J8
www.caitlinpress.com

Text design by Libris Simas Ferraz / Onça Publishing
Cover design by Sarah Corsie
Front cover images A-00238 and C-07093, and back cover image A-00934
        courtesy the Royal BC Museum and Archives
Edited by Meg Yamamoto
Printed in Canada

Caitlin Press Inc. acknowledges financial support from the Government of Canada and the Canada Council for the Arts, and the Province of British Columbia through the British Columbia Arts Council and the Book Publisher's Tax Credit.

Library and Archives Canada Cataloguing in Publication

Title: The eventful life of Philip Hankin : worldwide traveller and witness to British
        Columbia's early history / Geoff Mynett.
Names: Mynett, Geoff, 1946- author.
Description: Includes bibliographical references and index.
Identifiers: Canadiana 20230205836 | ISBN 9781773861197 (softcover)
Subjects: LCSH: Hankin, Philip, 1836- | LCSH: Vancouver Island (B.C.)—Biography. | LCGFT:
        Biographies.
Classification: LCC FC3844.25.H36 M96 2023 | DDC 971.1/202092—dc23

The Eventful Life of Philip Hankin

Worldwide Traveller and Witness to British Columbia's Early History

"I have had many ups and downs and have travelled several times around the world and held various positions in many parts of the globe, and although I have been somewhat of a rolling stone, yet, I have gathered some moss."

Philip Hankin, *Memoirs*

Geoff Mynett

CAITLIN PRESS
2023

To all Teachers of History and those who help us understand
what happened in the past and why it matters

Philip Hankin. Image C-07093 courtesy of the Royal BC Museum and Archives

Contents

Preface

Philip Hankin was penniless, starving and exhausted. He had tried his luck at prospecting for gold in the streams of the Cariboo region of British Columbia but had failed miserably. Only a few months before, he had been a lieutenant in the British Royal Navy. Now here he was, in the summer of 1864, at rock bottom. Yet within five years he would be the colonial secretary for the Colony of British Columbia and, for a few months in the summer of 1869, the administrator of its entire government. How could this meteoric change in his circumstances have happened?

His odyssey began in England in 1836. In 1849, when he was thirteen years old, his father sent him into the Royal Navy.[1] He first came to the Colony of Vancouver Island in 1857 on HMS *Plumper*, which had been sent to survey the coast. In 1864, after twists and turns, driven time and again off course, he went to the Cariboo to look for gold in Barkerville but returned penniless. Later that year, he was appointed superintendent of police for the Colony of Vancouver Island. Two years later, the Colonies of Vancouver Island and British Columbia merged and he was out of a job. In late 1868, he was appointed colonial secretary of the Colony of British Columbia. In the interregnum between the sudden death of Governor Frederick Seymour in June 1869 and the arrival of Seymour's replacement, Anthony Musgrave, in late August, Hankin was the administrator of the government of the colony. After British Columbia joined the Dominion of Canada in 1871, once again he was out of a job.[2] He then retired with a government pension.

In 1914, when he was seventy-nine, Hankin started to write his memoirs. He professes not to have kept a diary or journal and to have written it entirely from memory. On occasion his memory did let him down but nevertheless the memoirs are a lively account of the early days of British Columbia's history. He gave the memoirs to his friend E.L. Brittain of Ottawa. As a result of the efforts of Major General G.R. Pearkes, member of Parliament for Nanaimo, the original manuscript was given for safekeeping to Willard Ireland, provincial archivist in British Columbia. A shortened transcription from the original was serialized in the Victoria *Daily Colonist* every Sunday from June to October 1954.

Hankin's interest in writing his memoirs seems to have waned after he wrote of his time in British Columbia. He compresses the following fifty years of his life into one chapter. For a biographer, this is frustrating. It is also frustrating that he tells us so little about his family. Three of his brothers were also in the colony in the early 1860s, two of whom being original partners of Billy Barker of Barkerville. When Hankin was living in India, two of his other brothers and numerous cousins were also there. Moreover, he mentions his beloved wife only when writing of his loneliness after she died. Perhaps he was merely being reticent about family matters. He died in 1923, having drawn a pension for over fifty years.

I have referred to him as Hankin throughout this book except when writing of him as a child or in family situations where there might be a possibility of confusion with his siblings. Any unattributed quotations in this book are from his memoirs.

People wrote, and presumably spoke, about Indigenous people in colonial times in terms that today we rightly consider offensive and unacceptable. Their use in this book is confined to quotations. Not to record them as written would be dishonest to the story.

Hankin wrote in his memoirs that he had been a rolling stone all his life yet had gathered some moss. In this book I have attempted to find the moss and tell his remarkable story.

1

A Victorian Childhood

1836–1849

" I was born at the Village of Stanstead in Hertfordshire, on the 18th of February, 1836," Philip Hankin wrote eighty years later, "and the old nurse said, as she held my form and felt the house shake with the fierce night storm: He is born in February, I pity the child; his life, like the night, will be strange, and wild."

These words echo the opening lines of Charles Dickens's *David Copperfield*, which was written a few years after Hankin's birth. Dickens was one of his favourite authors and his novels played a small part in his life's story. Like the fictional Copperfield, Hankin was thrown away at a young age, the former to a brutal school and then to wash bottles in a grimy warehouse and the latter to the no-less-brutal Royal Navy. Necessarily—for he was writing his autobiography—Hankin was the hero of his story. But his old nurse was right. His life was indeed strange, with many twists and improbable coincidences. At times, it was also wild.

───────

Stanstead Abbotts is a small Hertfordshire village on the Essex border.[3] Rural then, less rural now, the countryside had not yet been chewed up by the new railway lines. Trains, which soon arrived, allowed people to travel easily outside their own villages for the first time. In the years between

1838 and 1850, three main railway lines cut through Hertfordshire and two branch lines were established. Philip was born as the railway age was beginning.

The Hankin family had lived in Stanstead Abbotts for over three hundred years. Family graves filled the churchyard. Philip's father, Daniel, was a local squire and farmer, perhaps more of the latter than the former. With the exception of groceries and beef, the farm provided the family's food. Chickens, ducks and geese pecked in the adjacent farmyard until their time came for the pot. Daniel kept six or seven dairy cows and also a few sheep. Pigs provided bacon and pork. The kitchen garden supplied vegetables, as well as strawberries, raspberries and gooseberries. This, naturally, did not stop the boys from raiding their neighbour's orchard for apples, pears and walnuts.

Philip had numerous brothers and sisters.[4] They grew up with the strictness of a Victorian home indoors and the freedom of Victorian children outdoors, roaming the woods and fields at will. Daniel paid the children a penny for each dozen eggs they collected that had not been laid in the henhouse. He also paid them twopence for a dozen sparrow's eggs, fourpence a day for rolling gravel in the yard and threepence a pound for fish they caught in the River Lea, which flowed along the bottom of their garden.

This pastoral scene suggests a golden Victorian childhood for the Hankin children. However, Daniel was a Victorian father and the home was not warm and loving. This rankled Philip. Seventy years later, it still hurt. He wrote in his memoirs:

The four younger children were always brought in to the dining room for dessert, first having had their faces well scrubbed with hot water and soap, and very rosy and shiny they looked, and nicely dressed in little white frocks and pink or blue ribbons. My Father was always very fond of the newest baby, but never cared for any of us after 4 or 5 years of age and so at last we didn't care for him. I remember once, when I was about 5 years old, running to say "good night" and put up my little face to be kissed, but my father pushed me away saying, there, that will do, run away, I never kiss boys. I have never forgotten that little incident—and I never in all my life kissed my father again.

I think little children are often very sensitive, and their feelings are much hurt by unkind treatment. There are times when petty slights are harder to bear than even a serious injury—for life is made up not of great sacrifices or duties, but of little things, in which smiles and kindnesses, given habitually, are what win and preserve the hearts of even little children: for as Tennyson truly says, "Kind hearts are more than coronets, and simple faith than Norman blood."[5]

Daniel managed the farm and farmhands while Philip's mother, Elizabeth, managed the household and the indoor servants. Her father was employed in the Treasury in London, where he held a good appointment. Philip recalled that many of their servants had been with the family for over twenty years and that his mother gave them their wages. He recalled, "My mother used to sign their names for them, and they were told to touch the pen and that was supposed to make the signature the same as if they had written it with their own hand. I don't know if it really did so, but at all events they thought it did, and so did my mother, and everyone was quite satisfied."

His father's sister Maria lived with them. The children loved her because she was kind to them. Philip writes of her with an affection entirely lacking in his description of his parents:

We always called her "Ria." She was a sister of my father's and had never married and when my grandfather died, Ria was left to her brother's care, and he gave her a home and £25 a year for her dress. Although poor old Maria had never married, I believe she was once engaged, but unfortunately had tumbled downstairs over a slop pail, which a careless housemaid had left on the top of the landing—and dislocated her knee and was lamed for life, so the young man to whom she was engaged broke off the match. She had always to walk with a stick.

She was a sweet-tempered little woman, with very black hair and eyes, and wore her hair in two little corkscrew curls, each side of her face, and a tiny knob at the back of her head. She was very sallow and looked as if she had been boiled in coffee. ...

I remember she had a very rough kind of wooden bath chair, and in the summer we all used to push her in the chair and go in the Easeny Woods, taking tea and a seed cake with us, and have a kind of picnic, making a little fire in the woods to boil the kettle. We had always to lift the chair over the stiles. It used to be great fun.

As children, Hankin wrote, he and his siblings were instructed not to ask for anything at the table. This puzzled him because he was also told that those who don't ask don't want. Their usual breakfast was milk with bread and butter. "I remember," he wrote, "my younger brother and I were always given an egg for breakfast between us, and he generally contrived to get hold of it first, and with one spoonful he managed to get the yolk entirely out and left the white for me." This would have been his brother Charles, two years younger, later to be one of the original partners of Billy Barker in the Cariboo.

Philip recalled Christmas dinners, when the family dined at four so that all the children could be present. Every December, one of Daniel's friends used to give them a cod's head and oysters for a sauce. The taste of that oyster sauce lingered with Hankin and found its way into his memoirs. Occasionally their neighbours, the two spinster Misses Soames and their bachelor brother Mr. Soames, would come to dinner. They came in a "chariot," which impressed Philip as being very grand because his father had only a pony carriage.

Philip's father had the habit of asking his children what they would do when they grew up and told them in no uncertain terms that he expected them to work for their living. This frightened Philip, who wrote, "I was then only five and I quite expected any day to be turned out of the house."

When Philip was twelve years old, the day arrived when his future career had to be decided. Daniel often said he would not have "a lot of idle, lazy boys living at home and doing nothing." Philip had to work. What would he do? Philip thought of all the raisins and almonds in the grocer's shop and said he would like to be a grocer. Obviously that would not do. Think again. "So, I replied, well, a doctor," he wrote. "No, said my father again. A pretty doctor you would make. You would kill all your patients."

Daniel consulted his good friend Sir Henry Ward, who was at the time first secretary of the Admiralty and so in a position to help.[6] Sir Henry offered to find Philip a position in the Royal Navy. The next day Daniel said, "Philip. I have decided what to do with you. You are to go into the Navy."

"No," Philip replied. "I don't want to go to sea. I would rather be a Grocer."

"Don't talk nonsense," replied his father. "You've got to go, whether you like it or not. So that's settled."

Philip would, of course, have to pass the naval entrance examinations before being accepted for the navy. Clearly it was thought he was not yet ready because he was sent for additional instruction to a clergyman near Harwich, who "rejoiced in the very English name of John Bull, the Rev. John Bull." This was a happy time in Philip's young life. John Bull was a kind old man with a gentle wife and two children a little younger than Philip. He also had three other pupils. "I had not much to do," Philip wrote, "and on fine days we all worked in the garden. We had to learn, each day, a few verses of the morning Psalm, and I have never forgotten them and he certainly taught me the rule of three, and the first four rules of arithmetic. I was not bothered with Euclid, which I never could make head or tail of and I used to get terribly beaten at various schools I had been at for not understanding it. The value of 'X' was a great trouble to me and always made my head ache."

When Philip was thirteen and deemed ready, his father took him to the naval base at Sheerness. There a doctor looked at him. "He gave me two thumps in the chest, told me to cough and say 99," Philip wrote. "I was then declared to be free from impediment of speech, defect of vision, rupture or any other physical insufficiency, and fit for service." The clerk on board HMS *Ocean* then examined him, obviously wanting to go on shore because he hurried through the formalities. He made Philip write a few lines from dictation without making any mistakes. After Philip had satisfactorily completed the dreaded rule-of-three sum, the clerk told him he had passed the examination with very good results.

A few days after this, Philip received a letter from the Lords Commissioners of the Admiralty, addressed to Philip J. Hankin, Esq. How important this must have made the thirteen-year-old boy feel! The letter informed him that the Admiralty had been pleased to appoint him as a naval cadet to HMS *Castor*, a ship bearing the broad pennant of Commodore Christopher Wyvill, and about to sail as the flagship to the Cape of Good Hope Station.[7] It directed him to proceed at once to the naval base at Chatham and join his ship, which was being fitted out there.[8] His appointment was announced in the newspapers on May 12, 1849.[9] The newspapers spelled his name as Hawkin, but no matter. It wouldn't be the last time his name was misspelled.

This news not unnaturally caused great excitement in the Hankin home. Philip was going to sea, and far away to the Cape! His problem now was that he had to acquire his uniform in a hurry. On no account, Daniel pronounced, could the Admiralty instructions be disobeyed. He decided they should both take the next train up to London to visit Messrs. S.W. Silver and Company, the naval outfitters in Cornhill, to find out if they could acquire at least part of his uniform immediately. In a couple of days, a uniform and a cap arrived at Stanstead, with the remainder to follow shortly. This uniform, Philip recalled, did not fit well because it had been made to allow for growth. The trousers were too big and buttoned up somewhere under his armpits, but that was apparently thought to be good because, Philip was told, he would soon grow into them. They were also far too long—a foot too long, his memory told him. They would have felt baggy and uncomfortable.

Philip's father insisted that he walk through the village in his new uniform wearing the smart cap with a gold band round it. Although he felt proud of his uniform, he did not like parading around merely, as he saw it, for the amusement of the village boys. All the servants came out into the garden to see Master Philip dressed up in his new uniform. Altogether, he said, it was rather an ordeal.

The next day they set out for Chatham. Daniel took Philip, with his trousers drawn up to his armpits and cuffs flopping over his shoes, on board his ship, HMS *Castor*. He asked to see the first lieutenant, who happened to be the commanding officer on board at the time. He told him that Philip had come to join the ship as a naval cadet. "All right," said the first lieutenant, "he is like a young dog and has all his sorrows to come."

Someone took them to the midshipmen's mess. There they saw one or two midshipmen asleep on the lockers, which were also used as seats. "The mess place was a long narrow room," Philip wrote, "quite dark, but had three tiny scuttles and three candles on the table, stuck in empty beer bottles, which gave a very faint light. One of the elder midshipmen was very polite, and offered my father a glass of ship's rum and some ship's biscuits, which he called 'hard tack.' We each took a small glass of rum and some of the hard tack, which I noticed was very full of weevils, but I was told when you threw the biscuit into your cup of tea it was all right, as the weevils were soon killed."

Daniel then got up to leave. In getting up from the table, he knocked his head against the beams, exclaiming "Jaw, bless my heart alive," Philip wrote. "He managed to crawl up the ladder to the upper deck saying, 'Well, goodbye, Philip,' and presented me with 10 shillings as a parting gift, and disappeared over the ship's side."

Philip's childhood thereupon ended abruptly. His new life in the Royal Navy now began.

2

Hunting Slavers on HMS *Castor*

1849–1852

Philip Hankin's career in the Royal Navy started inauspiciously. His first experience on board abruptly introduced him to the ways of the real world. He wrote in his memoirs:

> The Midshipman who had been so friendly then came to me, and said, Now look here, youngster, I promised your father I would look after you, and help you along a bit, and I will keep my word. He seemed a rum old cock, and I don't suppose he is very rich as I noticed he only gave you ten bob [ten shillings], and I want you to lend that to me tonight, as I am going on shore and have mislaid my purse. I said, I should be delighted and gave him at once my ten shillings, which I never saw again. He quickly took possession of the money and vanished over the side, telling me the tea hour was 4 o'clock, and that I must look out sharp, as if I was late it would all be gone.

A few days later, a fierce-looking man with a large, hooked nose and a red face came aboard. This was Captain Christopher Wyvill. Hankin was unlucky in this commanding officer. He was, in fact, unluckier than he knew. On May 5, 1849, the *Hampshire Telegraph* reported that Sir Thomas Pasley had been appointed to be the captain of HMS *Castor*.[10] By May 12, this had changed. Pasley was now to go to the Pembroke

Dockyard as superintendent and Captain Wyvill was to take over command of the *Castor*.[11]

HMS *Castor* sailed at the end of June.[12] The steam frigate *Sampson* took the ship in tow as far as Plymouth, where it cast off and charted a course for Cape Town. They sailed first to Funchal, in Madeira, and then on to Tenerife, where they obtained water and provisions, fresh beef and vegetables. Then they set off for the naval base on Ascension Island. "At this solitary island," Hankin wrote, "we got plenty of turtle instead of beef, which was served out to the ship's company, and we youngsters caught a great many fish of various kinds, which made a pleasant change after salt junk."

One of the midshipmen on board was George Sulivan.[13] Approximately three years older than Hankin, Sulivan already had one term of service under his belt. Hankin shared many of Sulivan's experiences on the *Castor*. Sulivan wrote that the routines of the Royal Navy had changed little since Horatio Nelson's day. For most of the time, the ship sailed under canvas. Although still made from wood, many ships in the Royal Navy were now being fitted with steam engines, funnels and propellers, but these were used only when absolutely necessary. Why use expensive coal when wind was available for free? The boatswain's pipe woke the crew at four or five in the morning, when they had to clean the decks. They had regular cutlass, musket and gun drills. Their life was spartan and their pleasures few. Among these pleasures was the grog distributed daily at noon and six. Every Sunday, the midshipmen and naval cadets had to go to school in the commodore's fore cabin. Here the ship's chaplain, Rev. Henry Jones, a Welshman with long red whiskers, taught them navigation.

On August 30, sixty-eight days after leaving England, they reached the naval base at Simon's Bay (Simon's Town) in the Cape Colony, in southern Africa.[14] Sir Harry Smith, governor of the Cape at the time, was upcountry dealing with the Eighth Xhosa War but a crisis erupted in Cape Town that necessitated his return.[15]

The *Castor's* arrival at Cape Town coincided with the news that the convict ship *Neptune* was bringing almost three hundred civil and military convicts from England to the Cape, which had been designated as a

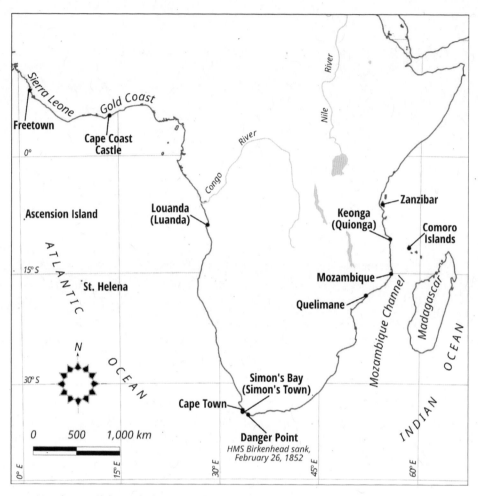

Map showing Philip Hankin's travels in the Royal Navy while on the East Africa and West Africa Stations on HMS *Castor* and HMS *Plumper*. Map by Morgan Hite of Hesperus Arts, Smithers.

penal colony. This was met with a storm of near-universal opposition, including that of Sir Harry, who was imperiously commanded by the British government to obey his instructions.[16] Two members of the executive council resigned, as did their replacements. A dozen magistrates resigned.[17] There were even angry calls for the colony to declare its independence from Britain.

The *Neptune* arrived in Cape Town on the evening of September 19. "The fact of the vessel's arrival was announced to the citizens of Cape

Town next morning (Thursday) by the striking of the gong of the Town-house, and the tolling, at half minute times, of all the church bells," the *Hampshire Advertiser* reported. "The people, though greatly excited, were sufficiently calm and collected to move prudently."[18] Sir Harry came close to insubordination by disobeying instructions that he should order the convicts to be brought ashore. He also refused demands from the colonists that he send the *Neptune* back to England with the convicts on board, saying, correctly, that he did not have the power to do this.

Sir Harry decided to keep the convicts on ships in Simon's Bay, well guarded by the guns of the *Castor*, until the matter could be sorted out. Most remained imprisoned on the *Neptune* but some were sent to wait on HMS *Seringapatam*.[19] The *Castor* remained in Simon's Bay to make sure the convicts did not escape.[20] It was not until February 1850 that the British government backed down and decided the convicts should be sent to Van Diemen's Land, which was then the name for Tasmania. There, it was hoped, they would be more welcome.

On February 22, 1850, the day after the *Neptune* left Simon's Bay with the convicts on board, HMS *Castor* commenced a long cruise in the waters around Zanzibar and Mozambique.[21] There it joined HMS *Pantaloon* and HMS *Dee* already patrolling on station in the Royal Navy's long war to end the traffic in slaves.

Slavery was abolished step by step. Lord Mansfield's judgment in the *Somerset* case in 1772 made slavery illegal in England and forbade the sending of a person to another country for enslavement. This meant that if a slave escaped from a ship in an English port, he or she was free and could not be handed back to any person who claimed ownership. In 1807, the British government passed the Slave Trade Act, which made the slave trade illegal in British possessions overseas. This was supplemented in 1833 with the Slavery Abolition Act, which made the purchase and ownership of slaves illegal within the British Empire. Of note also is the Act Against Slavery passed by the legislature of Upper Canada in 1793. This statute, which banned the importation of slaves, and which, in a compromise measure, emancipated slaves over the age of twenty-five, was the first legislation of a British colony to abolish slavery.

After the 1807 statute, the British government directed the Royal Navy to intercept slave ships and liberate slaves. It established the West Africa Squadron to patrol the three thousand miles of African coast to enforce its ruling. "At first, the Royal Navy tried to end the traffic by interception at sea," the historian Jan Morris wrote, "and a ramshackle squadron of frigates, sloops and gunbrigs, all the Admiralty could spare, pottered up and down the West African Coast, or, later, in and out of Zanzibar, in pursuit of slavers. This was a job the Navy loathed, despite the bounty paid—£5 a head for each liberated slave or £2/10s if he died before reaching port. The slave ships were generally faster and better sailers than the elderly warships of the patrols and the Navy's captains were hamstrung by legalism."[22] When the navy saw a slaver, the "captain had to ransack his locker for the necessary regulations, for his action depended upon the slaver's nationality."[23]

The British government also tried to strangle the slave trade by diplomatic means. In 1853, the British parliamentary committee into slave trade treaties reported, "By these Reports [reports submitted to the committee] it appears that there were in 1849–1850, twenty-four treaties in force between Great Britain and Foreign civilized Powers for the Suppression of the Slave Trade; ten of which give the right of search. ... There were also at that time forty-two treaties for the suppression of the Slave Trade existing between Great Britain and native chiefs on the Coast of Africa."[24]

Ramshackle or not, between 1808 and 1860, the West Africa Squadron captured 1,600 slave ships and freed 150,000 slaves destined for markets in the Americas. Half of all naval spending by Britain during the 1840s and 1850s went toward trying to catch slavers. In this period—1808 to 1860—many thousands of British sailors died of disease or during hostilities in the campaign to free slaves.[25] However, the naval officers had few illusions. They knew they intercepted only part of the trade. Reportedly, a quarter of all Africans taken as slaves to the Americas arrived there between 1807 and 1860. Slave ships picked up their human cargoes on the African coast and carried them on the notorious Middle Passage to

Rio de Janeiro, New Orleans or other places in the Americas. Those in the trade sold the unfortunate human beings at auction there and made large profits. The Royal Navy had an unending struggle.

As pressure on this trade from the Royal Navy grew in the Atlantic, so the trade in East Africa across the Indian Ocean to Arabia and India increased. The navy expanded its efforts into the Indian Ocean and established a squadron at Simon's Bay in the Cape Colony. This was the naval base to which the *Castor*, with Hankin and Sulivan aboard, was assigned. The small number of ships based there also patrolled the South Atlantic. At this time, Zanzibar was the centre of the slave trade in the Indian Ocean, although the trade was reportedly directed out of Oman. The British entered into a number of treaties with the sultan of Zanzibar to limit the trade in slaves. These treaties gave the navy rights to stop and search ships, but they knew all too well that not many people, from the sultan down, paid much attention to the laws or treaty obligations.

There were many reasons why the suppression of the slave trade was difficult. Whatever the legal and treaty requirements were, both the sultan and the Portuguese authorities clearly paid little attention to them. The trade was too lucrative to give up. Moreover, catching slave ships was not easy. Many of the vessels the slavers used were Baltimore clippers, fast ships built in Chesapeake Bay with two masts and hulls designed for speed. Slave-ship captains, when they saw they were being chased, used to increase their speed by throwing slaves overboard. You could always tell, one horrified navy lieutenant said, by the number of sharks that suddenly appeared.[26]

Ominously, the *Pantaloon* captured three empty ships in 1850.[27] In fact, the navy often caught slavers only when they were empty of their cargoes. When the navy did catch slave-laden ships—by guile, entrapment or navigational skill—the British officers and men who went on board were sickened by the conditions. One captain said he dreaded sending men on board a captured ship because of the risk of catching a pestilence and of the effect this would have on the crew's morale.[28]

In the Indian Ocean, the *Castor* stopped numerous dhows and other ships. When officers went on board, they often found it difficult to know who the slaves were. Unlike in the Atlantic, slaves in the Indian Ocean were not shackled to bolts on the deck. Most Arab dhows took on a few slaves as a matter of course. By taking slaves on board on the mainland and then to a slave market such as Zanzibar, members of the crew could supplement their income. Passengers also routinely took a couple of slaves with them on board to sell on arrival in order to pay for their passage. Every dhow probably had slaves on board, it was thought, often successfully disguised as crew. The slave traders enforced obedience by telling the slaves, many of whom had never seen a white man before, that the officers and crews of the navy were pirates who would undoubtedly eat them. Without trustworthy interpreters, the naval officers could not interrogate "passengers" or "crew" or read any papers presented to them as proof of their status.[29] They knew all too well that local interpreters were often paid well to mistranslate any answers that could have been incriminatory.

It should not be thought that all was light and virtue in the Royal Navy. Approval of emancipation was not universal. Some captains owned slaves on their own properties in the Caribbean. On occasion, it was suspected that a captain or mate was less than zealous in suppressing the trade or "let slip" information that allowed slave ships to evade capture.

Moreover, even after release, slaves faced an uncertain future. With the slaves' home villages burned to the ground at the time of capture, the navy didn't always know what to do with the ones they had liberated. They brought some to the Caribbean, where their working conditions were in some cases little better than those of slavery. Some were taken to Sierra Leone on the west coast of Africa. After slavery became illegal in England in 1772, a number of ex-slaves in that country and also a thousand ex-slaves from Nova Scotia became the nucleus of the new colony there. In this group from Nova Scotia were three slaves once owned by George Washington.

One notable captain, who later played a pivotal part in Hankin's career, was Commander Joseph Denman. A noted and passionate antislaver, he was the son of the abolitionist Chief Justice Thomas Denman. Slavery horrified him. As commander of HMS *Wanderer* on the West Africa Station, he was in a position to do something about it. In one celebrated case in 1840, he attacked the slave centre at Gallinas in West

Africa, going ashore with three boatloads of sailors and marines to burn the warehouses and barracoons. (A barracoon was a type of barracks or compound used for holding slaves while they were awaiting shipment.) In this action he freed a thousand slaves. Denman's actions were probably illegal, but the navy had a Nelsonian tradition of turning a blind eye and perhaps quietly approved. He was so aggressive in freeing slaves, seizing slave ships and attacking slave strongholds that a Portuguese slave trader sued him personally for damages. This led to one of the last in a line of anti-slavery cases in the English courts, *Buron v. Denman*, 1848, which Denman won on the basis that seizing and freeing slaves were acts of state.[30]

Hankin took part in the *Castor*'s campaign to suppress the trade: boarding dhows, interrogating the crew and trying to ascertain if the vessels had slaves on board. The navy often raided coastal villages active in the trade. The *Hampshire Telegraph* reported:

> The *Castor*, 36 [guns], Commodore Wyvill, anchored at the Mauritius, on the 19th of September, after a very long cruise on the east coast of Africa. She left Simon's Bay, Cape of Good Hope, on the 22nd of February, since which the Commodore has visited the slave trading coast of Mozambique. All the rivers have been searched for barracoons and slave vessels, and the strictest possible inquiry been established as to the slave trade. It is thought the Commodore's visit will have a wholesome effect on the wretches who deal in humanity; certain it is, the *Castor* did not succeed in making a prize until she reached Cape Delgado, in May last; all of a sudden, two large slave markets were discovered, which the Commodore caused to be surprised, and destroyed by the *Castor*'s boats before the people were aware of her being on the coast.[31]

Hankin was with the *Castor* during one raid that took place on June 8, 1850. This was at the large village known as Keonga (Quionga), two miles up a river near Cape Delgado. Commander Benjamin Holland Bunce, captain of the *Castor*, who led the raid, reported to Commodore Wyvill two days later:

In compliance with your orders on 8th June, I proceeded with the barge, pinnace, and the 2 cutters belonging to the *Castor* and 2 cutters belonging to the *Dee* to the River Mozamba. ... The whole river side is so fringed with thickly-wooded mangrove bush that it is quite impossible to penetrate it. ... In a couple of hours the tide suited and we proceeded with the boats in line of battle and succeeded in shooting them into a small opening. ... I then placed the men in position and commenced burning the barracoons, stores, sheds, etc., kraals and everything connected with them. I had half a dozen men with potfires, whose particular duty it was to burn, and the whole place was in a blaze in no time. A dhow, of about 100 tons and upwards, measuring 52 feet in length... was aground, and concealed in the mangrove bushes. I placed 20 lbs. of powder under her bilge, the explosion of which destroyed her; a 6-pounder gun, intended, I suppose, for the protection of the establishment, stood on the brow of the hill, and pointed so as to command the pass through the mangrove bush... loaded and primed and a match burning beside it. ... The whole of the barracoons, and everything pertaining to them in the shape of the store-houses being in full blaze, the dhow destroyed, the gun dismounted, and hove into the mud, I re-embarked and in proceeding down-river a few straggling shots were fired at us from the mangrove bushes. ... None of our men were hit. ... These barracoons, store-houses, etc., were on a much larger scale than the ones at Masani [another slave centre the *Castor* raided] and capable of containing at least 4,000 slaves.[32]

Writing on July 9, 1850, to the secretary of the Admiralty, Wyvill said that this attack on the barracoons had done enormous damage to the slave trade and "had spread the utmost alarm and confusion in Zanzibar. Some merchants are ruined and have fled."[33]

These depredations on the barracoons and slave centres on the coast by the *Castor* and the *Dee* led to a diplomatic dispute with Portugal. While Wyvill engaged in epistolary battles with the governor of Mozambique over the interpretation of treaties and protocols, Viscount Palmerston, British foreign secretary, famous for acting decisively first

Burning of the slave establishment by British seamen and marines at Keonga (Quionga), in the Mozambique Channel, June 8, 1850. *Illustrated London News*, January 18, 1851, p. 44.

and apologizing afterwards, if necessary, was instructing the British ambassador to Portugal to calm the ruffled feathers of the Portuguese government. "In pursuance of the permission thus obtained from the Imaum, the boats of Her Majesty's ships *Castor* and *Dee*... discovered at a village called Keonga... another slave-trading establishment... and those buildings were destroyed. ... I have the satisfaction of informing you that their destruction is represented as likely to prove a serious check to the Slave Trade on that part of the east coast of Africa."[34]

Although other ships in the squadron had some success, the *Castor* had little luck in capturing slave ships. All the vessels it chased escaped and the *Castor* took no prizes. The ship visited all the great slave trading centres: Madagascar, the Comoro Islands, Mauritius, Zanzibar and Quelimane, a seaport in Mozambique. A Portuguese possession, Quelimane was a notorious slave market, being, Sulivan wrote, the most southerly of the major slave markets and one of the biggest. He noted that the lowest estimate of slaves shipped from Zanzibar alone, which represented under half of the total number shipped from the east coast of Africa, was approximately twenty thousand annually. The sultan of Zanzibar levied a tax of the equivalent of one pound for each slave.[35] This tended to make his support of anti-slavery measures half-hearted at best. These figures did not include a similar number that the Portuguese shipped to the Comoro Islands and Madagascar. Nor did they include those shipped to Arabia without going through Zanzibar. It was described as a river of slaves emptying out of the interior of Africa.

The sighting of a possible slave ship usually led to a chase. Hankin recalled one such occasion. In the middle of divine service, the look-out spotted a sail on the weather bow. This caused great excitement, and Commodore Wyvill, who was very keen to catch a suspected slave ship, called out, "There, that will do Mr. Jones. Grace of our Lord etcetera. Amen." Then in a stentorian voice he called out, "Hands make sail." Everyone immediately rushed on deck and into the rigging. Rev. Jones was left alone in his pulpit to finish the service by himself. Sadly, on this occasion, the vessel, which could be seen only by its top sails, escaped.

Divine service was held on Sundays on the main deck. Hankin was ordered to act as clerk or, as they called it, to "assist Mr. Jones." He hated this because he never knew exactly when to stand up and when to sit down. He used to repeat the responses in a loud voice because he remembered that the clerk at Stanstead Church used to call out loudly, "We beseech Thee, to Aid us, Good Lord." So he tried to copy him as well as he could. He remembered that one Sunday he did not stand up at the correct time when repeating the responses. Rev. Jones soon refreshed his memory by giving him a bang on his head with his prayer book and called out in a very severe tone of voice, "Stand up, Mr. Hankin."

"Of course, I jumped up very quickly for I could feel a lump on the top of my head like a pigeon's egg where he had banged me with his heavy prayer book," Hankin wrote.

Bangs on the head aside, Hankin had a healthy constitution. He did not fall sick as readily as others. This served him well in East Africa, in West Africa and later in British Honduras. The drinking water was often impure and many of the crew consequently fell ill with dysentery and other fevers. On April 29, 1850, the *Castor* visited Zanzibar, where many of the crew fell badly sick. Sulivan described the water at Zanzibar as particularly abominable and attributed much of the crew's sickness to this. It was on this visit that the sultan gave the commodore a white horse. This stayed on board for the nine months until they returned to the Cape. By then it had almost become a member of the crew, who tried to teach it to smoke a pipe. Sulivan wrote that they sailed from Zanzibar with bullocks, sheep and pigs on board, which made the main deck look like a farmyard. This was not, in fact, uncommon. Once, in addition to sheep and what was described as "etceteras," they had fifty bullocks tethered between the guns.[36]

Replenishing the water supplies on board was a continuing problem. They had to fill water casks whenever they could. Hankin remembered the watering parties that went ashore to do this. It was, he said, always a long day's work. The watering party was piped to muster on the quarterdeck at two-thirty in the morning, when the boats were got ready and provisioned for the day. A lieutenant was sent in command of the ship's pinnace with two cutters. A midshipman in each boat had the duty to ensure that everything was in proper order. At three o'clock they all had breakfast, consisting of cocoa and biscuit, and at three-thirty, long before daylight, they left the ship. They often had to pull the heavy boats ten miles to the shore, so that by nine or ten o'clock the men were very hungry again. Usually about that time, Hankin wrote, they all had dinner. Then at three o'clock in the afternoon they had tea and biscuit again, which was their last meal of the day. It did not seem to be of any consequence, he wrote, at what hour the men had their meals, so long as they had three meals in the twenty-four hours.

Hankin did not like Commodore Wyvill, who, it is evident, did not like Hankin. Having a commanding officer not liking him made his life on board extremely unpleasant. He recalled one incident during the long cruise in the Mozambique Channel. He wrote that it was always a great event to be asked to dinner in the commodore's cabin, but instead of this being considered a pleasant invitation, all the midshipmen and cadets dreaded it. One day at sea, Wyvill's steward came to him and said, "Mr. Hankin, the commodore's compliments and you are to dine with him today at 4 o'clock."

Hankin said this alarmed him very much because he had been a long time at sea and had had no opportunity of washing his clothes. Under shipboard conditions, it was impossible to keep a shirt clean. However, this invitation was equal to a command and he had to obey. He looked over all his dirty shirts. He selected the least yellow one and commenced to make arrangements for this formidable dinner:

> There were generally 5 officers invited at the same time, so as to make a party of six. The Commodore generally gave two dinner parties a week and once a week he dined with the ward room officers. Now, for my dinner preparations, I first of all brushed my shirt well with a clothes brush, then washed it in my hand basin, and ironed it out with an empty bottle, and made it as smooth as I could. Then I rubbed carefully any dirty spots over with chalk. The collar was the most difficult part, but when it was all finished, with a smart new necktie and with my best Sunday jacket, it really didn't look so bad.
>
> I remember when I entered the cabin I made a low bow to the Commodore and the Steward told me where to sit. There were present, Jenkins (the first lieutenant), Clatworthy, the purser, Campbell (the third Lieutenant), the Commodore's Secretary and myself. I was fortunately near the door, as will be shown afterwards. It was the Custom in those days to drink wine with one another and it would have been thought an insult to refuse.
>
> Directly after the Soup, the Commodore looked at me and called out: "Mr. Hankin, pleasure of a glass of Wine, sir?" "With pleasure, sir," I replied, and a large glass was immediately filled with very strong fiery sherry. I had never been accustomed to wine, but the Commodore said, "No heel taps, drink it off, sir, like a man," and setting me an example by finishing his own glass, I had to do

the same. Then each officer in turn asked me to drink Wine with him and I dared not refuse, and each time the Commodore's eagle eye was upon me as he exclaimed, "No heel taps, sir, by God, sir, no heel taps." So by the time the dinner was finished I had drunk at least five large glasses of wine, and I began to feel a sort of buzzing in the head, which was very uncomfortable. At length the dinner came to an end and the usual dessert was placed on the table, consisting of Bananas, Oranges, Nuts and raisins and ginger and a large decanter of port, also one of Sherry, which the Steward handed round, saying as he did so, "Port, sir, or Sherry?" As I began to feel so very uncomfortable through drinking so much Sherry, I thought I had better try "Port," when a huge glass was poured out for me, and following the example of the Commodore, we all raised our glasses and said "The Queen," when at that moment the commodore called out "No heel taps, gentlemen," and every glass was immediately drained of its contents. Then coffee was handed round, and afterwards Liqueur in the shape of Curacao and Maraschino.

By this time, I was beginning to feel very uncomfortable indeed and began to wonder how on earth I should ever get out of the Cabin. I managed to retain my senses and held on very tightly with one hand to the table, when I was aroused by the Steward's voice saying in my ear, Curacao or Maraschino? I felt that the first one would be the easiest to pronounce so I mumbled out "shure a sho," when, soon afterwards, came the ordeal of leaving the table. I knew I had to get on my feet, make a bow to the Commodore and leave the cabin.

Presently I saw the first lieutenant rise, whose example was followed by the other officers and, watching for a favorable roll of the ship, I let go my hold of the table and just managed to reach the cabin door, which was being held open by the sentry, when I tumbled flat down on my face for I was undoubtedly for the first and only time in my life "drunk." The kind-hearted sentry immediately picked me up and carried me below and laid me on my chest with a pillow under my head and in a few minutes I became unconscious.

In a very short time, I was roused from my slumbers by the Quartermaster shaking me and saying, "Mr Ankin, Mr Ankin" (the H in my name was invariably forgotten) "there's the Commodore a-waitin' for you to muster your Quarters." "Oh dear, oh dear, what shall I do," I murmured out. "Oh, lemme go shlepp Quartermaster." However, this apparently was not to be thought of for a moment and the kind old man, after dabbing me in the face with a wet towel, exclaimed, "Oh, you're all right, sir, make a heffort, and come on deck, or there'll be an ell of a row." So I did my best, though I felt I was far from being "all right," but I managed with the help of the Quartermaster to crawl up the ladder and onto the Quarterdeck, and the first thing I saw was the old Commodore, with a very red face, sitting in the weather hammock netting, holding onto the back stays, with his eagle eye upon me.

I was literally terrified, and made a desperate effort to keep on my feet, but at that moment the ship gave an unexpected lurch to windward, which caused me to lose my balance and I fell on my nose! But I was soon brought to my senses by hearing the Commodore exclaim, as he called to the Commander, "Captain Bunce, Captain Bunce, look at that young gentleman, look at him, he's drunk, a disgrace to the service. By God, he's drunk. Put him abaft the Mizzen mast, with two Sentries over him with fixed Bayonets, and make him walk up and down until 4 o'clock tomorrow morning to get him sober."

And away I was marched and my sentence duly carried out. The sentries being relieved at midnight and, fortunately for me, Lieutenant Campbell, who was a very kind officer, allowed me to sit down during the middle watch. My headache had gone by 4 o'clock in the morning, but I was very tired, and was allowed to go to my hammock, and sleep until seven.

I was never asked to dine with the Commodore again and I was very glad for it, for he never liked anyone who, as he said, "couldn't stand his liquor," which I certainly could not, at least, not the quantity I had been forced to drink, for I was not 14 years of age and not accustomed to anything but a very little light beer. My leave was stopped for a fortnight after our arrival at Simon's Bay and there my punishment, which I had certainly not deserved, ended.

The *Castor* did not feed its midshipmen and cadets well. Hankin related he was often desperately hungry. He recalled that during their cruise, the provisions, at all events in the midshipmen's mess, were growing short. In one middle watch, some of them put their heads together and pondered ways to fill their stomachs. Through the perpendicular bars of the store room door, they had seen a tempting-looking ham on the shelf. They could see it was very close but still out of reach. The difficulty was how to get it through the bars. One night, it occurred to Hankin that they could push a long boarding pike through the bars, spear the ham and bring it back through. Then they could cut off a slice or two and put the ham back. What could go wrong? After one or two attempts, they succeeded in retrieving the ham but found it quite impossible to cut slices with the carving knife. They managed to scoop pieces out of the ham with their pocket knives. With some biscuit and rum and water, this, he said, made an excellent meal.

The difficulty now was to replace the ham on the dish in the store room. After their repeated attempts to push it back through the bars, the ham fell off the end of the pike on the deck with a bang. Hankin and his confederate fled. The next morning the steward found the ham on the floor. He put it on the table for breakfast and this caused "no end of a row." The two culprits sat very quietly and agreed with the others that it was a great shame. The caterer of the mess said he should report it to the commander and whoever was found guilty of stealing the ham would probably be dismissed from the service in disgrace. In about ten days, though, the crime, happily for Hankin, was forgotten.

———————

The *Castor* remained cruising the seas around Mozambique for approximately nine or ten months. The health of the ship's crew, though, was by now deteriorating. Approximately one hundred had been on the sick list from fever and dysentery, ten of whom had died. The doctor,

George Monro, informed Wyvill that if he did not wish to lose more men, it would be advisable to return to the Cape. They started back for Simon's Bay soon after. The commodore was "very sorry to give up his slave hunting and chances of making prize money but there was no help for it," Hankin wrote, and in about a fortnight's time they arrived at Simon's Bay, happy to be back. They arrived at the Cape on February 5, 1851.[37]

Being a midshipman or cadet had its expenses and Hankin was always short of money. The day after their arrival at any port, the usual bumboat men came out to the ship in their boats selling grapes, oranges and other fruits and demanding, of course, greatly inflated prices for everything. Like those of all the other officers, Hankin's clothes and uniforms had become exceedingly shabby. Now that he was back in port, he had to order a new uniform and engage a Malay as a washerman. This was a serious drain on his financial resources. With an income of three pounds, six shillings and eight pence a month, being the forty pounds a year allowed him by his father, he had a hard time making ends meet. A new uniform, he recalled, at that time cost him three pounds, ten shillings, and his monthly mess bill, including wine, cost him over two pounds. Fathers of other midshipmen and cadets gave their sons an annual allowance of fifty pounds, and that ten pounds made all the difference. The navy paid Hankin twenty pounds a year but deducted five pounds for Rev. Jones's naval instruction. His entire annual income was therefore fifty-five pounds. How could he keep clear of debt? In fact, he couldn't.

He wrote to his father begging for more money. His father sent him ten pounds with a severe letter saying he should be ashamed of himself. He should think of his mother and sister and not be so selfish. Rather sourly, Hankin commented that his father kept four horses and he thought he might have managed with three and spared his poor son in the navy a larger allowance.

The allowance from his father was paid quarterly through the commodore's bankers. Consequently, Wyvill quickly learned that Hankin had dared to write home for more money. He sent a signal to the ship from his house on shore: "Send Mr. Hankin to me immediately."

Hankin described what happened next:

In a few minutes I landed and went to the Commodore's house and asked to see the Secretary, who said to me, "You'll catch it hot, you've been writing home for more money—you are to come at once to the Commodore."

I followed the secretary into the dining room, where I found the Commodore sitting at the dining table with foolscap paper, pens and ink in front of him. Said the Commodore to me, "How dare you, sir, write to your father for more money?" Then turning to the Secretary, he said, "Now, Mr. Pritchard, take down the evidence against this young gentleman. I'll teach him to write home for more money." "Take down the evidence against me" sounded dreadful, and I wondered what on earth would happen to me. I was made to explain exactly how I could possibly have spent such a large sum as £55 in a year, which I did without any difficulty, for I often was obliged to buy a new suit of clothes, for my jacket and trousers got very easily spoiled by constantly going aloft, for nothing takes the shine out of Cloth so effectively as tar.

After the evidence was all taken down, Wyvill delivered his judgment. He sent Hankin back to the *Castor* with a letter to Captain Bunce instructing him to send him on board the *Seringapatam*, a coal hulk, with an order to the gunner who was in charge of the ship that on no account was he to be allowed to go ashore, and that he was to live on ship's provisions and wash his own clothes.

If this was meant to be a punishment, it failed. In truth, Hankin had rather a pleasant time on the *Seringapatam*. He had a nice cabin and was comfortable and happy. The ship, an old twenty-six-gun frigate, was the one used to hold some of the convicts from the *Neptune* while they were in Simon's Bay. The gunner had his wife on board and she was kind to Hankin. Every Sunday she invited him into their cabin for dinner. He passed most of his time fishing from the ship and recalled he had good sport. He generally gave his catch to the gunner's wife as he thought it advisable to keep in her good books. After he had been six weeks on board, he went back to the *Castor*. The money he had been able to save, through living on ship's provisions and washing his own clothes, helped him pay off his debts.

Lady Smith, the wife of Sir Harry, the governor of Cape Colony, was kind and hospitable to the midshipmen at Simon's Bay. She used to invite two at a time to visit Government House for a week or ten days. Hankin said he was lucky enough to be invited twice. All the junior officers looked forward to these visits and greatly enjoyed them. There was no railway from Simon's Bay to Cape Town in those days and they used to travel there in a shaky cart with four small horses, taking four hours on the journey. At Government House, they enjoyed the dinner parties—no wonder after shipboard fare—and two dances a week, with feminine company to enliven their adolescent ardour. His favourite dancing partner was a Bonny Cloete, who lived at Wynberg. He never forgot her.

Lady Smith was in the habit of going out for a drive every evening in a large, rumbling old carriage, and her young guests always had to go with her, in uniform, and sit behind her in the dickey (a folding outside seat at the back of a vehicle). Hankin said he became acquainted with many of the charming families at the Cape and, of course, he met all the best people of the colony at Government House.

The story of Lady Smith is well known but repetition cannot spoil it.[38] In 1812, during the Peninsular War, Juana María de los Dolores de León and her sister, both orphaned daughters of Spanish aristocrats—indeed, they were direct descendants of the explorer Juan Ponce de León—were trapped in Badajoz, a strategically important city. British troops under Lord Wellington attacked and captured it. The British officers then lost control of their men, who proceeded to find the wine and sack the city, with readily understandable dangers to young girls. Sir Harry later wrote that Juana María and her sister, their homes destroyed, escaped from the blazing city to throw "themselves upon the protection of any British officer who would afford it; and so great, she said, was her faith in our national character, that she knew her appeal would not be made in vain, nor the confidence abused."[39] Here Juana María met Captain Harry

HMS *Birkenhead* troopship. This is the only known picture of the ship as it actually existed. The picture was owned by the late Mr. Barber, chief engineer, Royal Navy, a survivor, and was the work of a brother officer. Wikimedia Commons.

Smith of the Ninety-Fifth Rifles, and they fell in love. A few days later, with Wellington giving Juana María away, they were married.

Juana María was beautiful, amiable and plucky. She endured the hardship of the campaign with her young husband, riding with the baggage train, sharing his meals and quickly becoming the darling of the army. Wellington called her Juanita. For the next fifty years, wherever Harry Smith went, she went. "From that day to this," he wrote in his autobiography, "she has been my guardian angel."[40] To South Africa, to India (where he won fame as the victor of the Battle of Aliwal) and then to South Africa again, this time with the now Major General Sir Harry Smith as governor. The town of Ladysmith in South Africa was named after her. Indirectly, as a result of the famous siege of that town during the Boer War, so also was the town of Ladysmith on Vancouver Island.

The crew from the *Castor* assisted the regular soldiers during the Xhosa War. Hankin does not disclose what part he played in these affairs but later in life he mentioned that for his participation in this war he had been awarded the South Africa Medal.[41]

Hankin was with the *Castor* in 1852 when it assisted in the rescue of some survivors from the wreck of HMS *Birkenhead*. The *Birkenhead* had come from England with fresh troops for the Xhosa War. On February 26, striking a rock two miles offshore from Danger Point, it quickly sank, with troops and numerous wives and children on board. Many of the sailors drowned in their hammocks. The number of people on board—therefore the exact number of dead—was never definitively established.

Legend and the capacity of the English for portraying a disaster as a glorious triumph tell us that, there being enough lifeboats for only 138 people, the captain ordered women and children into them first, starting the "women and children first" tradition, which came to be known as the Birkenhead Drill. Colonel Alexander Seton, commanding the approximately 450 soldiers, then told them to line up on deck as if on parade and die like men. Kipling wrote a famous poem about their stoic heroism, "Soldier an' Sailor Too":

> Their choice it was plain between drownin' in 'eaps
> an' bein' mashed by the screw,
> So they stood an' was still to the Birken'ead drill,
> soldier an' sailor too![42]

Corporal William Butler, one of those rescued by the *Castor*, tells a different story: "As to the troops being paraded, it is imagination. She was loaded to the funnel. It was *sauve qui peut*. The last words I heard the Captain say were 'Soldiers and sailors, I've done what I can for you. I can't do more. Those who can swim do so; Those who can't, climb the rigging.' Then it was a rush. ... When the Captain told us to save ourselves, many of us jumped overboard. I had stripped. I got hold of a bit of wreckage, on which it took me about seven hours to reach the shore."[43] A number of people did attempt to swim to the shore. Many of them were snatched by the sharks. Many drowned in the kelp beds. The *Castor*, coming on the scene not long after, helped rescue twenty-five seamen, sixty-three soldiers and thirteen children.[44]

After Hankin had been on board the *Castor* for a little over two years, the Admiralty ordered four midshipmen to return to England and sent out four to replace them. Hankin and Sulivan were two of the fortunate ones chosen to go home. They took passage on board the *Megaera*, an aging vessel of about eight hundred tons employed in carrying troops. As there was no midshipmen's mess, they messed in the wardroom and were told they need not keep night watch. (So, perhaps for the first time in a few years, they were able to sleep through the night.) Sulivan distinguished himself by jumping twenty feet into the sea to rescue a seaman who had fallen off the main yard and could not swim, holding him above the water while a boat was lowered to rescue them. Hankin was happy and comfortable in this ship and thoroughly enjoyed the forty-day voyage back to England. The *Megaera* arrived at Plymouth on June 15, 1852, and the crew was paid off.[45] Hankin was discharged from the ship by request and Admiralty order.

The day after he arrived in England, Hankin received a letter from his father, directing him to return home to Stanstead as soon as possible. So home he went. He was sixteen. Not long after he arrived, his father had a surprise for him. Philip's mother, Elizabeth, had a hacking cough that would not go away. The dank climate in England was making her recovery difficult. To try to improve her health, Daniel told Philip, he had decided to sell his property and take the whole family to live in New Zealand, including the two sons in India, if they were inclined to join them. Daniel said it would probably take about eight months to sell the property and wind up his affairs. He believed he could raise thirty thousand pounds from the sale and that this would be enough to establish themselves in New Zealand. There the Hankin boys would really have to work and not be idle. What was Philip to do in those eight months? Unsurprisingly, his father had plans to keep him busy.

To Vancouver Island on HMS *Plumper*

1852–1857

Philip's father, Daniel, would not, of course, hear of his remaining at home doing nothing. Like it or not, Philip now had to find a job for eight months. By the end of this time, Daniel would have sold the estate and wound up the family's affairs. Then they would all emigrate to New Zealand to start a new life. Daniel spoke with his good friend and neighbour Nicolson Calvert. And yes, Mr. Calvert would be happy to offer Philip a job as a clerk in his brewery.

Calvert's Brewery, which the Calvert family had acquired in 1730, was based in London, at 89 Upper Thames Street. Reportedly founded before the reign of the Tudors, this brewery was one of the largest and most successful in the city. It was not a tumbledown, rat-infested tenement on the banks of the Thames like the one where both Charles Dickens and the fictional David Copperfield were thrown away as children to work. Rather, it sprawled over three acres of land on the riverbank between London Bridge and Blackfriars Bridge. Here were massive buildings, some ancient, some new. Lighters brought malt down from Ware in Hertfordshire. Huge winches raised malt up from these barges and lowered barrels of beer down into them. Almost a quarter of a mile of Archimedean screws moved the grain around. The grounds were a jumble of warehouses, vats, conveyors, machine shops, cooperages and stables for up to fifty horses and wagons. Above the counting house, where it is likely Hankin worked, were the elegant wood-panelled boardrooms and offices. There were three

View of the brewery and dwelling house belonging to Messrs. Calvert and Company, about 1820. Philip Hankin worked here for a time as a clerk. Source: Alfred Barnard, *The Noted Breweries of Great Britain and Ireland*, vol. 2 (London: Sir Joseph Causton and Sons, 1889). Chronicle / Alamy Stock Photo G36M5A

wells on the premises, one going down as deep as 438 feet to reach the clear, pure water the brewery needed. The enterprise employed over three hundred people and every year produced over two hundred thousand barrels of beer, stout and porter.[46]

Using the third-class season ticket on the railway that his father had purchased for him, Hankin went down to London. He found his way to the brewery and gave the manager a letter from Mr. Calvert saying he had been appointed as a junior clerk in the office at a salary of sixty pounds a year. He thought this was a very handsome salary and noted it was more than his pay as a junior officer in the Royal Navy.

Philip's duties at the brewery were not onerous. He had to be at the office every morning at eight-thirty, light the gas and sweep out one small room. Then he had to run messages, take orders for beer and make himself generally useful. Every second week he had to work late. This meant staying until nine in the evening and booking any orders for beer that came in, but as the housekeeper always brought him a tray with tea, bread, butter and marmalade, he did not mind this in the least. He compared her tea favourably with the navy tea, where he got only tea, coarse brown sugar, no milk, and biscuits full of weevils. For an officer of the Royal Navy with experience commanding seamen much older than himself and with the huge responsibilities of even a midshipman in a warship, being a junior clerk in a brewery might be thought to be a lowly position. But Philip didn't seem to mind, and he did enjoy being his own master.

He was satisfied with his new position but more so with his freedom in London. At home, he was at the beck and call of his father and, with a sick mother, would have had to take his part in raising his numerous younger siblings. He recalled in his memoirs that when he returned from London in the evening, his aunt Ria would sometimes accuse him of smoking. She would say in a pious voice, "Philip, you've been smoking!" He always had to tell her he had been in a smoking compartment on the train, and that was why his clothes stank of cigarette smoke. For a young man who had seen active and dangerous service on the rivers and ships of the Indian Ocean and had helped rescue the desperate men, women and children of the *Birkenhead*, such a life would have seemed trivial and constricting.

After Hankin had been living at home for five months and going to London to work at the brewery every morning, the doctor pronounced his mother's health was worse and that it was now unthinkable for her to travel to New Zealand. Daniel consequently had to abandon his plan of emigrating.

What should Philip do now? There must have been anxious family councils. It was soon decided—and it is hard not to believe that the imperious Daniel laid down the law—that Philip should return to the navy. Through the influence of yet another of friend of Daniel at the Admiralty, Hankin was offered an appointment as a midshipman on board either HMS *Agamemnon* or HMS *Sidon*. His choice. Both ships were at Spithead.[47] He chose the *Sidon*, a paddlewheel steam frigate of twenty-two guns. Commissioned to her in December 1852, he was ordered to go aboard at once.[48] Announcing his appointment, the *Morning Post* called him Hawkins. Such mistakes were common when clerks had to transcribe names from handwritten lists. Soon, Hankin wrote, he fell back into the old routines of the navy and ceased to remember that he had ever been a brewer's clerk.

Hankin was now seventeen and an experienced young officer. There were even several cadets junior to him on the *Sidon*, three of whom later became admirals. He had the good fortune to be midshipman of the watch under a man called Frank Thomson, who was a sub-lieutenant on board, or mate, as it was then called. They became good friends. Hankin used to go with Thomson to visit his mother at her home in Southsea. She was, Hankin recalled, a "dear old lady" who always gave him a warm welcome and "wore black, with a large white cap, with strings hanging down the back." She used to play the flute while her son accompanied her on the piano. Thomson became commander of Queen Victoria's yacht, later captain of the *Challenger* and later still captain of the Queen's yacht *Victoria and Albert*. Hankin and Thomson used to go to dances in Winchester together. At that time they also used to go to the many dances being given in the then-fashionable town of Ryde. Hankin loved dancing and was good at it. Even when he was seventy-nine, he admitted he was never able to resist the "Blue Danube" waltz.

In February 1853, after he had been on the *Sidon* for a few months, his mother's health deteriorated.[49] He wrote, "My dear mother became much worse, and came with my sister to Ryde for change of air, but she was not comfortable in lodgings and found herself getting rapidly worse instead of better. So she returned home and three weeks afterwards she died." Although Philip was still on the *Sidon* at Spithead, and could easily have obtained leave, his father would not allow him to come home to see his mother before she died. He would, his father said, "only be in the way and could do no earthly good." Fifty years later, Hankin still felt the hurt. "She was a good Christian woman," Hankin wrote, "and for 25 years had been a most devoted wife and mother. And she had not the slightest fear of death, for when the summons came she was ready, and prepared." She was forty-nine years old.

The *Sidon* was an old ship and spent much of its time puttering around Portsmouth. Being on board wasn't very exciting and Hankin soon grew restless. When Captain George Goldsmith eased the ship out to journey to Spithead, only a few miles away, some machinery broke and the ship had to go to dry dock for lengthy repairs.[50] It was that kind of ship. Hankin wrote:

> I had now been ten months at Spithead, and was getting rather tired of it, and longing for a change. So I wrote to the Admiralty, making application for a sea-going ship and in a very short time I was appointed to the *Plumper*, a small screw steamer, barque rigged, and carrying 6 32-pounder muzzle-loading guns. She had an auxiliary screw and under favorable circumstances could steam six knots. We fitted out at Portsmouth, it was therefore very easy for me to join her. I was very sorry to leave the *Sidon*, and all my messmates. Less than a year after this, the Crimean War broke out and the *Sidon* went to the war, and when before Sevastopol, a shell burst on board and killed and wounded 22 men at the foremost Main deck quarters, where I should have been stationed—if I had been in the ship—so perhaps after all it was fortunate for me that I was not on board.

Hankin was appointed to HMS *Plumper* on August 1, 1853.[51] The *Morning Post* now called him P.J. Hankeir. Very soon after Hankin went on board, his new captain, John Wharton, was married. His bride, Matilda Gomm, was conveniently the niece of the commander-in-chief of the East Indies Squadron.[52] This occasion, happy for the bridal couple, was to have less than happy consequences for Hankin a year or so later. Far too soon for his marital bliss, Wharton had to leave his bride and take his ship to sea.

The *Plumper* steamed out of Portsmouth Harbour in mid-September 1853.[53] As soon as they were clear in the channel, they lifted the propeller, raised the sails and set course for Sierra Leone, where they arrived after about twenty days. This would be their base while on the West Africa Station. "The capital, Freetown," Jan Morris wrote, "became the principal base of the Royal Navy on the West African coast."[54] Sierra Leone, Hankin said, was a lovely spot with beautiful tropical vegetation. He always had the happy disposition to look on the bright side. Others with less hardy health called it the White Man's Grave. Statistically, they were right.

Under Captain Wharton, the *Plumper* was a happy ship. Both the captain and the first lieutenant, Mr. Didham, were kind and pleasant to Hankin. The second lieutenant, Edward Shaw, taught him seamanship—for free, unlike Rev. Jones on the *Castor*—and how to moor and unmoor a large ship, shift topsails and such nautical accomplishments. The first part of his tour of duty went well and he enjoyed the ship and his colleagues.

The *Plumper* cruised along the coast of West Africa for eighteen months, visiting Liberia, Accra, Cape Coast Castle and Lagos, and then went on to Ascension. Always they were striving to disrupt the slave trade and liberate slaves.

Cape Coast Castle was one of the many forts on the Gold Coast, in what is now Ghana. For the 170 years before the British first established a colony there in 1821, it had been a major slave trade centre. Here as many as a thousand slaves at a time were collected and held in underground dungeons while awaiting passage to the auction blocks in South and North America. One of the most active land-based anti-slavers on the coast was Sir William Winniett, governor of the reconstituted Gold Coast colony.[55] He came from Nova Scotia and at the time was one of the most senior "colonials" in a position of responsibility. He bought slave trading castles along the coast to damage the trade and he negotiated numerous anti-slavery treaties with local potentates. He had died in Cape Coast Castle in 1850, not long before Hankin arrived on the coast. The vigorous governor of Sierra Leone at the time Hankin was on the coast was an affable Irishman named Arthur Kennedy. It is unlikely that such a junior officer as Hankin would have had occasion to meet him. A decade later, though, Kennedy played a pivotal part in Hankin's life story.

The pleasantness on board the *Plumper* could not continue. Captain Wharton, longing to return to his new wife, requested to be relieved of his command. The Admiralty gave its consent. On April 7, 1855, it appointed Captain William Haswell to take over command of the *Plumper* while the ship was at Ascension Island.[56] Hankin wrote:

The change was not for the better, for Haswell was a tartar, who used to shake his fist within an inch of your nose and tell you he would make you jump before he had done with you. I think everyone on board hated him, and it was quite impossible to please him. I remember he used to wear white spring side boots with patent leather tips to them, and he would go up the rigging into the fore and main tops to see if he could find anything out of order, and he would rub his hand underneath the gun slide, to see if he could find any dust there. He certainly was a martinet, but the ship was as smart as paint and polish could make her. I was now a sub-lieutenant, or a mate, as they used to be called, and had charge of a watch. ...

As soon as Captain Haswell had taken over command from Captain Wharton, we made sail for Lagos, and were soon cruising about again at various places on the West Coast of Africa, hunting for slavers. We were in 3 watches—4 to 6, and middle 6 to 8, and morning afternoon, and first, and often being on duty from noon to 4 o'clock, we would have sail drill—shifting topsails, top yards until 7:30 p.m. Then I had the first watch to keep, from 8 p.m. until midnight.

How I hated it all. The hot climate, and many men ill with fever, the terrible monotony of the life, and the constant bullying of the Captain nearly drove me wild. As I had now been some time on the coast, I wrote home to my father's friend, Mr. Clifton, at the Admiralty, to ask him to try to get me appointed to some ship in the Crimea, for the war with Russia was now in full swing and at length a letter came from the Admiralty to say that I was to go back to England, if I could be spared. So Haswell sent for me into his cabin. He told me that he had by that mail received a letter from the Admiralty to say that I was to be sent home immediately, if I could be spared and then I should be appointed to some ship in the Crimea. Then the Bully went on to say, "So you thought you would get out of the ship, did you? Would you like very much to go, Mr. Hankin?" "Yes, sir," I replied. "Very much indeed." I was asked again—"Yes sir, very much indeed," I again answered. "Well, sir," he said, as he shook his fist in my face—"You won't go, sir. I'll see you damned first. Now go back to your duty."

So there was an end for ever of all my hope of my being able to leave the *Plumper*. Some months afterwards, a brig called the *Sappho* commanded by Captain Moresby arrived at Lagos, and from there [was] ordered to Australia. I tried to join this vessel, and persuaded Captain Moresby to try to get leave from Haswell to let me go. If he had known of the fate of the *Sappho*, I am sure he would have been only too pleased to have let me join her, for she sailed to Australia and was never heard of again!

While the *Plumper* was anchored off Sharks' Point at the mouth of the Congo River, Haswell ordered Hankin to take a small boat on an expedition upriver. He set off in the whaleboat with a month's provisions and five Krumen to go some two hundred miles up the river to see if any suspicious-looking vessels were anchored off a place Hankin called Punta da Legna.[57] This was a trip he enjoyed, and it was a great escape from the bullying captain. He recalled he shot plenty of parrots, some monkeys and curious birds, "many of which proved excellent eating."

No other white men were sent with him, he wrote, for they caught fever so easily and many on board were already ill. He, however, kept his good health and "it was as good as a picnic. I used to sleep every night in the stern sheets of the Whale boat, with the awning spread and serve out Quinine Wine every morning at 7 o'clock as a preventive against fever. At the expiration of the month, I returned to the Ship, and Haswell seemed much disappointed when, after 14 days, the Doctor reported I was quite well."

The *Plumper* was stationed for a while at the mouth of the Congo and also at Saint Paul de Louanda. Now spelled Luanda and the capital of Angola, Louanda, at the time of Hankin's visit, was one of the largest cities in the Portuguese Empire. Technically, the slave trade was illegal there but the laws were not enforced with any noticeable diligence or enthusiasm.

Hankin wrote that here he met the explorer David Livingstone, who was about to start on his journey across Africa to Quelimane on the Indian Ocean. This journey, which was to make Livingstone world famous, was allegedly the first made by a white man across Africa. During this journey he reached, and named, Victoria Falls and tracked the Zambezi River for most of its course.

Livingstone invited Hankin to go with him. He jumped at the opportunity and was anxious to accept. He begged Haswell for permission but Haswell would not let him go. So he had to abandon his hopes for this journey, which he had found so alluring. A biographer of Livingstone wrote, "While Livingstone was at Louanda, he made several acquaintances among the officers of Her Majesty's navy, engaged in the suppression of the slave trade. For many of these gentlemen, he was led to entertain a high regard. Their humanity charmed him, and so did their attention to their duties. In his early days, sharing the feeling then so prevalent in his class, he had been used to think of epauletted gentlemen as idlers, or worse. ... Personal acquaintance, as in so many other cases, rubbed off the prejudice."[58] Here perhaps we see Hankin's charm at work.

In November 1855, the *Plumper* finally had some success when it captured a slave ship off Cabinda, freeing ninety slaves, whom they sent to Saint Helena.[59] The *Plumper* went to Saint Helena for a fortnight. This, Hankin said, was a delightful change after the heat and discomfort of the African coast. While on the island, he visited Napoleon's tomb. (Napoleon's body was not taken to Paris for reinterment in Les Invalides until 1861.)

Hankin stayed at a farmhouse on the top of a hill, where it was delightfully cool. This farm was owned by a Mr. Evans, who kept two or three cows. He had a nice vegetable garden and made a living from that. Lena, one of Evans's two daughters, gave Hankin a present of two pounds of nicely packed butter, which she asked him to take back to the ship. Perhaps there had been a romantic dalliance, at least on his part. He thanked her and imagined it was a token of love and affection. He was undeceived when a boat came alongside the *Plumper* soon after he was back on board with a highly scented note, which read, "Dear Mr. Hankin, I must write you a few lines before you leave to say how much I miss you, but I hope we shall meet again some day, and with Love and Kisses, I am always your loving Lena. P.S. Please don't forget to pay for the butter, 2 lbs [£] 4 shillings."

So much for romance, Hankin might have thought. "So I sent the money by the boatman," he wrote in his memoirs, "and I have never heard a word since from my loving Lena, and as that is now 59 years ago I don't suppose I ever shall."

The *Plumper* had been away from England for three years when, at last, orders arrived for it to return home. From Saint Helena they sailed to Ascension and from there, after having taken on board a supply of turtles, they sailed for England. They arrived at Portsmouth on November 30, 1856, after a twenty-one-day voyage.[60] "I shall never forget the bitter cold we experienced in a heavy gale off the Isle of Wight," Hankin wrote. "I had the middle watch to keep and only white trousers to wear and a Purser's Monkey jacket."

Safely anchored at Spithead, the *Plumper* was soon surrounded by boats, and the bumboat women, as they were called, climbed on board to sell their bread and butter, cold fried fish, smoked bloaters and other good things. "What a treat it all was," Hankin wrote, "after our miserable fare on the Coast of Africa, to taste good English bread and butter again." After the port admiral had inspected the ship, the crew, including Hankin, were paid off. The Admiralty sent the *Plumper* to the dockyards to be refitted for its next voyage with a chart room on its deck.

Hankin now had his examinations for lieutenant to pass. The first one, in seamanship, he passed creditably, with a first-class certificate, but he had two more to face, which he dreaded. He studied and trained on board HMS *Excellent*, at anchor in Portsmouth. One examination was in navigation at the Royal Naval College in the dockyard at Portsmouth. He got through this without much difficulty, obtaining a second-class certificate. The other was in gunnery.

While studying, he lived in lodgings in Portsmouth. These rooms were close to the Hard at Portsea, just outside the dockyard gates. (The Hard is believed to have acquired its name after a slipway for boats. Men created a slipway by dumping clay in the sea at low tide, then rolling it till it was hard.) His landlords here were Mr. Stone, a local tailor, and his wife.

The Stones used to take in boarders, all young naval officers who, like Hankin, were working for their lieutenant's certificates on the *Excellent*. The aspiring lieutenants used to go on board ship every day at ten o'clock and work at gun drill until three in the afternoon. Mrs. Stone, Hankin recalled, was very short and stout, and each lodger paid her two guineas for board. They all took their meals together with the Stone family, which, she said, "made it more 'ome-like." They always had herrings and coffee for breakfast, and dinner was served at four o'clock, when they arrived back from the *Excellent*. For supper, she usually gave them boiled rabbits with onion sauce, with a milk or suet pudding. It was certainly better, Hankin said, than the food in the midshipmen's mess.

Mr. Stone was very religious and always wore a frock coat and white necktie like a clergyman. He and Mrs. Stone had two daughters, Tilly, who married one of the naval lodgers, and Dora. "Dora was a little fat girl, about 12," Hankin recollected, "with rosy cheeks, and wore her hair in ringlets. She always stood on a chair to say Grace after dinner, making a little curtsey as she said Amen!"

———————

One young naval officer lodging with the Stones was someone who would change the course of Hankin's life completely. Hankin wrote:

> There was living at this time at Stones an officer named [Daniel] Pender, a very pleasant bright young fellow, and he and I soon became great friends.[61] And he told me he had just been appointed to the *Plumper*, my old ship, as an Assistant Surveyor, and they were now fitting out for Vancouver Island to decide the 49th parallel of Latitude, being the boundary line between British and American

territory, and also to survey the coast of Vancouver Island, which would take some years to complete.

Then he added, why don't you come with us? It would be a very jolly trip for you, and I know the captain, Richards,[62] very well and, if you like, I will speak to him about you. I'm sure he will be pleased to have you with him, and he is a very nice man. The next day, when I saw Pender, he said—"Oh, I have spoken to Captain Richards about you, and he told me he could not apply for you himself as you are not a surveyor, but if you can manage to get appointed, he will be very pleased."

This, I found out afterwards, was just a tarradiddle on Pender's part. Pender had spoken to the captain, it is true, but when he heard I knew nothing about surveying he told Pender he would not have me on any account.

Of course, I thought it was just the other way, so wrote immediately to Mr. Clifton at the Admiralty, saying Captain Richards had expressed a wish for me to join the Plumper, and asking him to try to get me appointed, which to my great delight and to Pender's dismay, he succeeded in doing.

It all happened very fast. His passing the lieutenant's examinations was announced on March 14, 1857.[63] His appointment to HMS Plumper was announced in the newspapers on March 16 (here he is called P.J. Harbin).[64] Since the Plumper was to sail—and did sail—for Vancouver's Island, as it was still called, on March 16, Hankin had to hurry on board to report.[65] He expected a warm welcome. In this he was much disappointed. Captain Richards was surprised at his appearance on board his ship and not at all welcoming. He asked "how the devil" Hankin had managed to get appointed, not being a surveyor. Then Pender confessed. He had not thought it possible that Hankin could get appointed and had merely told him what he thought he wanted to hear, not knowing that Hankin would call his bluff. With hours to go before departure and needing a sub-lieutenant, Richards had to accept the *fait accompli*, which he did with grace.

George Henry Richards had been second-in-command of the 1852 expedition to the Arctic searching for the lost explorer Sir John Franklin.

Philip Hankin as a young man, in approximately 1857. Image G-00361 courtesy of the Royal BC Museum and Archives

He was an excellent surveyor and, as a result of his surveying work around the coasts, should be considered one of the most significant people in British Columbia's early history. The *Plumper*'s officers included men whose names would become familiar on maps of the coast: Pender, Bedwell, Mayne and Hankin himself.[66] In 1862 Richard Mayne published his own memoir about his experiences on Vancouver Island.[67]

Richards soon got over his annoyance at Hankin's appointment and they all became good friends. Hankin liked people and seemed to have an ability to make people like him. "Captain Richards," he wrote, "was a splendid fellow, and a universal favorite with all. He was a fine Navigator, a splendid Surveyor and a very clever man, but most eccentric. He had a way of putting his hand with outspread fingers thro' his hair and making it all stand straight on end, which gave him a most comical appearance. He was one of the best, and kindest men, who ever lived. We all got on so well together, and the *Plumper* was decidedly a happy ship and very different to her last commission, the miserable three years I spent in her with Haswell, on the coast of Africa."

The next morning, the *Plumper* left Plymouth Sound under sail and headed for Lisbon, where they stayed for four days. Hankin had time to make a pleasant sightseeing jaunt to Cintra, a historic old town now known as Sintra. Then they departed for Rio de Janeiro. Soon after they left the Tagus River, the *Plumper*'s propeller shaft broke. No matter. The *Plumper* was a better sailer than steamer, and so they continued under sail. Hankin soon felt quite at home again. Having passed all his examinations and now a full-fledged mate, he was given charge of a watch.

On May 25, they anchored in Rio de Janeiro's harbour, which Hankin said he always thought was one of the most beautiful in the world. Here they repaired the propeller shaft but it took two months and they had the hardship of waiting in Rio for that time. In July, they resumed their voyage to Vancouver Island. "We steamed out of Rio harbour, found the new shaft worked well, lifted up the Screw and made sail for the Straits of Magelhan [Magellan] thro' which we intended to steam through on our way to Valparaiso."

They entered the Straits of Magellan early one morning and anchored off Port Famine. Some Fuegians came alongside the ship in a small canoe, "a man, two women and a child, and very dirty and filthy looking they were and nearly naked, with a skin of some wild animal wrapped around the loins," Hankin wrote. "We gave them some biscuit, for they looked half-starved, and a few matches, which they eagerly took. They had a scrap of fire in the canoe, which they never allowed to go out." Captain Richards took pity on one of the most miserable-looking women and gave her a pair of warm knitted socks as he said the poor creature's feet must be frozen by the bitterly cold weather. She gladly accepted the socks but Hankin doubted if she had ever seen a pair before in her life, for instead of putting them on her feet, she took two empty beer bottles, which she had in the canoe, and put one into each sock.

Bad weather slowed their passage and they did not leave the straits until the end of July. As soon as they were clear of land, they hoisted

Captain George Henry Richards, Royal Navy, the captain of HMS *Plumper* and HMS *Hecate*. He surveyed the coasts of Vancouver Island and the mainland before being appointed hydrographer to the Royal Navy. Image A-03352 courtesy of the Royal BC Museum and Archives

up the screw, raised the sails and continued under sail to Valparaíso, their next port of call. They arrived on August 28, after a difficult ten-day passage, the wind being against them.[68] After ten days there, during which Hankin and Mayne visited Santiago, ninety miles away, they set sail for the Sandwich Islands (Hawaii), then still an independent kingdom. "We had a glorious passage, got into trade winds, weather simply perfect, and studding sails set, always going from 7 to 8 knots, and for 3 weeks we triced [hoisted and secured] the ropes up and painted ship," Hankin wrote.

The *Plumper* arrived in Honolulu on October 16.[69] Captain Richards landed and called on William Synge, the British consul general, who was, Hankin recalled, a pleasant man with a charming American wife, a lady from Washington. The next day Richards was presented to King Kamehameha IV and arranged with Mr. Synge that on the following day as many of the officers as could be spared should also be presented.[70] At eleven o'clock, the chosen officers all landed in full uniform and went to the palace. Here Richards and these officers, Hankin, Mayne and Pender, had an audience with the king. Hankin wrote:

> His Majesty was very dark but a good-looking man with the man-
> ners of an English gentleman. He shook hands with us all with a
> few words of welcome, speaking in perfect English, after which we
> returned on board. The Queen, "Queen Emma," was not so dark as
> the King, and very good looking, with the most beautiful dark eyes
> and black hair. She had English blood in her veins for her father
> was a Dr. Rook, and her mother was an Hawaian princess. She had
> been very well educated by the Missionaries at Honolulu and spoke
> perfect English, and had charming manners. She once passed a
> week at Windsor Castle with Her Majesty, Queen Victoria.

Richard Mayne wrote that the king was "essentially English in his habits, dress, the fashion of his residence and in his system of government, which is enlightened and progressive. ... He speaks English and French fluently."[71]

The king invited Captain Richards to spend a few days at his country palace, about ten miles from Honolulu, and asked him to bring one officer with him. Richards chose Hankin. Of this visit, Hankin wrote:

We had a delightful time. There were plenty of horses at our disposal and we used to take long rides in the Country. The Palace was very handsomely furnished and everything was done in very good style. There were two English footmen in very smart liveries waiting at table. One stood behind the King's Chair and one behind the Queen's. There were also several smart looking young Natives, in a neat dark livery with black stockings, knee breeches and smart steel buckles. The dinner was excellent and plenty of good champagne. The Queen came in a very handsome evening dress to dinner with some beautiful jewellery, and I thought looked remarkably well.

Captain Richards told the Queen I was an excellent cook, and that I could make a delicious curry. Her Majesty laughed and said she was very fond of a good curry. So I asked if I might be allowed to go the next day into the kitchens and make a curry for dinner. The Queen seemed much amused and said, oh certainly, it was very kind of me and she would very much enjoy tasting one of my Curries. The next day the Curry was made and was much appreciated. I expect I may safely say that I am the only English Naval Officer who has ever made Curry for the Queen of the Sandwich Islands.

The *Plumper's* officers persuaded Prince Lot, the king's brother, to take them to a local feast and see a "Hula-hula, or native dance." Hankin noted that this dance was fast dying out since the introduction of the quadrille and champagne to the island. They all went there on horseback. He recalled that the ladies rode astride their horses like men but, "with long flowing habits made of gaily-coloured Cotton... and lovely wreaths of orange blossom and sweet-scented flowers twisted in their hair," they still looked very feminine. He described the scene: "The entertainment was held at a lovely spot, about ten miles from Honolulu. We all sat on the ground on mats and the dishes handed round by native servants. It was, I remember, an excellent dinner, but there were some rather curious dishes. One especially I recollect was roast puppy dog, which was considered a very great delicacy." These dogs, bred for the table, were never fed meat. The officers also feasted on "loo-ou" and poi. Hankin wrote, "The natives are all particularly fond of [the poi]... but I thought it tasted like sour paste." The good champagne was more to his liking.

After dinner a dozen dancing girls entertained them for an hour. "Their dances," Hankin wrote primly, "may be considered by some people not quite correct but certainly better than the tango."[72] The tango, he said, seemed to be designed to show as much leg as possible. His comparison of the hula-hula to the tango suggests that he had not spent all his time in Rio de Janeiro supervising repairs to the *Plumper*'s propeller shaft.

On October 23, 1857, the *Plumper* left the Sandwich Islands and set sail for the naval base of Esquimalt, at the southern tip of Vancouver Island. Here they were to join HMS *Satellite* in surveying the coast. Mayne wrote, "Sailed from Honolulu this day and on the 9th November entered the Strait of Juan de Fuca, which divides Vancouver Island from the mainland of the American continent. In making the Strait of Fuca, should the weather be clear enough for the navigator to see the Flattery Rocks, he will at once know his position. ... In fair weather the entrance to the Strait is plainly visible from them."[73]

As Vancouver Island became visible, Hankin had his first sight of the land that was to become so meaningful for him. Little did he know what surprises, challenges and opportunities were waiting for him there.

4

From Vancouver Island to the Mediterranean and Then Back

1857–1861

H MS *Plumper* arrived in Esquimalt on November 10, 1857. After the long journey from England, the officers and crew no doubt welcomed the sight of the rocky islands and deeply wooded shores of Vancouver Island. Hankin wrote in his memoirs:

> It was, I remember, a lovely Autumn day... when we anchored at Esquimalt, and found the *Satellite* there. She had been expecting us for a long time, not knowing that we had broken our shaft after leaving Lisbon and been detained two months at Rio. As we steamed into Esquimalt Harbor, the *Satellite*'s band played "Where Have You Been All Day?" I thought Esquimalt one of the prettiest places I had ever seen. The Maple trees were just getting their Autumn tints and a few little cottages with pretty English gardens were dotted here, and there, along the shores of the bay.

Hankin's colleague, Lieutenant Richard Mayne, wrote that the crew of the *Satellite* received them with rousing cheers. Mayne had visited Vancouver Island nine years before, during the Crimean War, when Esquimalt was being established as a supply port. "I was surprised," he wrote, "to catch sight of a row of respectable, well-kept buildings on the southeast point of the harbour's mouth, with pleasant grounds in front

Photograph of a painting by Lieutenant Bedwell of HMS *Plumper* at Discovery Island, with Mount Baker in the distance. Image A-00238 courtesy of the Royal BC Museum and Archives

of them. ... This was, we found, a Naval Hospital, erected in 1854, when we were at war with Russia, to receive the wounded from Petropaulovski [Petropavlovsk], and since that time continued in use."[74]

At this time the naval base of Esquimalt and the Hudson's Bay Company fort at Victoria were two small, separate communities located at the southern tip of Vancouver Island. Both had good harbours but Mayne wrote that Esquimalt Harbour was far better than the one at Victoria. "The entrance to Victoria," he said, "is narrow, shoal and intricate; and with certain winds a heavy sea sets on the coast, which renders the anchorage outside unsafe, while vessels of burden cannot run inside for shelter unless at or near high water. ... Ships of larger tonnage must always prefer Esquimalt."[75] Then, as now, the majestic mountains of the Olympic Peninsula in the United States across the Juan de Fuca Strait formed a snow-covered backdrop.

The *Plumper* arrived at Vancouver Island before the rush to find gold in the Fraser River changed everything. Hankin's and Mayne's accounts

View of Esquimalt, Vancouver Island, July 1858, engraved from art by Charles Christian Nahl (1818–1872). Image PDP00262 courtesy of the Royal BC Museum and Archives

of Victoria and Esquimalt therefore have a quaint "before the deluge" feel about them. They described a small, quiet English community where everyone knew each other.

Victoria was a Hudson's Bay Company post, still called Fort Victoria. The Company's fort stood roughly where Fort and Government Streets now meet. It was a compound built in the usual Hudson's Bay Company fashion, with palisades, a bastion or two, and large buildings inside. The houses of James Douglas, the chief factor and also governor of the Colony of Vancouver Island, and Dr. John Helmcken were a little to the south, approximately where the provincial museum now stands. (Dr. Helmcken's house is still standing.) Across the bay were numerous settlements of the Songhees Indigenous People. One large village lay on the point jutting out into Victoria Harbour. There was no road from Victoria to Esquimalt in those days, merely an Indigenous trail through the forests connecting the two communities. This was an hour's walk, more if you dallied to admire the view. Mayne noted that men walking back to Esquimalt occasionally lost their way and had to sleep in the bush all night.[76]

Hankin recalled that the Hudson's Bay Company managers were James Douglas, Joseph Pemberton, Benjamin Pearse, Dr. John Helmcken (who married Douglas's daughter Cecilia in 1852), William Tolmie, John Wark (or Work), Roderick Finlayson and Joseph McKay. Most of the managers were married and had large families. Helmcken, ten years older than Hankin, had already been living in the colony for some years. In 1856, he had been elected to the Legislative Assembly of Vancouver Island and he served as its first Speaker for ten years. He was later active in the involved politics of the union with the mainland Colony of British Columbia and then, later, the union with Canada. Rev. Edward Cridge, who several years later officiated at Hankin's marriage, was the chaplain to the Hudson's Bay Company.[77]

The Hudson's Bay Company managers, Hankin wrote, generally dined together at one o'clock in the fort's mess, with Douglas taking the head of the table. Mulling the business of the day, Douglas would often order that a bottle of sherry be opened as well as the Company's rum. The dinner was generally salmon, mutton and potatoes, with a plain pudding afterwards, "and very good it all was," he said.

One of the topics of their conversation would have been the presence of gold on the mainland, in British territory north of the border with the United States. As early as April 1856, Douglas had alerted the Colonial Office in London of the discovery of gold within British territory on the upper Columbia. And news was coming in of discoveries of gold on the Fraser River. What did these discoveries on the Fraser portend? The Hudson's Bay Company had always viewed the discovery of gold on its lands as a threat to its trading monopoly, with a consequent loss of profits. Although temperamentally wanting to keep the American gold seekers out, Douglas was practical enough to know that when the news became widely known, it would be impossible to prevent them from flooding in. But he would not make it easy for them and he raised all manner of barriers, including the need for licences and taxes.

Hankin recalled John Wark, the veteran chief factor in the Hudson's Bay Company service.[78] He had joined the Company in 1814. "He was an old man, about 70 at that time," Hankin wrote, "and his Wife had a charming family consisting of two sons and 6 or 7 daughters, all very agreeable and very good-looking girls. They lived at a place called Hillside

Fort Victoria. The captions read, left to right: "Officers' Mess Room & Church on Sundays"; "Lands & Works Office & our quarters from 1857 till 1859"; "Gate on Gov't. St. & leading up Fort St."; and "Chaplain's Quarters (Messrs. Staines & Cridge)." Image I-68037 courtesy of the Royal BC Museum and Archives

and many happy evenings have I spent there. Nothing could exceed their kindness and hospitality, and Naval officers were constantly there, and we generally managed to get up a dance."

Judge David Cameron and his wife, with their two daughters, lived at Belmont, close to the entrance to the harbour. The Skinners lived across the bay, with their large family of boys and girls. They too were most kind and hospitable and gave a generous welcome to the young officers. Hankin said he spent many pleasant evenings at their houses. Then there were the Langfords, an English family who lived at a nice farm at

Colwood, about seven miles from Victoria. One of their daughters married a Captain Jocelyn of the navy and another married John Bull, the senior surveyor of the *Plumper*.

This hospitality and conviviality was all very well, but Captain George Henry Richards had work to do. His first job was to establish the boundary line between the colony and the United States and to ascertain where it touched the coast. To this end he took the *Plumper* to Boundary Bay. The American surveyors had already arrived and made their assessments of the line of the forty-ninth parallel on the ground. Richards proceeded to make his own assessment. When the two surveying teams compared their calculations, they found there was only an eight-foot difference between them.[79] Richards directed Hankin to take a party from the ship to build an obelisk to mark the line where it reached the coast.[80]

On December 16, 1857, the *Plumper*, its mission accomplished, returned to Esquimalt. The crew moored the ship, both head and stern, sloped the awnings and made all snug. Since they could do no surveying during the winter, there was little to occupy them but to keep the ship clean and enjoy themselves. Young dashing naval officers were always welcome and made much of in a society where there appears to have been a surfeit of unmarried young ladies.

The two communities of Victoria and Esquimalt were so small that Hankin claimed he knew everyone. Approximately two hundred people lived in them and in the surrounding farms. He could certainly remember all the young ladies on the island at that time—two Miss Camerons, three Miss Langfords, two Miss McNeils, four Miss Warks, two Miss Douglases, two Miss Reids and three Miss MacKenzies. There were also several young married ladies who were always ready for a dance. And there were, Hankin wrote, "the papas and mamas who, if they did not dance, enjoyed the supper, and chaperoned their daughters. We managed to get a party altogether of about 40. It was very cold weather, but we were all young and kept warm by dancing."

They had many dances at the settlers' houses and thought nothing of walking there and back, four or five miles and often through deep snow, with top boots on and carrying their dancing shoes in their pockets, with the ladies doing the same. It was not uncommon for one or other of them to fall into a snowdrift, sometimes up to their hips. Hankin recalled one occasion, while he was coming home from a ball, when Anna Maria Tuso, a pleasant girl of about thirty, he said, with her mother chaperoning her, fell into the snow up to her neck in a deep ditch. As everyone laughed, Mrs. Tuso called out, "Oh, pull her out, pull her out," which, amid laughter, they did. Anna Maria was, happily, none the worse for her experience.

The naval officers reciprocated the hospitality given them by holding dances on board the *Plumper*. They always started to dance at 8:00 p.m., Hankin said, and kept the ball rolling till 3:00 a.m. By the time all the guests had left the ship, it was usually past 4:00 a.m. He recalled the Ross sisters. They were, he wrote, fine-looking girls with large black eyes and black hair and a good deal of Indigenous blood. They lived about ten miles from Esquimalt but could not refuse an invitation to a dance. They always came on horseback with their ball dresses fastened behind their saddles in a large bundle. They tied their horses up to some trees and changed their dresses in the bush. Then they would paddle out to the ship looking extremely smart.

The sailors also enjoyed themselves. On New Year's Day, 1858, the crew of the *Satellite* invited the crew of the *Plumper* to a feast on board. One of the *Satellite's* crew wrote:

> Two hundred and seventy sat down to dinner. We had all the ship to ourselves that day—the quarter deck for dancing. The table reached from end to end of the ship; any person could invite one or two friends, and we kept it up till ten at night. The whole affair went off in first-rate style—our men were allowed 1 quart of ale and a glass of grog each. ... It took us three days to decorate the ship; the quarter-deck was fitted out like a splendid ball-room, with flags of all nations. The gangways were covered with green boughs, with an entrance over the starboard gangway like a pleasant bower. ... We also had a public house, the Satellite Hotel, with a drawing of a Beehive, and this inscription:

Within this Hive we're all alive
Good liquor makes us funny.
If you are dry, step in and try
The flavours of our Honey.

Myself and the Quartermaster acted as landlords, and a pretty job we had of it, I can tell you. For seven hours, we were hard at serving our customers.[81]

The officers, it appears, were respectfully requested to stay away.

Though at the time obviously no one knew it, that winter was the last one for "old Victoria." Soon everything would change.

When better weather returned in mid-February, the officers and crew prepared the *Plumper* for the coming spring and summer of surveying. But first they went to collect their mail. Because there was no mail delivery at Victoria, it not being important enough, the officers used to go to Port Townsend in the United States once a month to collect their mail.

They also visited the small village of Seattle and San Juan Island. As a result of an ambiguity in the 1846 treaty that established the boundary line between American and British territories, there was a dispute about whether the island was British or American. This led to the famous Pig War that started in 1859 when an American named Lyman Cutler shot a Hudson's Bay Company pig that was rooting in his potato patch. After a short period of warlike bristling and growling, both sides settled down to amicable coexistence while the problem was being sorted out. In 1872, an arbitration commission, appointed by Kaiser Wilhelm I of Germany, awarded the island to the United States. Famous people were involved in this war that had no casualty other than one pig. General Henry Robert of *Robert's Rules of Order* fame and General George Pickett, who achieved fame in the American Civil War, were both stationed on the island.

Richards's primary task was to survey the coast. In this he was assisted by John Bull, the chief surveyor, and other surveyors on board.

By now, Hankin had learned enough surveying to be useful. After bad weather in late February and early March, they started their work in earnest on March 16, 1858. They soon found that the *Plumper* was not powerful enough to get through the three-mile-long Seymour Narrows between the mainland and Vancouver Island. On account of the strong currents there, Captain George Vancouver many years before had reportedly called it one of the vilest stretches of water in the world.[82] This was a serious impediment to their surveying work.

The tranquility of Victoria was shattered in April 1858. News that gold had been discovered on the Fraser River in attractive quantities had reached California. "By the time of the Fraser River Rush, San Francisco alone claimed to have more newspapers than London," Daniel Marshall writes in *Claiming the Land*, "and, as a consequence, along with the wire service and the mobility of gold seekers that was enhanced by steamboats, news of gold discoveries travelled quickly."[83] Gold fever, once caught, is contagious. Men—and undoubtedly some women—hurried north from California to the Fraser River as fast, it seemed, as they could. Many weren't sure where the Fraser River was, it was said, or how to get there when they reached Victoria. Everyone, however, knew that the first prospectors to arrive at the site of a new discovery would always be the most successful. Hence the scramble. The rush to the Fraser River had begun.

An article in *Harper's New Monthly Magazine* in 1860 described the excitement in the United States:

> A faint cry was heard from afar—first low and uncertain, like a mysterious whisper, then full and sonorous, like the boom of glad tidings from the mouth of a cannon, the inspiring cry of Frazer River! Here was the gold sure enough!—a river of gold!—a country that dazzled the eyes with its glitter of gold. There was no deception about it this time. New Caledonia was the land of Ophir. True, it was in the British possessions, but what of that? The people of California would develop the British possessions. Had our claim to

54°40' been insisted upon, this immense treasure would now have been within our boundaries; but no matter—it was ours by right of proximity![84]

On April 25, 1858, the SS *Commodore* arrived in Victoria from San Francisco with approximately 440 eager prospectors on board. The ship's captain was Jeremiah Nagle, destined to be Hankin's father-in-law. Margaret Ormsby, the pre-eminent historian of British Columbia, described the *Commodore's* arrival:

> The townspeople were just leaving church to return to their white-washed cottages when she entered Victoria harbour on Sunday morning, April 25, 1858. From their position on the hillside, they could see that her decks were crowded: with surprise and fascination they watched her approach the landing-place, make fast, and then disembark a stream of men, most of them wearing red flannel shirts and carrying packs containing blankets, miners' wash-pans, spades and firearms.[85]

That approximately 400 of them soon left Victoria in a hurry to go to the Fraser River—and it was not an easy journey—did not matter. The *Commodore* was followed by the *Golden State*, then the *Constitution* and then more ships. On May 8—only three weeks after the *Commodore* had docked—Governor Douglas estimated that 1,000 prospectors were already on the Fraser. Between May 15 and June 1, 10,000 men started up the Fraser River, and before the year was out, the figure had swelled to 25,000.[86]

As Victoria became more crowded, it became no longer agreeably English. Almost overnight it changed from a small, sleepy village into a bustling port with strong business connections to San Francisco. Within six weeks 225 new buildings had been erected, 200 of them being stores. Land prices jumped. An American company started a newspaper, the *Victoria Gazette*. New people were arriving, people with strange accents and strange ways, people who had little regard for the law of the land they thought was either American or soon would be, and certainly should be.

View of Victoria, Vancouver Island, July 1858. The Hudson's Bay Company fort, still with its stockade, is in the centre. The description reads, "The picture is taken from Deadman's Point, nearly south-west from the town. At its right is an arm of the estuary entitled James' Bay, on the south side of which may be seen the Governor's residence. The thorough-fare running along the northern bank of this inlet is known as Kanaka Road (now named Humboldt Street)" (*Victoria Gazette*, August 28, 1858, page 1). The sketch was made by F.W. Green of Lammot, Freeman & Green and was copied on wood by C. Nahl and engraved by S.F. Baker, both of San Francisco.

They came from goldfields in California where violence was accepted as a natural and efficient way to settle disputes. "Most of them were armed with bowie knives and revolvers," Ormsby wrote of them.[87] And they had experience using them. Among the *Commodore*'s passengers were also many French, German and Italian people. Added to those were thirty-five Black people from the United States, seeking refuge from slavery and the coming civil war.

Gold fever seemed to infect everyone. Captain Richards of the *Plumper* and Captain James Prevost of the *Satellite* became very worried that their crews would desert and join the Americans on the Fraser. Indeed, Prevost wrote that he had already lost twenty men.[88] They asked for and were granted permission to increase their crews' wages to stem the losses.

Despite his fears about a rabble of Americans with no respect for British law and order at all, Governor Douglas found that some of the arrivals who remained in Victoria were law-abiding, churchgoing men. Somewhat to his surprise, he changed his opinions, but only a little. He was alarmed by the possibility that scofflaw Americans might prompt annexation by the United States. He did everything in his power to keep the supply lines down the Fraser River to Victoria and away from the Columbia River, which flowed into the United States. Extending the long arm of British law formally over land where the Hudson's Bay Company had long informally held sway, the British government established the Colony of British Columbia on the mainland, with Douglas as its first governor. It was originally to be named New Caledonia but because there already was a New Caledonia, Queen Victoria decided it should be called British Columbia. Douglas imported policemen from Ireland and promulgated new mining regulations. Judge Matthew Begbie arrived to adjudicate the law in his inimitable way. Soon Colonel Richard Moody would arrive as lieutenant-governor and, with the force of Royal Engineers he brought with him, start the work of road building.

While these dramatic events were happening in Victoria and on the Fraser River, Hankin would have been on the *Plumper*, perhaps surveying the islands and inlets on the west coast of Vancouver Island. Doubtless he would have been aware of the changes but not, manifestly, of what they meant for his future.

At this point, Hankin's life took another turn. On June 5, 1858, his promotion to lieutenant was formally confirmed.[89] Although he would have liked to have remained with his shipmates on the *Plumper*, the Admiralty ordered him to return to England for reassignment forthwith. He wrote:

In April [1858] we left Esquimalt and visited San Juan Island and New Westminster, then only a very small village on the Fraser River, Cowichan and Barclay Sound and in October returned to Esquimalt, where I found my promotion to the rank of lieutenant, with orders to return to England at once. I was glad, of course, to get promoted but very sorry to be obliged to return to England, for I had been so happy with Captain Richards in the *Plumper*. And he had taught me surveying and made me his personal assistant, and I was often with him in his boat for two or three weeks at a time.

At night we used to anchor the boat in some snug little cove, the men slept on board, and Richards and I had two little tents on shore. He said I was a first rate cook and I always took care that we had a good supper at night. I generally made him a fish curry, of which he was particularly fond, and boiled potatoes which we could often buy from the Indians.

Admiralty orders could not be disobeyed. Hankin said farewell to Richards and his messmates with sincere regret. Richards told him he was going to apply for a larger ship that would be powerful enough to steam through the Seymour Narrows. He promised Hankin he would write to the Admiralty and ask for him to be sent out in it.

———

Hankin took the mail steamer to San Francisco and from there went on an American ship to Panama. He then crossed the isthmus by rail to Aspinwall, as Colón was called at the time.[90]

This railway line crossed the forty-seven miles of the Isthmus of Panama, halving the twenty-thousand-mile sea voyage from Victoria around Cape Horn to Southampton. The four-hour crossing, costing five pounds, was through dense and unhealthy forests. John Emmerson was one starry-eyed prospector who came from England in 1862 to pick up gold from the rivers and make his fortune. "A few miles of the line from Aspinwall runs through a swamp," he wrote. "The rest lies through deep cuttings and over embankments, with very many sharp curves and iron bridges. At intervals of four miles, there are neat and elegant wooden buildings, beautifully painted and ornamented, each with a sweetly pretty flower garden attached."[91] These were the houses of the managers. Admitting it may have been a slight exaggeration, Emmerson recounted that as many workers died from yellow and other fevers when building the railway as there were sleepers under the rails—about twenty thousand.

From Aspinwall, Hankin took the West India Mail steamship to Southampton. When he reached England, he found that his father and his new wife, Jane Elizabeth Reay, were now living at Pertenhall, in

Bedfordshire. Hankin went home for a few days. Within a week of his arrival, his father was fidgeting and continually asking him when he was going to sea again.

Hankin applied to the navy for another commission. On May 11, 1859, the Admiralty appointed him to HMS *Cadmus*, an eighteen-gun screw corvette, commanded by Captain Henry Hillyar, soon to leave for the Mediterranean.[92] (The newspapers, improving their spelling of his name, now listed him as T.J. Hankin.) The first lieutenant, Hankin said, was a pleasant man named De Kantzow, who later became an admiral. The clergyman on board was Rev. Henry Jones, with whom Hankin had served on board the *Castor* in the Indian Ocean and who had once banged his head with a prayer book. After a refit, the *Cadmus* left Portsmouth on June 22.[93]

The *Cadmus* cruised in the Mediterranean for eight months, generally under sail. It visited most of the naval stations there, including Gibraltar, Malta and Naples. The admiral on the station was Sir Arthur Fanshawe, and his flagship was the *Duke of Wellington*, a three-decker. Hankin said that when it was under full sail, the flagship was a fine sight, but it was soon to be a romantic picture of the past. The days of the Royal Navy under sail were fast coming to an end.

Hankin recalled one proud night at sea. He was officer of the watch. The whole squadron was under sail, going from Gibraltar to Malta. A signal was made to the *Cadmus* to take up her position on the admiral's bow. "It was the middle watch and a dark night," Hankin wrote, "but I put the helm up and wore round and took up my position as indicated by signal, and a signal was made from the flagship—'Well done, *Cadmus*, position very well taken up.' I felt very proud indeed, tho' the captain didn't even trouble to come on deck."

On one of the ship's visits to Gibraltar, Hankin joined the Freemasons. This was the Gibraltar Lodge of Friendship 325, now the Royal Lodge of Friendship 278. One of the oldest lodges in the world, it can trace its history back to before 1788. It has a strong connection with the military and boasts of four members who have won Victoria Crosses. He also attended the Lodge of Saint John and Saint Paul in Malta. Although his friend Daniel Pender and several other naval officers were active Masons in Victoria, Hankin does not appear to have been active when he was living there a few years later.

Throughout his service on the *Cadmus*, Hankin kept the memory of Vancouver Island alive in his mind. He had been happy there and formed the determination to go back. He began to think, though, that Captain Richards had forgotten all about his promise to ask for him for his new vessel. He wrote:

At last, I made up my mind that I would leave the Service, and so get out to Vancouver [Island]. I sent in a letter which had to go through the admiral requesting my discharge from the navy. The Admiral was so surprised that he thought I was out of my mind and made a signal for me to go on board the Flagship, which, of course, I did at once when he sent for me into his Cabin, and asked me what on earth I wanted to leave the Navy for! I told him I had no interest and promotion was very slow and I thought I could do better if I were to emigrate and go to San Francisco. "And pray, Sir, what do you propose doing when you get there?"

"Well, Sir," I replied, "I am young and don't mind hard work. I could get a situation as a waiter at once in one of the large hotels there, and with tips I could make 200 dollars a month, food included."

"What," said the admiral, "give up your position as a Lieutenant in the Navy and become a waiter? You must be mad. I will take you out of the *Cadmus* and appoint you as 4th lieutenant of the *Orion*, a fine vessel of 90 Guns and just going to Naples, and don't think anything more about such nonsense as becoming a waiter." It was very kind of the Admiral. So I thanked him and said, I would give up the idea, at present, of becoming a waiter and would join the *Orion* as he suggested.

Hankin then moved to the *Orion*, a "magnificent" screw-assisted two-decker under the command of Captain John Frere. "I remember he was a great Homeopathist, in which he believed implicitly," Hankin wrote, "and I thought it advisable to have some imaginary complaint, and become a Homeopathist also. So I bought a regular little chest of all kinds of Medicine—Pulsatilla, Belladonna, Nux Vomica, Aconite and many other little bottles. They all looked like little sugar plums. And they tasted so sweet, and pleasant, I found myself constantly eating them." Captain Frere, whom Hankin described as an extremely nice man, imagined he had found a soulmate and eagerly sought out Hankin to discuss his passion. More than once while on duty on watch, Hankin told Frere he had a pain in his stomach and needed to go below to take some pulsatilla. "Yes, do go... I dare say it will do you good," Frere would say, telling him to take his time. Then, while the kind but gullible captain stood on watch for him, Hankin would go below to drop a little pulsatilla into a bottle of pale ale, returning to deck half an hour later, maintaining, truthfully but perhaps not honestly, that he had taken the pulsatilla and was feeling much better. The captain would then return to his cabin, saying, "Well, good night, Hankin. There is nothing like Homeopathy."

In April 1860, on a journey from Malta to Naples, the *Orion* sprang a serious leak. The hold filled with four feet of water. Since the operation of the machinery in the boiler room only made matters worse, the ship was ordered to proceed under canvas to Plymouth for repairs.[94] It arrived on May 17 and the crew was paid off. Hankin then went home to his father.

When he arrived home he found, to his great delight, a letter from Captain Richards informing him he had applied for a more powerful vessel to be sent to take the place of the *Plumper* and that he had requested the Admiralty to appoint Hankin as its first lieutenant. The next day, May 19, Hankin received a letter from the Admiralty informing him he had been appointed as first lieutenant to the paddle steamer HMS *Hecate*, of eight hundred tons, commanded by Captain Anthony Hoskins.[95] He should join his new ship at once at Portsmouth and proceed to Vancouver Island.

At Portsmouth he found the *Hecate* almost ready for sea. He knew Hoskins, having served with him on the *Castor*, where he had been midshipman of Hoskins's watch. They sailed at the end of June 1860.[96] The *Hecate* followed much the same route the *Plumper* had, touching at Lisbon and Rio de Janeiro and then going through the Straits of Magellan to Valparaíso and the Sandwich Islands.

At the southern tip of South America, the *Hecate* steamed through Smyth Channel, through the Gulf of Penas, instead of entering the Pacific at Cape Pillar. This was an unusual route and a passage rarely taken, for it was narrow and intricate, but was, Hankin said, the most interesting. The water was deep and they could not drop anchor at night but always tied up to large trees that grew close down to the water's edge. The weather was bitterly cold because it was the middle of winter. One morning, the ship was surrounded with ice sufficiently thick to enable Hankin to walk on it around the ship.

The *Hecate* made a good passage to the Sandwich Islands. Here they were again made welcome. While they were in Honolulu, the officers—Hankin among them—attended the first fancy dress ball that had ever been held in the islands.[97] This was given by Robert Crichton Wyllie, the minister of foreign affairs, at the Court House. All the noble and great were there, including the king, who went dressed as an Albanian chief in a velvet scarlet jacket embroidered with gold, and with suitably imposing dagger and pistols. The queen went as Cybele, the great mother of gods of Greek mythology. Wyllie went as a Scottish laird, which perhaps he was anyway. The ballroom dazzled with Chinese mandarins, Mexican peasants, *ci-devant* French aristocrats, and Iago, Titania and other characters from Shakespeare. The blue and gold of the naval uniforms were, it was said, colourful accompaniments. A special quadrille was composed for the occasion. Since everyone declared it to be a great success, the king promised to hold another such ball the following November. Doubtless Hankin, not only because he was a charming young naval officer but also because he was an excellent dancer, would have been a great favourite.

The following day, Captain Hoskins and his officers attended court and were formally presented to the king. Hankin would no doubt have mentioned his previous visit to Hawaii. (Did the queen remember Lieutenant Hankin and request another of his curries?)

After only a few days' stay, the *Hecate* sailed for Vancouver Island and made a good passage to Esquimalt. There, the officers and crew of the *Plumper* were expecting them. Thomas Gowlland, the second mate on the *Plumper*, wrote in his journal:

> December
> We are all anxiously looking forward to the arrival of HMS *Hecate*, now due some days at Vancouver Island. Various bets are flying about as to the time of her arrival.

> December 23rd, Sunday
> At 6 p.m. when no one was thinking of her or looking out, a steamer was observed coming into the Harbour. Night glasses were immediately brought into requisition and the long-looked for *Hecate* was discovered in the Stranger steamer. We were of course all delighted and a party immediately manned a cutter and proceeded on board to inspect our Ship. We found her as far as her internal appearance and fitments went more comfortable and roomy than we had even expected and were quite charmed at first sight with our future home for the next 4 years. … The same officers take *Plumper* home except Hankin, who remains in *Hecate* as a 2nd Lt with a view of becoming a Surveyor.[98]

"How delighted I was to find myself back again," Hankin wrote, "and see the little *Plumper* at anchor in the harbor." He was back on Vancouver Island with his friends and wondering what changes he would find.

HMS *Hecate*, Lady Franklin and Hankin's Crossing of Vancouver Island

1861–1864

Back in Victoria at last, Hankin renewed his acquaintance with old friends and observed the numerous changes since he had left in mid-1858. The bastion around the Hudson's Bay Company fort had now been taken down and there were even suggestions that the rest of the fort be dismantled. New buildings, new sounds, new people. Victoria was no longer a quiet English village but a bustling town full of people of many different nationalities: Chinese people, called Celestials in the newspapers; Sandwich Islanders; eager prospectors and Black people from the United States; a large number from Europe on their way to seek their fortunes in the rivers and gold-bearing streams of the two colonies— all bustled through the streets. Songhees Indigenous people crowded the land on the western side of the harbour. Crime and every manner of vice were flourishing in the growing seedy districts.

The *Hecate* had come to replace the *Plumper* as the primary survey- ing vessel in the Colony of Vancouver Island. The *Hecate's* officers and crew changed places with those of the *Plumper*. Hankin remained on board the *Hecate*, where he now became second lieutenant. He was back with his old shipmates—Richards, Mayne, Pender and the others. Also on board was Midshipman Sulivan, probably a brother of Hankin's old messmate from the *Castor*, George Sulivan. In January, Captain Hoskins took the *Plumper* home to England, where she was broken up. Ships of wood such as the *Plumper* were obsolete, and the British navy, modernizing, was now building warships of iron and steel.

His mission being to survey the coast of Vancouver Island, Richards took the ship to visit Nootka, Clayoquot and Quatsino Sounds, as well as innumerable islands along the east and west coast. They steamed up the west coast of Vancouver Island, going on to the Queen Charlotte Islands (now Haida Gwaii). The *Hecate*, with its 240-horsepower engine, could easily steam through Seymour Narrows, making navigation of the east coast of Vancouver Island possible. Richards and his crew also surveyed the Fraser River in the mainland Colony of British Columbia.

Hankin remained on the *Hecate* for approximately two happy years. By now he was a competent surveyor and took his part in the ship's work. He later said he had sailed around Vancouver Island twelve times. He also developed a facility for learning local languages, a skill that would be of life-changing service to him some years later.

Not all Hankin's duties were nautical. In 1861, when Jane, Lady Franklin, arrived on Vancouver Island to visit her old friend Captain Richards, Hankin was pressed into another service. Lady Franklin was the widow of Sir John Franklin, the celebrated explorer who had disappeared in the Arctic in 1847. She had financed seven expeditions to find out what had happened to her husband. These expeditions, it has been said, led to a greater knowledge of the Arctic than those of her husband. She was now an international celebrity, one of those indomitable Victorian ladies who steamed their way through life like an ocean liner. Sophia Cracroft, her husband's niece, was travelling with her, and she wrote detailed letters about their travels to friends back in England. Lady Franklin was also accompanied by her maid, Sarah Buckland. Captain Richards was himself an Arctic explorer, having been second-in-command of the 1852–1854 expedition searching for Sir John and his ships.[99]

The SS *Oregon*, which brought Lady Franklin to Esquimalt, anchored at 4:00 a.m. on Sunday, February 4, 1861. Lieutenant Richard Mayne went to greet the two ladies and bring them to the *Hecate* for lunch. Thomas Gowlland, second master on the *Hecate*, described Lady Franklin as "a fine cheerful, amiable old lady of about 57—full of live [life] and Energy— very observant of everything and always wanting to know the why and wherefor."[100] Gowlland's assessment of Lady Franklin's age was a compliment to her vivacity because she was actually sixty-nine years old.

After lunch, Richards sent for Hankin and introduced him to Lady Franklin. Richards told him that during her stay in Victoria he was to "act as her A.D.C. [aide-de-camp] and look after her, and take her about anywhere she might wish to go," Hankin wrote. "And I was desired to take both Lady Franklin and her Niece in the Captain's Gig to Victoria, about a three miles' pull. In those days there was no road from Esquimalt, and the easiest way was to go by water." Here Hankin's memory may have been playing tricks on him because Miss Cracroft, writing at the time and therefore more likely to be accurate, said there was a road and they went from Esquimalt to Victoria by express wagon. This was a wagon with springs and a bench for three, pulled by two horses. This express transport service, costing one dollar each way, had been set up in the summer of 1858. Their conveyance—more of a cart than a carriage—jolted along the terrible track and around the numerous puddles and fallen tree trunks. On occasion, Miss Cracroft wrote, the horses' legs sank up to their knees in mire. Captain Richards walked alongside the wagon as there was not enough room in it for him as well as for the ladies' luggage.[101]

Hankin recalled that Lady Franklin was a wonderfully active old lady. Sophia Cracroft was approximately forty-five and a dedicated assistant and amanuensis. The officers saw the ladies safely established in rooms that were "the best in the place and really very tolerable."[102] Their rooms were in the house of Wellington and Sophia Moses on Fort Street. Miss Cracroft described them as a most respectable couple. Moses was one of the people of colour who had come to Victoria on the *Commodore* in 1858. Now he was a barber and ran the Pioneer Shaving Saloon and Bath House. Perhaps he was not quite so respectable as Miss Cracroft believed because the following year he ran away with another woman to the Fraser River gold diggings, perhaps to search for gold himself. He settled down as the noted barber in Barkerville. His abandoned and jealous wife tried to drown herself.[103]

Miss Cracroft wrote that Captain Richards had very kindly lent them as their escort "the 2nd Lieutenant Hankin, a very nice young man. ... He is a very natural nice fellow, with plenty of fun in him. Very lately, he got himself conveyed after an original fashion to a Ball at the Governor's on a wet night. He was of course in full uniform, so he rolled himself in a big blanket on the floor, & made 4 Indians pluck him up and carry him into the very hall of the Governor's house! He speaks fluently in Chinook, which is a very great comfort here."[104] Hankin wrote that he attended on them every day, taking them both out either for a short walk about the town or for a drive. He procured a gig for them. They then rode out to inspect the school for Indigenous children and afterwards visited their village. Miss Cracroft also noted that Lieutenant Richard Mayne sometimes escorted them, though Hankin, writing fifty years later, does not mention this. Captain Richards was, it seems, determined that Lady Franklin and her niece were to be well looked after.

Lady Franklin received many visitors. All the great and good in Victoria came to visit the celebrity in their midst. Governor James Douglas called on her, as did the chief officers of the Hudson's Bay Company. The ladies became acquainted with William Young, the colonial secretary, a person who features in Hankin's own story a few years later. Young showed them all round the Birdcages, as the government buildings in Victoria were called. Here they went to the upper gallery, from where they had a good view of the town and harbour.

The mayor, Thomas Harris, and his wife also called on them. A few days later a letter came from Mrs. Harris inviting Lady Franklin, Miss Cracroft and Hankin to lunch on the following day at two o'clock. Lady Franklin asked him who would be there. "So I told her," Hankin said, "only your Ladyship and Miss Cracroft, the Bishop, our host and hostess, and myself. And I added we can easily walk there, as the Mayor's house is not more than five minutes' walk from here. I was young in those days and full of fun, so I told Lady Franklin I could tell her exactly what the Luncheon would be like. Old Harris was a Butcher, with a bald head and very red face, and looked as if he had always been accustomed to good living, but no one could say they were a very refined sort of people, but kinder-hearted, or more hospitable, persons never lived."

Everything went off well. "They are plain, worthy people," Miss Cracroft wrote approvingly but a little patronizingly, "without any pretensions."[105] Soon after three o'clock, after the lunch speeches, Hankin escorted them back to their lodgings.

At the beginning of March, Lady Franklin and Miss Cracroft decided to visit British Columbia, the colony on the mainland, and travel up the Fraser River as far as Yale. Hankin was assigned to go with them. At this time, James Douglas was governor of both colonies, Vancouver Island and British Columbia. After Douglas, the most important person in British Columbia was Colonel Richard Moody, commander of the Royal Engineers there and the deputy governor of the colony.

They all went over on the paddle steamer *Otter* to the Royal Engineers' camp, which was located a mile from New Westminster, the colony's capital. They stayed several nights with Colonel Moody, who had the best house in the colony. Here they met not only Colonel Moody but also other leading citizens. Miss Cracroft's sharp eyes noted, and her pen described, the fierce animosity between the two colonies.

Leaving at eight-thirty on the morning of March 6, they started up the Fraser River in a little stern-wheel steamboat named the *Maria*, with Captain Irving in command. As they ascended the river, the stream became very rapid and it was all the steamer could do to stem the strong current. Hankin said that for so small a vessel the accommodation was surprisingly good. Each of them had a comfortable little cabin, although Hankin had to share with three others, including two officers of the Royal Marines who were on a sketching expedition. When the *Maria* tied up to the bank for the night, they stayed on board. "This is a primitive sort of way of securing a vessel," Miss Cracroft wrote. "We draw very little water & run close in under the bank—the men jump ashore with a hawser, scramble up to the top & pass it round one of the straight tall trunks which are crowded together there."[106] That evening by the riverbank, they made a merry party, Miss Cracroft wrote, "thanks to Mr. Hankin," who had "plenty of the midshipman left in his composition."[107]

When they reached Hope, Peter O'Reilly, the magistrate in town, came on board to have tea with them. "Mr. Hankin officiated & amused us infinitely by his love of jam and butter," Miss Cracroft wrote.[108] While waiting for the *Maria* to continue to Yale, O'Reilly showed them around Hope. He also explained to them the methods used by many prospectors in town to search for gold.

After arriving at Yale, they again remained on board for the night. The next morning they landed and walked around the small community, sightseeing and meeting the residents. These included Rev. William Crickmer, the local clergyman. "He seems active," Miss Cracroft noted tartly, "but not especially clever."[109] Crickmer thought he should invite Lady Franklin for tea to meet the respectable citizens in town. About twenty-five to thirty people crowded into his house, including at least two wives and one daughter, while Mrs. Crickmer, a pretty woman, Miss Cracroft said, who carried a baby on her hips, made tea. "The providing tea was no light matter," she wrote, "& we had ample entertainment in Mr. Hankin, who began by helping Mrs. Crickmer to make it, in the smaller room, and ended up by sending her to entertain her company, while he not only made but brought in the tea. Imagine him in Lieut's uniform bearing in a big tray loaded with cups which he gravely handed round to us all, men included, for they sat quiet to be helped, and he declares they believed him to be hired, livery & all, for the occasion. But I can't write half the fun he got out of the evening party—which at last came to an end by our going back to the ship to sleep."[110]

Hankin had charm, a great sense of fun and a taste for practical jokes. He certainly had a mischievous streak in his character. That night at Yale, he played one of his tricks on Lady Franklin's maid, Sarah Buckland. Miss Cracroft wrote that on the boat that night she woke to the sound of Buckland screaming, followed by peals of male laughter. Hankin had, it turned out, borrowed an Indigenous ceremonial mask from a fellow passenger and placed it in Buckland's bed, with the sheets pulled up under its wooden chin. Then he waited for Sarah Buckland to find it. For Hankin and fellow passengers, her horror and screams were fine rewards for such a prank. What Buckland thought of Hankin for his practical joke was not recorded but may be imagined.

Yale, in about 1865, where Hankin brought Lady Franklin. This was also from where he started his walk to Barkerville. Image A-03584 courtesy of the Royal BC Museum and Archives

The next day, Mr. Allard of the Hudson's Bay Company placed a "large and commodious canoe at their disposal manned by a dozen stalwart Indians dressed in uniform," the *British Columbian* said, "and [they] proceeded to pay a visit to the Grand Falls, in what has hitherto been called, the Little Kanyon. At the falls, Her Ladyship witnessed the passing of a canoe over the ways around the falls, and was thereby enabled to form a faint idea of the hardships encountered by the Fraser river boatmen in reaching the mines."[111] At the narrowest part of the canyon, they saw a big banner with the words "Lady Franklin's Pass" on it—this was Crickmer's doing—but the name did not stick.

The boat downriver was leaving at noon. An hour or so before departure, Rev. Crickmer called on Hankin and told him the citizens wanted to present an address to Lady Franklin and asked him what time would be agreeable for her to receive it.[112] Precisely at 11:00 a.m., Crickmer, together with the whole town of Yale—Miss Cracroft put it at twenty men—made an appearance on board and presented the following address, which was slowly read by Crickmer in a very loud and distinct voice:

> May it please your Ladyship—We, the inhabitants of Yale, representing well nigh every nation under heaven, esteem the present as the proudest moment in the annals of our Country, and in the existence of our town—for today is our town of Yale for ever linked in history with the name of one, the memorial of whose abundant kindness and wifely devotion will never die, at whose immortal Veneration Princes bow down, and Kings and Queens of the earth may envy, but never win. From the bottom of our hearts, do we pray God to bless your Ladyship with many happy days and when called by God's good providence from the holy church militant to join the heroic in the Church Triumphant, may the grave be transmuted, by the touch of living faith, into the gates of everlasting life, and a glory more lasting, than the perishing Laurels of earth, for ever crown the double brows of the noble pair, whom the whole civilized world of Christendom delighted to honor.

Hankin said he thought this such a magnificent piece of oratory that he asked Lady Franklin if he might make a copy of it. She said, "No!" (It is not likely that Hankin was serious in his praise of such hyperbole.) She was sure he would only laugh at it, but he obtained her permission to read it over. It made such an impression on him that fifty years later he still remembered it verbatim. To be fair to Rev. Crickmer and perhaps to raise a doubt about Hankin's memory, it should be added that the account of this address in the *British Columbian* was considerably less florid. Hankin may have "improved" Crickmer's speech by constant after-dinner retelling. Hankin said that, when relaxing after dinner over cigars and port, Captain Richards would often call to him, "Now, Hankin, give us the address to Lady Franklin."[113]

Back at Colonel Moody's camp near New Westminster, Governor Douglas, who was visiting and staying with Moody, invited Lady Franklin and her companions, together with Moody, to a dinner at a restaurant in New Westminster. Afterwards they attended the gala performance for the reopening of the Pioneer Theatre. The Robinson Dramatic Troupe, a touring group of four actors and two actresses, was presenting "petite comedies, dramas, and farces and delighting the inhabitants by their humorous representations."[114] They performed *Pas de Fascination*, the pantomime *The Clown Outwitted* and the play *Family Jars*. Little Miss Susan and Master William performed the double sailor's hornpipe enthusiastically, for which encores were demanded, and Mr. Robinson brought the house down with his impersonation of a gruff old landlord. (This evening may perhaps have reminded Hankin of the Crummles family and the Infant Phenomenon in Dickens's *Nicholas Nickleby*.) "Everything was burlesque," Miss Cracroft wrote, "and we laughed as much as ever I did in my life." She wrote that the clown in one of those make-fun-of-someone-in-the-audience moments fixed on Hankin as his mark "amidst shouts of laughter from the whole house at Mr. Hankin."[115] With her memories of the mask in her bed, perhaps no one laughed so loudly at his discomfiture as Sarah Buckland.

The party stayed for a few days at the Royal Engineers' camp in New Westminster while they waited for the steamer from Victoria to arrive. While they were waiting, Colonel Moody showed them round the barracks, the workshops, the well-stocked library and reading room and the map-making room. On the last evening, the officers put on a performance in Lady Franklin's honour. This was a revue with musical items and short plays. Both Lady Franklin and Miss Cracroft had been teasing Hankin, saying that as a sailor, surely he could dance a hornpipe for them. What type of sailor was he, anyway? The orchestra consisted of seven members. The actors, Miss Cracroft wrote, were exceedingly good and some of the soldiers had shaved off their moustaches to play the female parts in the playlets. The curtain went down and when it went up again, "Mr. Hankin bounded on the stage in full sailor's summer costume (all white & blue), flung down his hat, folded his arms & danced his hornpipe *beautifully*. You can imagine the reception he got from the astonished audience, who knew nothing of his intention. He was encored & very good-naturedly came on again."[116]

Soon after they arrived back in Victoria, Lady Franklin and her companions left the colony.

After the excitement of Lady Franklin's visit, Richards and his crew resumed their work of surveying the coast. On August 20, 1861, the *Hecate* sustained damage after running aground near Cape Flattery on the American shore. "My morning watch and one of the densest fogs prevailing I ever remember seeing," Second Master Thomas Gowlland wrote. "By our reconning [reckoning] we ought to have been close in to the South Shore of Vancouver Island. ... We were just sitting down to it [breakfast] when a bump, crump and crash warned us that breakfast would be a myth; up we all rushed and there was the poor old Ship in a rock amidships, and rocks all around her close to the gangway."[117] Although they managed to free the ship and reach Esquimalt, it soon became clear that the damage was more serious than originally thought. Richards, consequently, took the *Hecate* to a dry dock in San Francisco for the necessary repairs. Back in Esquimalt by the beginning of December, Richards sat down to plan the surveys of the Alberni Canal and Barclay Sound for the following year.

In addition to surveying the coast, Captain Richards wanted to explore the interior of Vancouver Island. This was a jungle of mountains, forests, deep valleys and lakes, known only to the Indigenous people who lived there. He wrote to the governor:

It has been my desire, and practice, whenever the more immediate duties of the Maritime Survey would permit, to gather as much information as possible of the interior of this island, as well as the adjacent Continent, and with this view, parties have from time to time been equipped and despatched from the *Plumper* and *Hecate*. ...

HMS *Hecate* at Esquimalt, Vancouver Island. Image PDP05357 courtesy of the Royal BC Museum and Archives

It may not be out of place here to inform Your Excellency that the survey of the greater part of the Western Coast has been completed, and several new harbours and anchorages discovered, which when published for general information will I trust prevent a recurrence, or lessen the frequency of disasters which have annually befallen vessels navigating in this boisterous neighbourhood.[118]

In May 1862, Richards directed Hankin and Dr. Charles Bedingfield Wood to cross the island from Kyuquot Sound to the Nimpkish River on the northeastern coast and rejoin the *Hecate* at Fort Rupert.[119] The two men set out on May 25 and made one of the early crossings of Vancouver Island from west to east, that is, by non-Indigenous people. They were not, though, the first. The previous year Hankin's colleague, Richard Mayne, had made a crossing from the Alberni Inlet to Nanaimo, but this had not received so much publicity.

Richards chose Hankin for this expedition partly because he could speak several Indigenous languages. In previous expeditions of the *Hecate* on the west coast of the island, he had acquired enough of the local languages to enable him to act as interpreter. Wood was impressed by Hankin's ability to learn these languages. "I beg leave to offer my testimony," he wrote in his report to Richards, "to the great energy displayed by Lieut. Hankin who, with his previous knowledge of Indian dialects and without an interpreter, within a few days made himself sufficiently master of the Cayuket [Kyuquot] language as to make our Indians perfectly understand his and my wishes in our progress across the Island."[120] Hankin's proficiency in languages would have life-changing consequences for him three years later.

Hankin did not mention in his memoirs—or perhaps deliberately left out—an embarrassing incident that happened to them on their way by canoe to Kyuquot Sound. Richards, with a touch of criticism, wrote about this incident in his own journal:

May 25, Sunday. Mr. Hankin and Dr. Wood went to Kayuquot by canoe, with a view to crossing the I^d [Island] to Nimpkish river where I purpose meeting them with the Ship on the 16th June.

June 1, Sunday. … Mr Gowlland tells me he met Mr Hankin and Doctor Wood in difficulties. It appears that the Ehasset [Ahousaht] natives who took them from here with the understanding that they were to convey them to Kyuquot, landed them about 3 miles from this and then left them, and laughed at them, saying they were quite far enough. They had been paid 5 blankets and other things for the service. Then Dr. [Wood] and Mr. Hankin, not liking to return, managed with difficulty to get a very small canoe with 2 men to carry them and their traps to Kyuquot, and were fortunately met by Mr. Gowlland on the way and taken by him to the Kyuquot village among the I^s [islands].

And fortunate it was further, for the canoe was so small and the weather so doubtful that in all probability they would have reached nowhere but for this fortunate meeting. Mr. Gowlland from his acquaintance with the Kyuquot people was able to help them considerably and I hope he has ensured their reaching Nimpkish.

I made a point of finding the natives who had behaved so knavishly and obliged the Chief of the Ehassets to return the blankets paid by Mr. Hankin, who protested himself much annoyed at the behavior of his people. After getting the blankets back and making them understand my disapproval of their dishonest proceeding, I made the Chief a present of the blankets so received, or part of them. I have rarely known an instance of this nature. Mr. Hankin was wrong to pay them beforehand, and all arrangements of this kind should be made thro' the Chief.[121]

In his official report to Richards, which was published verbatim in the *Daily British Colonist*, Hankin wrote:

We arrived at Kayuket Island the following day at Noon, where I found a very large Indian settlement, called by the natives "Actiss." There are between 700 and 800 people living here, and they are a finer looking race than any other Natives I have seen on Vancouver Island. ...

We found the Natives here most civil and obliging. They helped us to pitch our tent and carry our traps out of the canoe. I had afterwards occasion to remain with these people several days, & although they had both temptation and opportunity, it is worthy of remark that not the smallest trifle was stolen from us. On one occasion I lost a meerschaum pipe, which was afterwards found and returned to me.

With the exception of occasional visits from trading schooners, they had seen but little of the Whites; but two of them had visited Victoria and they had returned with such wonderful accounts, that many others were eager to go, & their anxiety to see the *Hecate* was intense.

I found my Knowledge of the Barclay Sound language most useful to me. In fact, without it, we should have been quite unable to proceed, for they were totally ignorant of Chinook.[122]

Hankin and Wood started their journey across the island the next day, taking with them seven Indigenous packers to carry their tent, food and other gear and also to act as guides. However, they travelled for only a day in rain so heavy that the packers refused to go any farther, forcing Hankin and Wood to return to their starting point. Discouraged, they concluded they had to give up the expedition and wait for the *Hecate* to pick them up.

Hankin wrote:

During my stay here, my time was principally occupied in improving my Knowledge of the language, and adding considerably to my already extensive vocabulary.

In the evening, I would get up games among the Indians, leaping, jumping, racing etc. by which they appeared much amused. They also had one or two games of their own, which they showed us. One especially, a trial of strength, appeared to be a favourite. 50 or 60 of them, with their naked bodies, & faces daubed with red and black paint, would seize a long pole, and then, using it as a battering ram, looking more like demons than men, would, with tremendous yells and shouts, charge against some 150 others, who with their united strength would endeavour to rout the Invaders. Another, more quiet one, was sticking a feather in the ground, when an Indian standing on one foot would stoop down &, without touching the ground with his hands, extract the feather with his teeth. This feat I tried several times, and generally tumbled, when a hearty laugh was raised at my expense.

During the day, an intelligent Indian would draw for me on the sand the trail across the Island to Nimpkish, putting in the lakes and rivers, and telling us their native names. Several would volunteer their services for this office, and it was amusing to see their disputes about the differences of the distances they had marked.

On the 3rd day of our stay here, it struck me that it would still be possible to cross the Island in time to meet the ship at Fort Rupert by the 15th, according to my instructions, if I could but get Indians to accompany me.[123]

After speaking with the Chief, though, Hankin realized that if he wanted to cross the island he would have to increase the packers' pay. "I was, therefore, obliged to increase each man's reward by 2 blankets, or give up entirely the idea of going, and, feeling that the latter course, for the sake of saving the expense of half a dozen blankets would be absurd, I held out the reward of 5 blankets and a shirt to each Indian, and before evening 6 volunteers, stimulated no doubt by the additional bribe, offered their services, which were immediately accepted."[124]

On Hankin's stipulation that there would be no turning back, they set off again. Because they did not have enough bearers, Wood had to leave his collecting equipment behind, which more or less destroyed his ability to achieve his scientific objectives for the journey. His disappointment during the crossing was alleviated, though, when he realized that he was not, in fact, finding any plants or animals he had not already seen. Like Hankin, he was impressed by the size of the trees. "I measured," he wrote, "a prostrate one blown down by the wind, some 60 ft. from its roots, where it had a circumference of 75 feet."[125]

This was a difficult and, at times, hazardous journey. With the help of their guides, Hankin and Wood found their way through the forests, waded across icy rivers and paddled lakes, not without risk to life and limb. For much of the time it rained, although on the first day the weather was fine. Hankin wrote:

It was a beautiful clear morning, & with a fresh breeze from the S.W., we rapidly arrived at Tarshish, and by 5 o'clock the same evening, camped some four miles up the river, on the north bank. Here, the Indians hid their Canoe in the bush, being unable to proceed further by water on account of rapids and falls. We had some difficulty in proceeding even thus far by canoe, and in one place had to make a portage of about 200 yards. On examining our stock of food, we discovered that we had barely enough to last us across, even with the strictest economy, having but 15 lbs of flour, a few beans, and a small quantity of preserved meat. After our first disappointment at having to retrace our steps, we had been too lavish of provisions, not thinking to make a 2nd start, and I had given both flour and meat to Kai-ni-nitt the Chief, at Kayuket, but having my gun with me, and plenty of powder and shot, we anticipated Venison Steaks in abundance, but in this, were disappointed. ...

The Indians assured me that Elk, about this part of the country, were very numerous. We certainly saw plenty of tracks, although we did not meet the animals themselves, but, considering so large a party cracking through the bush, one could hardly expect it. The land on either bank of the river was very thickly wooded, rocky with small hills of from 100 to 250 feet.[126]

Largely because of the heavy rain, they had difficulty crossing the rivers. Dr. Wood recounted in his report that the eight of them crossed one forty-yard-wide river by all holding on to one long stick. Not long before, an Indigenous man had drowned trying to ford it. "In this," he wrote, "we were very nearly carried away by the force of the current, two or three of our members being floated off their legs. The united strength of those who had more secure footing or less depth of water, for the river was extremely uneven, enabled them to regain their feet still clinging to the stick and we were quickly on the opposite bank, on touching which the Indians cheered, we also joining having got over our first difficulty."[127] In describing this brush with drowning, Wood does not mention if Hankin (or himself) was one of those who lost his footing.

They also had a problem crossing at least one of the lakes they came to. Hankin wrote:

We were disappointed at not finding a canoe of any description here, but we observed a large log lying on the beach, which after some trouble we succeeded in launching, and having packed our traps on it, commenced to paddle across the Lake but we had scarcely left the shore when we found our most extraordinary craft to roll so heavily as to keep us in momentary expectation of its completely capsizing.

We found it impossible to proceed in this way, so we paddled to the bank as quickly as possible, and obtained a smaller spar, to act as an outrigger, which we lashed to the Big one with strips of Cedar bark, and then with a blanket for a sail, began to make satisfactory progress. We continued proceeding in this manner until 11 p.m. when the wind began to freshen considerably, and a disagreeable sea getting up, rendered ours anything but an enviable position, so I persuaded the Indians to paddle in shore, and tie up to a tree for the night. We now contrived to snatch a couple of hours sleep and were off again at 3 a.m. the following morning and by 9 o'clock had arrived at the Nimpkish river. We found the stream far too rapid to venture down it unless in a good Canoe; so we here discarded our log and took to the trail following a general Northerly Course. The land on both banks of Lake Karmutsen [Nimpkish Lake] is densely wooded, with mountains on either side varying from 1,800 to 2,000 feet in height.[128]

Eventually they reached Fort Rupert, where Hamilton Moffatt, the Hudson's Bay Company factor there, and his wife entertained them hospitably. When they reached and boarded the *Hecate*, Captain Richards gave them a "warm and hearty welcome," Hankin wrote in his memoirs. "I don't think he ever expected to see me again, for crossing the Island had taken longer than he thought. The Bush was very thick, and we had many big logs to climb over, Rivers and Lakes to cross and to climb over two mountains some 3,000 feet high."

Hankin and Wood rewarded their Indigenous packers, who had behaved so well, with six red blankets each, which they bought from the Hudson's Bay store. They also gave them a bag of ship's biscuits. After a few days' rest, the Indigenous packers returned to their homes by canoe, going round the north end of Vancouver Island.

The *Hecate* then returned to Esquimalt, going through Seymour Narrows down the east coast.

Notwithstanding his charm, intelligence and usefulness—not to mention his ability to cook a fine curry—Hankin did manage to annoy Richards from time to time. On one occasion he knocked over Richards's sextant and chronometer "and nearly broke his leg." Richards wrote in his journal testily that this "would not have been half so bad as damaging the instruments."[129]

Friday was an Indigenous man whom Hankin had befriended. He had come on board and been taught some English and some navigation. He had been on board for a year and had even gone with the ship to San Francisco. Richards loftily said Friday was useless as a crew member but it would be of benefit to him to learn English customs. Hankin had argued that Friday was grateful for all this attention and held him up as an example of how Indigenous people could show gratitude. He was upset when Friday took off for a year without permission and delighted when he returned to the ship. Richards wrote:

> Three days afterwards, his eyes [Hankin's] were opened. Friday told him early that he had made a great deal of money thro' being with us formerly; that he could now pilot vessels into Barclay Sound and that the little English he had learned was a fortune to him. He had now come to perfect himself in the language—nothing else—and as soon as that was accomplished, he was off like a Shot. Mr. H. was much cast down by what he qualified as the slight ingratitude of Friday, but for myself I cannot see anything unnatural in the lad's behaviour. All his friends are at Ohiat (Barclay Sound) and why should he stay with us save for his own advantage.[130]

In mid-1862, the Admiralty ordered Richards to bring the *Hecate* back to England, where it was to be decommissioned and broken up. It directed him to return westward across the Pacific, taking his time, and to survey sections of the Australian coast on his way. Daniel Pender, the senior assistant surveyor and Hankin's friend from their days at Stone's boarding house in Portsmouth, was left behind to finish the surveying work on the *Beaver*, an old paddlewheel steamer belonging to the Hudson's Bay Company.

Hankin was so charmed by Vancouver Island that he decided to leave the navy, find some employment and end his days there. Captain Richards wrote to the Admiralty on his behalf, but the answer came back that he could not be spared. Hankin was ordered to remain on the *Hecate* until she returned to England, where his discharge would be granted.

The *Hecate* left Vancouver Island on December 22, 1862, but not before a round of tributes in the newspapers and addresses of gratitude. "Captain Richards has always taken a deep interest in everything that pertains to the welfare of these colonies," the *Daily British Colonist* said, "and his unusually accurate surveys demonstrate that beyond a doubt."[131] A six-stanza poem was composed for the newspaper to commemorate the ship's departure. One of the better stanzas reads:

> Oh, yes, my brother *Colonist*,
> We can fancy all this here;
> But the *Hecate*, she's a going home
> And we're a staying here.[132]

Lady Franklin had commented on the close relationship between the crews of the naval ships at Esquimalt and the churches there. Men from the ships swelled the church choirs, where, she said, they sang very well. Miss Cracroft noted that Hankin had been coaching the crew of the *Hecate* in singing lessons on its way out from England. Before the *Hecate* departed, a deputation of seamen and marines went to Rev. Charles Wood and presented him with a ship's Bible to thank him for his services as chaplain to the *Hecate* during the ship's time in the colony.

Second Master Gowlland wrote that the people of Victoria offered the officers a ball to commemorate their stay and wish them well, but Richards had turned this offer down, which caused some offence. When the *Hecate* departed, Gowlland wrote, "Sailed at 7:30 a.m. from Esquimalt Harbour, all the ships cheering as we passed them steaming out. ... Poor

Dan Pender... accompanied us to Albert Head. ... Not a dry eye in the boat amongst them, and [they] attempted to give us 3 feeble cheers choked with sobs—but it was a complete failure."[133]

They sailed first to San Francisco and then down to Acapulco. The voyage home turned out to be a healthy one, but it was here at Acapulco that the ship had the only fatality on its voyage, when a seaman died of fever. The *Hecate* then sailed on to Honolulu, arriving on March 17, 1863. Here Hankin renewed his acquaintance with many old friends.

A few days later, the ship had some excitement when a lookout spotted a fire on the *Florence*, an American bark in Hawaiian waters. A boat under the command of Hankin's fellow lieutenant, Henry Hand, immediately pulled over to it and quickly suppressed the flames. Robert Wyllie, the foreign minister, formally thanked them for saving the ship from total destruction. The captain of the *Florence* told him, he wrote, "that he never saw anything to surpass or even equal the perfect coolness and presence of mind of your first lieutenant and the admirable discipline of the men under his command in their prompt and efficient execution of his orders, all most wisely directed to the extinguishment of the fire."[134]

The *Hecate* and Captain Richards had other duties to perform in Hawaii. The ship sailed to Maui to visit the king and queen and brought them back to Honolulu. The king asked Richards to survey Honolulu harbour and make some recommendations to improve its safety, which he did. Richards was also invited to the British Consulate in Honolulu to chair a meeting of the subscribers for some form of monument to Captain Cook. What could he suggest? He proposed that the most appropriate monument would be a lighthouse at the entrance of Honolulu harbour.

Sailing from Honolulu on April 21, the *Hecate* journeyed through the South Pacific islands to Sydney, where it arrived on June 26. On its way, it visited, among others, Fanning's, Humphrey's and Reardon islands. Several of these islands they visited had recently been raided by slavers, who had seized all the inhabitants and destroyed their villages.

The *Hecate* spent a few months surveying the east coast of Australia. Richards was asked to visit Rockingham Bay in northern Queensland to see whether it would be a good place for a settlement. He wrote in his report, "Tuesday, August 18. I went to look at the mainland opposite our anchorage, with a view to ascertaining its eligibility as a townsite, and also to examine one of the rivers in the hope of getting some new palms. I was accompanied by Lieutenant Hankin and Dr. Wood. We ascended streams, marked fresh water on the chart seven or eight miles from our anchorage.[135]

After returning to Sydney, the *Hecate* left Australia and headed to Batavia, the capital of the Dutch East Indies. They then went through the Torres Strait to Java. They spent a week there, a visit Hankin described as delightful. He went with Richards to Buitenzorg, now known as Bogor, a city in West Java. They stayed three days at the hotel there. "There was a large marble swimming bath, which we enjoyed immensely," Hankin wrote, "beautiful public gardens, and the climate was delightful."

The *Hecate* carried on to Timor, where they found a Dutch man-of-war. They now had to observe diplomatic courtesies. The Dutch captain came on board the *Hecate* to make the requisite call on Captain Richards. Richards, though, spoke no Dutch and the Dutch captain spoke no English. How could they communicate? Richards had an idea. About two years previously, Hankin had mentioned to Captain Richards that he could speak a little Dutch, having picked it up when he had been at the Cape in the *Castor*.

When the Dutch captain came on board, Richards summoned Hankin to act as interpreter, ordering him to put on his dress uniform and epaulettes, cocked hat and sword and come on deck immediately. Hankin had no illusions, though, about the difference between a smattering and a proficiency in speaking a foreign language. When he arrived on deck, he found Richards and the Dutch captain bowing very low to each other and making curious steps forward and backwards as if they were dancing a kind of Dutch hornpipe. Hankin wrote:

Immediately I appeared on the scene, Richards said to me, "For goodness' sake, say something to this Dutch Captain, he doesn't understand a word of English, and I don't know what to do with him." I replied, "Really, Sir, I can't speak Dutch." "Nonsense, you told me you could. Say something at once. One looks a perfect fool standing here." After meditating a few moments, I suddenly remembered I could say in Dutch: "Give me some bread, please." "Well, say it," said the Captain, "that's better than nothing," and so I said to the Dutchman, "Give me some bread please," and we all took off our cocked hats and made a low bow.

"Now," said the Captain to me. "Say something else directly." "Oh dear," I replied, "I really can't say anything else," when I suddenly recollected I could say "Give me an orange, please," which I did, and we all bowed to each other again and kept walking round and round in a circle. "Well, that's all right," said the Captain, "but you must say something more" when I remembered I could say "eighty-eight" in Dutch. "Well, that sounds very well," said the Captain, "say it two or three times over. It's much better than standing there looking like a fool." So I repeated, "Give me some bread, give me an orange and eighty-eight," when we all bowed again, and walked several times round the circle, when at last the Dutch captain said something in Dutch, which I told our Captain meant goodbye, though I had not the slightest idea what it was, and then he went into his Gig, which was alongside the Ship waiting for him.

In about half an hour, Richards returned the Dutch captain's visit, ordering Hankin to go with him as interpreter. Directly they got on board the Dutch man-of-war, the scene—Hankin called it ridiculous— was played again. "We first of all made low bows to each other, taking off our cocked hats, and walking round and round. 'Now go on, Mr. Hankin,' said the Captain. 'Say that give me some bread thing again.' Then they all bowed and smiled. 'Now that eighty-eight. ... Ah, that's the best of the lot. And it sounds quite Dutchy.' When we got on board the *Hecate* again the Captain said, 'It wasn't so bad as they could not say a word of English so we could say something in Dutch!'"

Richards reported to the Admiralty, saying he had duly returned the visit, and that most friendly relations existed between the Dutch captain and himself. Tongue in cheek, Hankin wrote, "I have no doubt the Dutch Captain did the same to his Admiralty. I think I did a great deal towards the friendly relations, and perhaps prevented war, between England and Holland!"

Soon they left Timor and carried on through the straits of Sunda, passing the volcanic island of Krakatoa, which would erupt so dramatically twenty years later. Then they set a course for the Cape of Good Hope. This would have been a long sail to Simon's Bay, where they arrived on November 11.[136] This was familiar ground to Hankin and his visit there must have brought back many memories.

Up until now, their voyage had been leisurely. At the Cape this all changed. When Richards opened his dispatches, he learned that the British government had appointed him hydrographer of the Admiralty.[137] The notice of his appointment was accompanied by orders to return to England as quickly as possible to take up his new position. This meant loading the ship with coal and using the steam power of the ship's boilers. "In those days Men-of-War never got up steam," Hankin wrote, "unless on some special occasion, when it always had to be noted in the log-book. Vessels invariably made passages under their own sail. There was great excitement on board and we filled up our Coal bunkers, also carrying many sacks of Coal on deck, and, as soon as we were ready, we went to sea and shaped a course for Madeira."

On their way north, they stopped at Ascension Island and then went on to Madeira. Here Hankin read in an English newspaper that Arthur Kennedy had been appointed governor of the Colony of Vancouver Island, to live in Victoria, and Frederick Seymour had been appointed governor of the Colony of British Columbia, to live in New Westminster. Hankin would not have had any idea how much this news would affect him a few years later.

They remained for only twenty-four hours at Madeira. They quickly refilled the ship's coal bunkers and left at once for Woolwich. The *Hecate* arrived back in Plymouth in the first week of January 1864.[138] It was then decommissioned, and the crew were paid off. Hankin wrote that he was very sorry to leave the ship and say goodbye to all his messmates, for they had spent many happy years together and were always the best of friends. Hankin might have reflected that he had now circumnavigated the globe.

Richards offered to find Hankin an appointment in charge of the meteorological station at Valencia and said he would gladly do anything he could to help. Hankin, though, was determined to leave the navy and return to Vancouver Island. He asked Richards "as a great favour" to try to get him his discharge from the service. "I longed to go back to Vancouver Island and try and get me some employment there," he wrote. "My service on the Coast of Africa with Capt. Haswell had given me such a dislike of the navy that I determined to leave it altogether and devote my energies to private enterprise or some branch of the public service." Richards wrote to the Admiralty as promised and Hankin was released from the Royal Navy after fifteen years of service.

Richards, however generous and helpful, was sharp enough to be objective. He made the following comment on Hankin's file with the navy. "Knows French, Italian and 3 Indian languages. ... Not fit to be a 1st lieutenant. Honest, good with men. No great ambition."[139] The truth was that Hankin had not wanted to go into the navy in the first place. He had served under several captains who had made his life unpleasant. He never developed that love of naval customs and traditions that made a committed sailor. He had also evidenced a lively sense of fun that some might have confused with irresponsibility. Besides, the pay was bad.

He went home to see his father, who was now living at a place called Stiffkey in Norfolk. "I did not meet with a very kind reception as my father was naturally annoyed at my having left the Service. However, he let me have £100 with the full understanding I was never to expect another farthing from him as long as I lived."

Now, for the first time in his life, Hankin was entirely his own master.

6

Looking for Gold in Barkerville

1864

W hat Hankin really wanted to do was to return to British Columbia. Having said goodbye to his father—perhaps a little frostily—he went to London. There he spent a few days in lodgings and bought some clothes appropriate for his journey. Then he went and booked a third-class passage on one of the West India packet steamers to Aspinwall (Colón), at the eastern end of the Isthmus of Panama. A journey in steerage, with emigrants and others going out to the goldfields, would certainly have been rough, chaotic even, to someone used to the order and structure of the Royal Navy. Fortunately, he was able to make friends with the ship's officers after a few days. When they learned he had just left the navy, they were kind enough to invite him to mess with them. This was far more agreeable.

After a three-week journey to Aspinwall, he took the train across the isthmus to Panama City. He would have recalled this journey from west to east from not so long before. The crossing took four hours in a slow and crowded train, and what with the heat, hordes of mosquitoes and flies of every kind, he recalled it as not being in any way enjoyable.

Arriving in Panama, he found the American steamer to San Francisco had just left. Consequently, he had to stay at the only hotel in town for twelve days. It was a very dirty place, he said, full of mosquitoes and other insects. At length, the steamer from San Francisco arrived. Since it was going to stay in Panama for only two days, he quickly booked a passage going north, well aware how fast his hundred pounds was disappearing.

The year 1864 was a momentous one for him. He was only twenty-eight. His robust health had enabled him to withstand numerous fevers and other diseases the tropics had hurled at him. He also had an adventurous disposition. When he left the navy, he said, he had made up his mind always to make the best of everything. He said he was "quite prepared to rough it." Little did he know how much he would need this happy frame of mind for what was coming.

In the heat, he slept each night on deck, much preferring that to sharing the stuffy crowded cabins for third-class passengers below, where there was not a breath of fresh air. John Emmerson, the Englishman who had come out to try his luck at prospecting for gold two years before and had made a similar voyage, wrote that the water they were given to drink on board was almost always smoking hot and the iced water at the bar cost twenty-five cents a glass. Hankin recalled that the food was really bad. People dined at noon, all standing up at a swinging table. The knives and forks were chained to the table lest they be stolen. In those days, rough miners and all kinds of loafers were making their way to the goldfields in California and the Cariboo. Emmerson wrote, "An extensive whole-sale business was carried on in the pilfering line. Pockets were picked of money; gold and silver watches abstracted; carpet bags plundered of their contents and the bags thrown in the sea."[140] With good reason, the steamship company was obviously taking no chances.

In a fortnight, the ship reached San Francisco safely. Fortunately, Hankin did not have to wait long for a passage to Vancouver Island. The following day he was able to find a small vessel starting for Esquimalt. "I took passage by her," he wrote in his memoirs, "and I was [soon] glad to find myself once again among old friends, and in the Country where I had already spent many happy days."

Almost certainly Hankin arrived back in Esquimalt on March 31, 1864, on the SS *Sierra Nevada*, having left San Francisco on March 21.[141]

His name on the passenger list is set down as Phillip Hawkin, but the chances of it being someone else would seem low. Interestingly, another passenger on board was someone named Chas. Hawkin. This could perhaps have been Philip Hankin's brother Charles, who had made money as a partner of Billy Barker in the Cariboo and who visited San Francisco on occasion. Hankin does not mention his brother in his memoirs, but he could have made arrangements to meet him in San Francisco or they could, by lucky accident, have bumped into each other there. Or it might have been someone else who really was named Hawkin.

Arriving in Esquimalt, Hankin found the *Beaver*, with his old messmate Daniel Pender in command, at anchor in the harbour and immediately paid him a visit. He soon saw that he must "bustle round" and look for employment of some kind or he "should soon be getting hungry," he wrote. "I found most of my old friends very kind, and seemed pleased to see me again, but no doubt there *was* a difference between being a Lieutenant in the Navy and a working man trying to make a living." However, he was fully prepared for this. He was determined to work hard and not refuse any offer that came his way. "I also determined," he said, "that I would never be seen in a drinking saloon, or be persuaded to play cards."

By this time, however, he had very little money left. He started knocking on doors. Finding a job in Victoria, though, was easier said than done. He had no luck at all. "After trying at many places in Victoria, and not being successful in getting any employment," he wrote, "I made up my mind to go to the newly-discovered gold mines at Cariboo, on the mainland about 500 miles north from Fort Yale."

He took a third-class passage on the *Eliza Anderson*, one of the steamers sailing between Victoria and New Westminster, at that time the capital of the Colony of British Columbia. Here Frederick Seymour presided as governor. From there, Hankin went by a little sternwheeler to Fort Yale, where he no doubt recalled his visit with Lady Franklin and Miss Cracroft three years before. Now he had to get to the fabulous rivers of gold in the Cariboo to make his fortune. Wagon or foot? He wrote:

There was a rambling old waggon with 3 wooden seats and with 4 scraggy unbroken horses, which was called "the stage coach" and a passage by this from Yale to Quesnelle [Quesnel] could be had for 50 dollars and it generally took 4 days, travelling also by night. And from Quesnelle it was 30 miles to Williams Creek, where there was a very small town called Barkerville. But to this place there was only a trail over the mountains and one was obliged to go on foot. As I had not the half of 50 dollars left, I had to abandon all idea of going by Coach and made up my mind to walk, like many other poor people did.

Many of the would-be millionaires set out on that walk to Barkerville. John Emmerson a year or so before was one, but he eventually gave up in despair without reaching his destination. When Hankin decided he would walk, he was undertaking a famously difficult hike. But he was young and healthy and he felt up to the challenge. "From there [Fort Yale] I was obliged to walk the rest of the way to Cariboo," he wrote. "I carried a pair of blankets on my back and a haversack full of bread, cheese, and some cooked meat, and off I started. I could always get plenty of water to drink, either from the Fraser River, or from numerous little springs on the way."

With the road up the Fraser Canyon having been finished in all its perilous glory in September 1863, Hankin almost certainly would have taken that route. The other way was up the lakes and through Lillooet, which would have meant backtracking and would have cost too much. With the miles falling away behind him, he would have trudged through communities such as Lytton, Clinton, 70 Mile House and Soda Creek. "I completed the journey in 20 days," he wrote. "There was always a small rest house, which was called a Hotel, every 20 miles or so, and if I could not reach one by dark, I slept anywhere by the road side, wrapped up in my blankets, with my boots and coat for a pillow—and slept soundly too after walking all day. ... Sometimes I would overtake some man, also going to Cariboo to try his luck, and we would keep together for a bit and be a little Company for each other."

Fortunately, it did not rain, which would have made his trek miserable. It was May and so not cold. He generally awoke about five every morning and, after washing in the nearest stream, packed up his blankets and marched on. He wrote that he "kept splendid health and always slept like a top and always managed to get a meal of some kind at one of the road-houses. It generally consisted of beans and fat bacon, with bread or biscuit, and thick coffee, sometimes with milk and sometimes without milk." Every house was what was called a "dollar house." Whatever the meal consisted of, and whether it was good or bad, he said it always cost a dollar. He related that, being young and having been in the fresh air all day, he enjoyed it all and always had a healthy appetite.

Finally, he arrived in Barkerville. There he found a busy ant-like settlement, mostly log cabins, all inhabited by miners and hangers-on. All were hoping to make their fortunes. Some of them owned good claims and were taking out a considerable amount of gold. Others were struggling mightily. Hankin had walked into town at about four in the afternoon with only half a dollar left, feeling very hungry and tired. He wrote that there was several feet of snow on the ground still, it being at a higher elevation, and so by now he was probably also cold.

As I had no money to go even to the smallest Hotel, to get a bed of any kind was an impossibility, so I walked into one of the small saloons, and sat for a long time in front of the stove, and invested my last half dollar in some bread and butter and hot coffee, which I thoroughly enjoyed, as I had eaten nothing for 12 hours and walked some 30 miles. I stayed until 7 or 7:30, when it was getting dark, and time I began to think where I would sleep for the night. I knew I should not be allowed to stay in the public room all night, and sleep on the floor which I would gladly have done, so I went out into the cold, and walked some distance down the creek to see if I could find a hole to sleep in.

Fortunately, though, the night was fine and clear, and it was not too cold because there was not a breath of wind. He eventually found an old empty shed where he decided to pass the night. He crept in, wrapped himself up in his blankets and in a few minutes was fast asleep. He got up early the next morning and wandered lower down the creek, wondering where he could get something to eat. He said he now "had not a farthing of money left."

He wrote that at this point he began, for the first time, to feel rather down on his luck. What was it his fellow officers had said when he had told them he was leaving the navy? "Remember, Hankin, that there's no pipe to dinner on shore." He was now beginning to be convinced of the truth of this. He said he did not for a moment regret leaving the navy but did occasionally wish he was on board the *Hecate*, with all his old messmates around him, having a good dinner. "Suddenly a little drop of water, very like a tear, trickled down my cheek," he wrote, "but this was soon brushed away, and saying to myself, 'Cheer up old boy. Never say die while there's a shot in the locker,' I walked a little further." But here he was, hungry, penniless, at rock bottom.

Here, however, is an unsolved puzzle. Two of Hankin's brothers, Charles and Graham, had come out to the colony in 1858. It is possible that a third brother, Thomas, had travelled with them. Thomas was certainly in the colony by 1861. Both Charles and Thomas served as officers of the Gold Escort, which had been set up to take gold from the Cariboo to New Westminster, in 1861 and 1862. In early 1864, though, Thomas was serving with the police in Victoria. Charles and Graham had been in Barkerville in the early days and were among the seven original partners of Billy Barker, who had found a rich claim and given Barkerville its name. Indeed, for a while Charles was secretary of the Billy Barker Company. Unlike Barker, Charles appears to have been able to hold on to his mining gains.

At the time Philip was in Barkerville and feeling down on his luck, it is possible that Charles and Graham were also there. If so, Philip's time there may have been a happier experience than his memoirs suggest. But were they there at that time? Charles Hankin could have been in Victoria or San Francisco spending his earnings. In his memoirs, Hankin was noticeably reticent about family matters. The puzzle remains unsolved.

Hankin related he was now hungry, broke and feeling sorry for himself. He wondered what on earth he was going to do next. He wrote:

Walking a little further, I came to a man, about 30, winding round a windlass, and heaving a large bucket full of mud and gold dust out of a shaft, when this was thrown into what was called the dump box, and then thoroughly washed with water separating the gold from the earth. The man who was winding up the bucket looked desperately ill, frequently stopping to take breath, and the perspiration streaming down his face, and was evidently in a deep decline. I said, "Well, mate, that seems pretty hard work, and you are not looking very well and have a nasty cough. I am young and strong, and have nothing to do, so let me help you." He looked at me for a moment and said "I guess you are not accustomed to this Kind of work and you couldn't wind up that heavy bucket full of mud from the bottom of our Shaft." "Oh, do let me try," I answered. "I'm sure I could do it. I'm very strong." He, poor fellow, looked fit to drop with fatigue. So I took the handle of the winch out his hand and managed to lift the bucket without much difficulty.

It, at first, was rather hard work, for the shaft was a deep one, but after a bit I got used to it, and insisted on the poor man resting, while I continued his work for him, for a couple of hours, when another man came to take his place. It was now about 4 o'clock, and I was feeling desperately hungry, when my friend said to me: "Well, mate, where are you going to? 'Ave yer got a claim here?" "No," I replied, "I've no claim, and as I've only just arrived on the creek, I've no friends, no money and I'm very hungry." "Well, come along with me," he said. "I lives in a cabin nearby. You've been real good to me, and I'm sure the boys will be mighty glad to see you. We can give you a bit of supper, and if you've nowhere to go, you can get some fir boughs and make yourself a bit of a bed underneath my bunk."

Hankin gratefully accepted this offer. The man lived with four other prospectors in a comfortable log cabin consisting of one fair-sized room, about fifteen feet long by twelve feet wide, with five bunks round it like a ship's cabin. Opposite the entrance door was a fireplace with large logs on the ground, which were burning brightly. A kettle was hanging from a hook over the fire. In the centre of the room, he wrote, there was just enough space for a plain wooden table and a bench that would seat six persons all round it.

Some meat and vegetables, which Hankin said smelled most appetizing, were stewing in a large pot over the fire. In half an hour's time, the rest of the boys came in and they all sat down to a good meal, consisting of tea and damper with butter, and a kind of Irish stew.[142] Not having tasted food for twenty hours and being young and healthy, he would no doubt have feasted on this and enjoyed it hugely.

He got up at three the next morning without being called, lit the fire, cleaned up the shack and by six had a good breakfast prepared for his new friends. They were all very pleased when they turned out of their bunks to find everything cleaned up and breakfast quite ready before they went to their work. As he had no money to give them, he felt he had to do something in return for their kind hospitality. He stayed in this shack and paid his way by his cooking and assistance.

After some weeks of this, Hankin began to think he should find employment that paid him money, for although he had plenty of work, he was not being paid. The men said he was well worth his keep. "But of course they could not afford to give me any wages," he wrote. Just about this time, he said, a claim nearby began to pay very well as the owners were taking out three hundred ounces of gold every day. Being able to read and write, he managed to find a job as secretary and treasurer to their company at a salary of fifteen dollars a week. His duties were to see that the gold was carefully weighed each day, keep the accounts and pay the dust every evening into the bank. He now began to feel that he was really getting on all right and said goodbye to the men in the log cabin, who, he recalled, were sorry to part with him.

Hankin decided to move to a small hotel. Here he had a tiny bedroom, which held a small bed, one chair and a little washstand with one small towel hanging over the back of the chair. It was many weeks since he had enjoyed the luxury of a bed and, even though it was only a straw

Barkerville, Williams Creek, Cariboo, before the fire that destroyed most of the town on September 16, 1868. Hankin spent a few months here in early 1864 and tried his hand at mining.
Image A-00355 courtesy of the Royal BC Museum and Archives

mattress, he found it agreeably comfortable. The sheets were clean and there were two good blankets. "For this room," he wrote, "I paid one dollar a night, and I had 2 meals a day for 50 cents each meal. I washed all my own clothes and paid out for my board and lodgings 14 dollars weekly, leaving me one dollar over from Salary and every Saturday I treated myself to one very bad cigar and one glass of rum and water, and the two together cost me exactly a dollar."

He described the three or four small public houses that advertised themselves variously as "hotels," "drinking saloons," "billiard tables," "hurdy-gurdy girls" and "dancing." To these establishments the miners would go every evening to gamble, drink, dance and "make things hum" until three in the morning.

After a month, though, the claim he was working for ceased to pay as the prospectors of the company lost the lead: that is, the vein of gold-bearing rock ran out. As the claim was now not yielding any gold, there was no money to pay his salary and he lost his job. He now had another "What now?" moment.

One person he met in the Cariboo was a G.C.B. Mathew, who held a small government appointment. Hankin had known him in former days at Victoria. (In one of those coincidences that do occasionally occur, Mathew later died in British Honduras and Hankin was appointed to take his place as colonial secretary.) Since Hankin was not doing well in Barkerville—actually his visit had been a disaster—he decided to return to Victoria and look for a job there. "I did not at all like the idea of walking to Fort Yale again," he wrote, "where I could catch the steamer for New Westminster, for it was a long and lonely tramp. However, Mr. Mathew very kindly lent me $60, which I am glad to say I was able to repay before 6 months."

He left Barkerville at five in the morning, with a small knapsack containing some bread and cold meat, and started on the trail through the woods to Quesnel, a distance of thirty-five miles. He arrived about five in the evening. He recalled he was wearing a rough red flannel shirt and a pair of long wellington boots with the legs of his trousers tucked inside, as miners wore them. It was a lonely walk, and he did not see a human being or an animal and very few birds. By walking from Barkerville to Quesnel, he saved ten dollars.

He wrote:

I remember when I arrived at Quesnelle, there was a dance going on at the little Inn and the guests were Miners in their red shirts, and top boots, with their trousers tucked inside, a few hurdy-gurdy girls, and about 15 or 20 Indian [women], who were supposed to be quite in society. Altho' I felt pretty tired after my long walk, I could not resist, after I had some supper, going to the dance. The [women] had moccasins on their feet and generally wore a short red or blue petticoat made of Serge, and some who did not quite belong to the upper ten, wore a blanket! They had learned a little

English and all the men could speak Chinook more or less, which was the lingua franca of British Columbia, and Vancouver Island.

The party was most amusing. 25 cents (about a shilling) was the entrance fee and there was a kind of Master of the ceremonies, who called out the figures saying "first gent to the left with the left hand round, back again and turn, balance in line." It was really wonderful what good time they all kept, and how serious they all were about it. All the girls were either Kitty or Polly—and when the Quadrille was finished "Waltz up to the bar" was shouted out in a very loud voice—when everyone did so at once, and we all had a drink, and your partner generally took lemonade or ginger ale. Fifty cents was charged for each drink, whatever it might be; so one can easily understand that a good profit was made. Sometimes Champagne was ordered—I should be sorry to say what it was made of, but it always cost $10 a bottle.

I recollect asking one of the Kittys in Chinook to dance with me and she drew herself up in a very dignified manner and said, "Halo introduce," which signified I had not been introduced to her! And I couldn't keep [from] laughing, which made her very angry. What fun it all was, and how I enjoyed everything! But I was young and full of life and spirits and altho' I had only a few shillings in the world I had splendid health, which was better than money.

Finding he could get a seat in the wagon that ran from Quesnel to Yale for forty dollars, he booked a passage for the next day. The wagon, or Royal Mail cart, as it was generally called, was a rough, shaky conveyance, drawn by four unbroken horses, containing three rough planks, four seats and three persons on each seat. The middle seats were the safest; someone on the outside always ran the risk of falling off. As the middle seats were all taken, Hankin had to be content with an outside place.

They travelled day and night for three days. He said it was difficult to keep awake. The man in the middle slept quite soundly by simply resting his head on his neighbour's shoulder. The wagon stopped at occasional rest houses for about twenty minutes either to give the horses food and water or to obtain fresh ones. Hankin would then get down from his hard seat and lie down on the ground or the floor of the little inn and fall instantly into a sound sleep. Soon, though, he was roused from his slumber by the driver calling out, "All aboard boys! All aboard." Then he had to hurry to climb back on the wagon and reclaim his seat or the wagon would start without him. "I never in my life," he said, "remember feeling so tired or such an intense longing for sleep."

They reached Yale at four o'clock on a Wednesday afternoon. He went at once to a small hotel, which he remembered was called the Royal, and ordered a bed. They gave him a small room with a comfortable bed with clean sheets. "I could hardly manage to undress myself," he said, "and the instant I was in bed I fell asleep and never moved for 27 hours. I don't think anyone knows what a dreadful thing it is to suffer from want of sleep unless they have experienced it."

When he surfaced from his slumber, he started in the sternwheeler downstream to New Westminster, arriving the following day. On board the steamer, he met Archdeacon Henry Press Wright from New Westminster, where he lived with his wife and daughter.[143] Hankin wrote:

> I had known him slightly in former days when I was in the Navy. "How are you, Hankin," he said, and shook hands with me, adding "I'm afraid you are not one of the lucky ones" and continued, "come and stay for a few days with me at New Westminster and have a bit of a rest before going over to Victoria to try and get some employment." "It is very kind of you, Mr. Archdeacon," I replied, "but I have no clothes except what I stand up in, and I am not fit to sit down at table with Ladies." Wright brushed that excuse aside. "Stuff and nonsense," he replied, "Don't think of that. I am sure Mrs. Wright will be very pleased to see you."

Hankin could not resist such an invitation. He stayed with Wright and his family for two days. "Mrs. Wright and his daughter were both very good to me," he wrote, "and made me feel quite at home. I shall never forget their kindness as long as I live, for there is an emanation from the heart in genuine hospitality, which cannot be described but is immediately felt and puts the stranger at once at his ease."

Archdeacon Wright seems to have made a habit of helping out those who, like Hankin, were down on their luck. John Emmerson, walking the same route, had not reached Barkerville but had turned back, bereft of all hope and all money. Wright noticed his distressed appearance on one of the ferries on the lakes south of Lillooet and not only loaned him a sovereign but also gave him a letter of introduction to the Hudson's Bay Company manager in Victoria, who gave Emmerson a job as a blacksmith.[144]

At the end of those two days, Hankin left the kind archdeacon's house and crossed over the strait to Victoria, where he arrived with about seven dollars in his pocket, "which was every farthing [he] had in the world."

His problem could not be avoided any longer. He badly needed a job—anything to earn money to keep body and soul alive. He slept that night at the cheapest inn he could find. The next morning he called at a dozen or so places and asked for work of any description, saying, "I would do it better, and for half the money anyone else asked." But still, those few dollars in his pocket would feed him for only a few days. What then?

7

Hankin Becomes Chief of Police for the Colony of Vancouver Island

1864–1866

Jobless and penniless, Philip Hankin trudged from one door to another asking for a job. This would have been dispiriting. But at length, his luck turned.

One door he knocked on was that of Montague Tyrwhitt-Drake. At that time Tyrwhitt-Drake was the senior partner in Drake, Jackson and Aikman, the principal law firm in Victoria. He had himself tried his hand at prospecting but, after making only two or three dollars a day, had decided that law was a more reliable profession. Perhaps he saw something of himself in Hankin because he gave him a job for twenty dollars a week. Like Hankin, he came from Hertfordshire, which could only have helped. (In 1866 Tyrwhitt-Drake also gave a job to Hankin's brother, Graham.) The firm had chambers at the corner of Langley Street, in Bastion Square. True, it was only a temporary position, but it was a foot in the door. Hankin was to fill the place of one of the clerks who had fallen sick. He confessed that, though it was scarcely Christian, he earnestly hoped the clerk would not recover.

The work was not hard, Hankin said, and the pay was good. He had a knack of soothing ruffled feelings and making people like him. An intelligent worker, he made sure he was attentive to his responsibilities. He noticed the other clerks were in the habit of going out for their lunch at about a quarter to one and coming back at two-thirty. They called this the lunch hour, to which they said they were entitled. He realized his employer would also notice this. So he always brought some bread and cold meat in his pocket for his lunch so that he should not have to leave the office until the evening. He was grateful for his job and wanted to get ahead.

Alas for his unchristian hopes, the clerk recovered within a month and so Hankin had to relinquish the position. Tyrwhitt-Drake, though, had observed his diligence. Saying he was sorry he had to let him go, he offered to provide him with a written reference.

Hankin was again out on the street job-hunting. But this time he had experience at the law firm and a useful reference from Tyrwhitt-Drake. He had managed to save a few dollars and could afford enough to eat and a bed to sleep on. But he wanted a little more comfort and thought that a home of his own would be good. Since he could cook well—as the queen of the Sandwich Islands could attest to—he thought he could manage. "I at once rented a tiny furnished cottage, for about $15 a month," he wrote in his memoirs, "and commenced my housekeeping. The little house consisted of one bedroom, one living room and a tiny kitchen, with a small American stove, and a little outhouse for wood. I soon got everything clean and tidy, and I bought some common soap and a scrubbing brush, and scrubbed the floors of the two rooms and the kitchen thoroughly with soap and hot water." He was never, he said, one of those men who required two dinners a day:

I used to go every day to the Butcher and buy about 50 cents worth of meat, sometimes the best end of the neck of mutton, and, with a few onions and potatoes, would make myself an Irish stew for dinner, which was always at one o'clock, and at 6 I would take my last meal, consisting of bread and butter with tea, or cocoa. ...

The way I lived, was, at all events, much better than anything I had been accustomed to in the Navy, when the last meal was always at 4 o'clock, and then only tea, with coarse brown sugar and biscuit, which was full of weevils. After my supper, before going to bed, I always scrubbed out the sitting room and kitchen and the common deal table [made with soft, low-quality wood] with hot soap and water, and washed up everything, and by 9 o'clock I was in bed and soon asleep. I did not know a single game of cards, neither could I play Billiards, so I had no temptation to visit any of the gambling or drinking saloons.

He met many other young men who were also looking for jobs. He observed that these often frequented saloons to strike up friendships with businessmen, merchants and well-to-do people and play billiards with them to pass a pleasant evening. These gentlemen, Hankin said, could have given them a helping hand, had they been so disposed, but "one does not, as a rule, feel inclined to give a young man a place in your office, with whom you have been playing cards or Billiards until perhaps one o'clock in the morning." So he took good care never to be seen in any of the saloons either by day or by night.

Finding a job, though, was not easy. He spent whole days tramping round Victoria, knocking on doors and trying to persuade someone to hire him. He found he lacked many of the required qualifications. Being an ex-naval officer got him only so far. His perseverance, though, eventually paid off. With his reference from Tyrwhitt-Drake in hand, he called on the colonial secretary and asked that his name be registered as an applicant for employment in the civil service.[145] After waiting a couple of weeks, he received a letter that offered him a junior clerkship in the colonial secretary's office, at a salary of eighty dollars a month.[146] "How happy I felt, and how rich!" he wrote. "Eighty dollars a month—equal to £192 a year! More than I had earned as a Lieutenant in the Navy."

He started his new job the next day, again being careful to be the first person to arrive in the office in the morning and the last to leave at night. As before, he always took his lunch with him so he did not need to leave the office for the so-called lunch hour, which, he again noticed, was nearer two hours than one. By this means, and being bright, efficient and polite, he was able to make himself useful around the office, quickly becoming familiar with the files. He soon attracted the notice of the colonial secretary and made progress. By his diligence and responsibility, he established himself firmly in his new job.

He now began to think of finding a better home for himself than his little shanty. It was, he said, rather lonely coming home after a long day at the office and cooking his dinner with not a soul to speak to. Consequently, he and the chief clerk, a Mr. Nesbitt, agreed to share accommodation and they soon found a small furnished cottage for twenty dollars a month.[147] This consisted of a bright and cheerful sitting room, two bedrooms, a kitchen and also a garden, well stocked with vegetables. The cottage was built entirely of wood, as were all houses at that time in Victoria. There was a charming balcony covered with honeysuckle and climbing roses. Here Hankin and Nesbitt used to sit in the evening and, perhaps over cigars and brandy, solve the problems of the world. Here also Hankin would have learned from an insider about the politics of the colony—the gossip, the ins and outs of the administration and the difficulties the governor was having with the penny-pinching legislative assembly.

Neither of them had time to do any housework, so they hired a Chinese handyman, who did all the cooking and washing and kept the house and garden in good order. Their monthly expenses were now rent, twenty dollars, handyman, twenty dollars, and food, forty dollars, for a total of eighty dollars. They shared everything, paying forty dollars a month each. As Hankin's salary was eighty dollars, he had a good margin left. "Now I could buy some decent clothes," he said, "and I looked up some of my old friends I had known when I was in the Navy. They were all pleased to see I was making headway and I was often asked out to a high tea, with a little dance afterwards, at various houses."

———

The British government had appointed Arthur Kennedy as governor of the relatively unimportant but undoubtedly argumentative Colony of Vancouver Island in late 1863. He arrived in the colony the same year as Hankin.[148] In the Colonial Service he had been a governor in Sierra Leone, at the time Hankin was stationed there in the navy, and also in Western Australia. He had built a reputation for administrative reform and for cleaning up corruption. In these previous positions, though, Kennedy had not had to deal with an elected assembly and when he came up against one in Vancouver Island he didn't know how to handle it. This deepened the rift after he arrived in Victoria and attempted to govern

Arthur Edward Kennedy, the affable governor who appointed Hankin superintendent of police for the Colony of Vancouver Island.

Wikimedia Commons

in the way he had been accustomed. The problem was that the governor had to administer the colony, but the legislative assembly had control of the finances. Kennedy tried hard, but the assembly opposed him seemingly on every point and grumbled about his attempts to govern. Almost as soon as he arrived, the assembly refused to approve his salary or to pay for the costs of an official residence. The relationship went downhill from there, with Dr. John Helmcken being one of his most vocal adversaries.

Kennedy has been criticized for having achieved little of note as governor. This is unfair: the fractious members of the legislative assembly blocked most of what he was trying to do and then blamed him for doing nothing. He failed in his attempt, for example, to ensure that Indigenous land could be acquired only by fair compensation. He did, though, shake up the civil service, firing those he thought were dishonest or incompetent and replacing them with new men.

At this time, Frederick Seymour was governor of the mainland Colony of British Columbia. Seymour was the grandson of the Marquess of Hertford and an aristocrat, even if his father had been illegitimate. His father had little money to give him either as an inheritance or for an education. Frederick was fortunate, therefore, that his elder brother, General Sir Francis Seymour, had been a friend and equerry to Prince Albert, Queen Victoria's husband. After the prince's death in December 1861, he had become a groom-in-waiting to the Queen. He was consequently well placed to obtain a post for his younger brother in the Colonial Service. Frederick bounced around the colonies, from Van Diemen's Land

(Tasmania) to a series of ever more senior appointments in Antigua and British Honduras. In September 1863, he had been appointed governor of British Columbia, the so-called gold colony on the mainland, partly because he was believed to have had experience with what were at the time dismissively called savage tribes. In accepting the appointment, Seymour wrote to the colonial secretary, the Duke of Newcastle, "The prospects of a change from the swamps of Honduras to a fine country is inexpressibly attractive to me, and I trust, in the bracing air of North America to prove myself worthy of your Grace's confidence and kindness."[149]

In 1864, when Seymour arrived in New Westminster, the competition between the Colonies of Vancouver Island and British Columbia was at its

Frederick Seymour, governor of the Colony of British Columbia, who at first refused to swear in Philip Hankin as colonial secretary even though Hankin had been appointed by the British government. Image A-01752 courtesy of the Royal BC Museum and Archives

height. He quickly absorbed all the resentments and prejudices of the mainland toward the island colony. The two colonies were not only physically but also temperamentally apart, each with a fierce rivalry amounting to animosity toward the other. The waters between the two colonies formed not only a physical but also a psychological barrier between them. Hankin said that only very seldom did he see any of the New Westminster officials in Victoria.

Working in the colonial secretary's office, Hankin soon became acquainted with Governor Kennedy, for whom he had nothing but praise.

"He was one of the most delightful men I ever met," he wrote. "He had been in the Army, and was a very fine handsome man, and looked every inch what he was—a thorough Gentleman. ... I was frequently asked to dances at Government House, and always thought it a great honour to go there. I was always a good dancer and used to enjoy these parties very much." Kennedy, who recognized Hankin's ability and charm, was soon to make use of his services in a significant way.

The admiral commanding the Pacific Station at this time was Joseph Denman, the aggressive anti-slaver from the West Africa Station.[150] He had lost none of his passionate fervour for the suppression of slavery. It is possible he saw little difference between the Indigenous slave-owning communities on the Pacific coast and the Indigenous slavers on the West African coast.[151] Slavery had to some extent been part of the culture of the Indigenous people on the coast for generations. Although it is hard to assess how widespread it ever had actually been, by 1864 it appears to have declined substantially. Nonetheless, the authorities in Victoria, the church and Admiral Denman would have viewed it with abhorrence.

In his book *Gunboat Frontier*, Barry M. Gough describes the actions the civil and naval authorities in Victoria took to eliminate slavery, piracy and the trade in liquor on the coast. James Douglas, the old Hudson's Bay Company trader and governor, had successfully applied moral suasion and force of example. Naval officers followed his policy of non-interference in Indigenous institutions and trusted to negotiation and persuasion to provide remedies. The missionaries buttressed their efforts. In writing of Captain George Henry Richards on the *Hecate*, Gough describes him as one of the naval officers who had an intelligent and sensitive approach to Indigenous people. "Richards," Gough writes, "provides the best example of a naval officer determined to resolve white-Indian conflict on the northwest coast. His competent and sensitive opinions, views he shared with many naval officers, led him to the belief that most of the difficulties lay with the whites, not with the Indians."[152] Gough cites the example of Richards ransoming a female slave for one hundred blankets.

Slaves or captives were freed usually one or two at a time, given protection and frequently returned to their home tribes.

Governor Kennedy, a seasoned soldier and colonial administrator, was inclined to take a more vigorous and assertive approach than Douglas. Both he and Denman were not, for example, going to tolerate what they saw as piracy by Indigenous people who they believed still practised slavery. This lay behind their actions in the *Kingfisher* affair.

Sometimes called the Ahousaht affair, the *Kingfisher* affair occurred in the late summer of 1864. No one comes out of this with credit. Although the salient facts are clear, some ambiguity arises from accounts that differ on the details and the sequence of events. Hankin's own recollections, written approximately fifty years after the affair, differ in some ways from the official record. He describes an incident that was relatively benign, which is not at all what contemporary documents reveal. In his memoirs, Hankin also gives the impression that his was the restraining voice, the one trying to limit the punitive actions of the warships. It should also be borne in mind that the accounts we have are mostly told from the perspective of the non-Indigenous participants.

The *Kingfisher* was a small trading sloop that plied the waters off the west coast of Vancouver Island. In August 1864, members of the Ahousaht Indigenous People, led by a Chief called Cap-chah, lured the *Kingfisher* into an ambush off Flores Island in Clayoquot Sound and took it to Matilda Creek. There they pushed two members of the crew off the vessel and drowned one by holding his head under the water. The other managed to clamber back on board, where five men held him while the sixth knifed him in the stomach. An Indigenous member of the crew was held on shore for a few days and then his head was split with an axe. The attack was so sudden and unexpected that the crew, including Captain James Stephenson, were all murdered without having time to make any resistance. The ship was then stripped of everything worth stealing, set on fire and scuttled in deep water.

A bloody proceeding, no doubt, but the response of the colonial authorities might well be thought to have been disproportionate.

The news of the murders was brought to Victoria by some Indigenous people from Alberni who were no friends of the Ahousaht people. After HMS *Devastation* had made an unsuccessful investigation, Governor Kennedy asked Denman to send a warship to Clayoquot Sound to investigate the matter further and to apprehend the murderers. With his history of aggressive actions in freeing slaves off the west coast of Africa, Denman was a believer in swift and decisive use of force to maintain law and order. Gough writes that Denman had the reputation of being a ruthless fighter for just causes.[153] In the *Kingfisher* affair he would justify his reputation.

Denman decided to take command of the expedition and arrest the murderers himself. He asked Governor Kennedy if he knew of anyone who could speak the local Indigenous languages to take with him. "Certainly," said the governor in Hankin's telling of the story. "I have... Mr. Hankin. He was formerly a Lieutenant in the Navy and was out here for several years in the *Plumper* and *Hecate*, surveying the Coast. He can speak Chinook and knows something of the Nootka Sound language." Hankin was thereupon directed to report to Denman on his flagship, HMS *Sutlej*, and to assist him any way he could. The superintendent of police, Horace Smith, as well as Denman's wife, Grace, went with them.

On October 2, the *Sutlej* reached Clayoquot Sound and anchored off a large Ahousaht village. Denman sent for Hankin and asked what he should do. Should they fire on the Indigenous village as a reprisal? Hankin said he begged the admiral not to do this. He wrote:

> If he would allow me, I would land in the ship's Dinghy with only two men. I had some trouble to get the Admiral to consent to this, as he said we should all be most certainly shot, but I said, No, I would not be shot, just landing in the way I proposed and firearms would be no use to me whatever. For we could see with our glasses all the Indians, about 2,000 of them, all in their war paint and evidently very excited. The Admiral said I must take at least a Revolver and a ship's Cutlass, but I protested strongly, for I said I should be certain to trip over the Cutlass. They were nasty, heavy, clumsy things and it would only be in my way, and as for the pistol, what was the good of it against 2,000 men. I said I wanted nothing but my walking stick, but I knew the Indian character. I

felt sure they would not fire on me alone. So at last the Admiral consented to let me go, and when within a few feet of the shore, I jumped overboard and waded ashore, telling the boat to push off and wait for me.

Hankin said he walked straight up to the assembled Ahousaht people and managed to make them understand what the big ship had come for. If they did not give up Cap-chah and the other murderers responsible for killing the *Kingfisher's* crew, there would, he told them, be trouble. The admiral would fire his big guns and destroy their village. Many of them would be killed. They answered, he said, that as the murderers had escaped into the forest, they could not give them up.

Hankin then returned to the ship and reported to Denman the results of his visit. He said that he and another interpreter, his old friend Friday, had found out what had happened on the *Kingfisher* and who the murderers were. The admiral asked again what he would advise being done. Should he destroy the village now? Hankin said he recommended landing a party to surround the village, taking as many prisoners as they could and holding them as hostages until the murderers surrendered. Denman's official report says he ordered HMS *Devastation*, which had also come up with the *Sutlej*, to destroy several of the villages but not to fire on anyone unless fired upon first.

On the morning of October 7, Lieutenant Hugh Stewart, accompanied by Hankin, landed with twenty sailors and forty marines and, hacking their way through the tangled forest and swamps, attempted to capture the murderers by surprise. All went well until barking dogs gave them away. The inhabitants all took to the forest at once. The marines were eager to have a shot at them as they ran away, but Hankin said he restrained them. They found items stolen from the *Kingfisher* in all the houses. Hankin took up a position on top of a rocky hill about a hundred feet high, in order to see what was happening and to give the necessary directions. "Two or three bullets," he said, "whizzed by me." After one of the men was slightly wounded, Lieutenant Stewart then gave orders to return fire, and three—some reports say ten—of the villagers were killed. But the forest was very dense and the remainder all made their escape.

By this time it was daylight. Not an Indigenous inhabitant was to be seen. Denman ordered *Sutlej*'s guns to open fire and destroy the villages. In all, they destroyed nine villages and sixty-five canoes and killed fifteen Indigenous people. "The recent action of our war vessels in shelling the Indian villages," the *Daily British Colonist* said, in an assertion that few today would agree with, "was conducted according to the strict rules of civilised warfare. Mr. Hankin and the Indian Friday warned the natives in every instance and were only molested but once, when an Indian rushed at Mr. Hankin with a knife; the weapon was, however, quickly wrenched from his hand by his intended victim."[154]

In the wreckage of one village, the bluejackets found a young girl orphaned by the bombardment and brought her back to the *Sutlej*. Grace Denman, the admiral's wife, adopted her and called her Margrette (Maggie) Sutlej Davis. This adoption was entirely in accordance with the Victorian assumption that the child, being raised in a Christian home, would then have an opportunity for a better life. It has, though, been widely criticized as the theft of a little girl from her own people and is today widely condemned. Poor little Maggie reportedly died off Valparaíso two years later.[155]

Denman eventually did succeed in arresting all the murderers except Cap-chah. They were brought to Victoria in irons.[156] Hankin was given credit for capturing one of them. In London, both the *Illustrated London News* and *Frank Leslie's Illustrated Newspaper* reported that "Mr. Hankin and his Man Friday again landed and approached this man quietly, without exciting his alarm, but presently made him a prisoner, believing him to be one of the murderers, and brought him safe on board."[157] At the trial, Chief Justice David Cameron ruled that since the witnesses were not Christian they could not swear on the Bible. Consequently their evidence could not be believed. To Denman's fury, the accused murderers were thereupon released. Denman had reason to be angry. Cameron, who was often criticized as chief justice because of his lack of legal training, had overlooked an 1843 statute that permitted such evidence.[158]

The admiral was pleased, though, that none of his men had been killed in the operation. He wrote an official report to the governor, in which he said, "I cannot close my letter without expressing very strongly the great assistance I have received from Mr. Hankin, whose coolness and presence of mind have been of the greatest value. ... He is also an excellent interpreter and with the aid of Friday, the means of communication have been all I could desire."[159] Hankin merely noted that it did not seem that he had done anything to deserve such praise. His training in the Royal Navy and, in particular, his knowledge of languages, though, had certainly helped. Hankin wrote that he had spent a pleasant ten days on board the *Sutlej.* He received the greatest kindness from everyone, the admiral asking him to dinner almost every night.

Back in Victoria, Hankin resumed his duties as a junior clerk in the colonial secretary's office. But Governor Kennedy had his eye on him. In October, in a report on the policing situation in the colony, he reported that Hankin had been extremely useful to Admiral Denman, adding "Mr. Hankin was recommended to me by Captain Richards, under whom he served in the Royal Navy. I hope to put Mr. Hankin in a better position when a suitable opportunity arises."[160] Hankin's star was clearly rising.

In July 1864, Kennedy had written to Edward Cardwell, the colonial secretary in London, saying that there was a need to reform the police in the colony. "The whole police force in this Island," he wrote, "consists of eight constables, two sergeants and one superintendent."[161] Outside Victoria, there were no police at all. The need for better policing was manifest. The quiet English village of Victoria had changed into a raucous little town with, in some areas, a wealth of bars and brothels. The Cormorant-Fisgard district was described as a devil's kitchen of thieves, renegade whisky traders, over two hundred prostitutes and roving sailors off the ships looking for action.

Kennedy was also well aware there was corruption in the Vancouver Island police. In November 1864, Superintendent of Police Horace Smith was charged with receiving bribes from saloon keepers to turn a blind eye to gambling.

"I am proprietor of the Fashion hotel," a man named John Keenan said in court. "I have paid money to the accused. ... The arrangement made with Sergeant Blake was that when the game was going on they would pay him $5 a night."[162]

Real estate agent Victor Foucault, night watchman John Taylor and Lewis Shapard, who owned the Confederate Saloon, all testified they had paid bribes to Smith. Foucault confessed to having paid Smith $200 to have an Indigenous woman, who had been taken away from him by another policeman, returned to him. Kennedy accepted Smith's resignation the day before he was going to dismiss him for "having received numerous bribes to permit gambling in various public houses and for other immoral purposes. ... The proceedings in this case have made it clear that the Police Force has been corrupt and inefficient from a period anterior to Mr. Smith's entering it, and that Mr. Smith, the sergeants and privates of the Force have been compensating themselves for insufficient salaries by receiving bribes on a large and systematic scale."[163] Clearly, vigorous reform was needed.

Kennedy sent for Hankin, still a junior clerk, and offered him the position vacated by Smith. The salary would be $1,200 a year, with free living quarters, coal, gas and a servant. Hankin realized this was an excellent opportunity and accepted it gratefully. His appointment, Kennedy wrote, was received by the public with general satisfaction.

The appointment was gazetted on December 23, 1964.

His Excellency the Governor has been pleased to appoint Philip James Hankin, Esquire, to be Superintendent of Police, vice Smith, resigned.[164]

This was an extraordinary promotion and prompts the question: Why did Kennedy reach down to a newly hired junior clerk in the colonial secretary's office for such an appointment? There is no clear answer, but Kennedy obviously knew of Hankin's experience of commanding men in the navy. Hankin had performed well during the expedition to Clayoquot Sound, for which Admiral Denman had given him a glowing recommendation. Helpfully, despite his rough time in Barkerville, he was also a gentleman. He could speak the languages of many of the Indigenous offenders and criminals. Most importantly, perhaps, he was an outsider at a time when Kennedy needed an outsider to clean up the corruption and cronyism in the police.

So, how did he do, this twenty-eight-year-old superintendent of police? Very well, it seems. In 1974, Robert Louis Smith wrote of Hankin's work as superintendent of police in an article entitled "The Hankin Appointment"—although it was not this appointment he was writing about. "Hankin addressed himself to duty with zeal and a certain puritanical spirit. He dismissed insubordinate constables and, in a proposal to his superiors, set out standards of qualification and performance for the men. Hankin patrolled the coasts, parleyed with Indians,... conducted meteorological readings and a census, managed the chain gang and supervised the Victoria Jail. ... Both public and private sources indicate that Hankin was an efficient and honest officer."[165]

With the experience and discipline of the Royal Navy behind him, Hankin set about his work with honest determination. He seems to have been one of those who, mischievous and fun-loving by nature, respond well to the challenge of being in authority. He found the "jail in a filthy state, and no kind of discipline." He had it thoroughly cleansed. Using a great quantity of coal tar and whitewash, he got the whole place thoroughly clean and in order. Within days of his appointment, he had started to install new drains to improve its hygiene. "My best officer was a Sergeant McBride, who had retired from the army," Hankin wrote in his memoirs. "He was a splendid fellow, and always loyal and true and we got on very well together. His son, is now [written in 1914] Sir Richard McBride, and is now Premier of British Columbia."[166] When asked to inspect the cleaned-up prison, Kennedy heartily approved of his actions.

Improving the state of the town jail was one thing; keeping prisoners inside was another. In February 1865, a sailor, serving a two-month sentence, was trusted enough to be appointed Hankin's valet de chambre. One evening when Hankin was dining out, he helped himself to Hankin's Sabbath suit, shorts, collars and necktie, as well as three gold watches and ninety dollars. He then shinnied down a drainpipe and made his way to Esquimalt, where, respectably well dressed and with money in his pocket, he had no trouble taking passage to the safety of Portland.[167]

In June 1865, Hankin made an official visit on board the gunboat *Forward* to the Indigenous communities on the west coast of Vancouver Island, including Clayoquot Sound. Part of the reason behind this was to assess the consequences of the *Kingfisher* affair. He found the people there friendly and eager to trade. He even coaxed Cap-chah out of his hiding place and calmed his fears about being arrested. The people were in the process of building new canoes, even though several of the villages were still in the ruins the *Sutlej* had left them in. Although the visit was amicable and many protestations of friendship and loyalty were made, Hankin was the pointed end of colonial governance. He promised friendship, goodwill, protection and trade—unless the Indigenous people misconducted themselves, for which there would be punishment. Nevertheless, his charm offensive appears to have worked—at least in the government's estimation. His report was sent to the Colonial Office in London, where the file on him was growing.

Hankin enforced the laws rigorously, particularly those against rum-running. He dismissed officers who didn't meet his standards. On July 5, 1865, for example, he dismissed Constable Dobbs for being too intoxicated to go to work.[168] And on July 29, he dismissed Constable Erickson for being impertinent to his sergeant, for having disobeyed orders and for stirring up mutiny among the other constables. Since Erickson had been reported for disobedience and impertinence twelve times in the previous six months, the dismissal sounds amply justified.[169] Later, when the legislative assembly for political reasons reduced the police budget, he had to tell Sergeants Wilmer, Ferrall and Blake that he could not afford to pay them any longer and had to dismiss them.[170]

With a small force of five men to police the whole colony and run the jail, which at the time had what were described as fifty to sixty desperadoes in it, Hankin clearly had a difficult job. In Victoria alone he had to police eighty-five bars and twenty-six wholesale outlets.

Hankin clearly managed to find time for romance. He became engaged to Isabel Nagle, known as Belle and Bella to her family. She was the daughter of Jeremiah Nagle, who had come to Victoria in 1858 as captain on the *Commodore* with that first shipload of prospectors. An experienced mariner, he had wisely stayed in Victoria, where he had become harbour master and a magistrate.[171] He had a spot of trouble when he was fired for some mishap with his expenses but that allegation was later determined to be unfounded.

Philip and Isabel set their wedding date for August 3, 1865. In late July, alarmingly, Admiral Denman sent Hankin on a mission to Nootka Sound, and it was uncertain when he would be back. "Fortunately," Isabel's sister, Susan Nagle, wrote in the diary she kept, he "got back in time for the original wedding date, which was the third of this month. They were married [in the Nagle family home] at half past eleven. ... We had breakfast directly after and then danced for a short time, but it was too warm to do more than a few Quadrilles and Lancers. At half past four the bride and groom started for their cottage at Esquimalt and we accompanied them on horseback. ... We remained at the cottage for a short time & continued our ride. On our way home we stopped at Richmond and had ice cream, raspberries & cream."[172]

Isabel Hankin, Philip Hankin's wife. Image G-00046 courtesy of the Royal BC Museum and Archives

Hankin also found time for amateur theatricals. He took a small part in the farce *High Life below Stairs*, performed at the Victoria Rifle Volunteers concert in March 1866.[173]

That October, Hankin and Isabel went to the first ball given by the governor in the new ballroom at Government House. All the great of both colonies were there, including Admiral Denman, William Young (the colonial secretary), Henry Pellew Crease, John Helmcken, William Fraser Tolmie and Montague Tyrwhitt-Drake, as well as Philip's brother Charles. With an excellent seven-piece quadrille band providing lively dance music, the over four hundred guests were, the *Daily British Colonist* reported, "in the full spirit of enjoyment, though with somewhat damaging effect from the members who participated in female attire."[174] That is to say, so exuberant and crowded was the party that the girls' ball gowns were crushed. They all went for supper at one in the morning. "Dancing," and we may assume that Hankin, who was an avid dancer, enjoyed this, "was maintained without the least flagging until half past three, when the National Anthem was sung in chorus."

As a result of Admiral Denman's report, the Lords Commissioners of the Admiralty sent Hankin a letter reinstating him in the Royal Navy with the rank of lieutenant.[175] Kennedy, not wanting to lose him, requested that he be given leave of absence from the navy for a year in order to remain as superintendent of police. He was already too useful to be let go.[176]

The assembly was quibbling over the police budget and wanted to reduce it. Kennedy wrote to Edward Cardwell in February 1866 to complain about this threat to the colony's policing. Among his points were:

15. It is obvious that a total of five policemen for the whole Colony, affording one at a time for duty, is virtually to leave whiskey selling to Indians, drunkenness, and prostitution unchecked. ...

16. Now that Lieutenant Hankin, R.N., the Superintendent, has brought it to a state of efficiency and decency, the Legislative Assembly see fit to reduce it [the police force] to a standard both as to pay of officers and numbers which renders it useless or compels the members of it to the same means for a subsistence.

17. The number of prisoners undergoing sentence in the gaol varies from 50 to 60—desperadoes of all nationalities—and the absence of any force beyond a gaoler and a few warders to suppress any outbreak is courting a danger which will more than probably occur.[177]

Hankin's firm and efficient hand did not make him friends. The fact that he was Kennedy's protégé set many of the leading citizens firmly against him. Any reformer, especially one only twenty-eight years old, who had been in the colony for only a few months, was bound to upset people. His charm and self-assurance could easily be seen as arrogance. He ruffled many feathers and these would still be ruffled when he returned a few years later in another capacity.

This feeling sometimes found expression in the press. In July 1866, the *Evening Telegraph* complained of his imperious and arbitrary conduct toward both policemen and prisoners. That summer, in an attempt to embarrass Kennedy politically, the legislative assembly appointed a committee to investigate the management of the police department.[178] An ex-constable named McEwan told the inquiry that Hankin had asked a cook at the jail to prepare some meals for him and that he had also asked prisoners to make some furniture for his house. He complained that Hankin had called some constables "a lazy, idle lot." Their offence? When asked to cart off a drunk from a street, they had refused to put the drunk's feet on their shoulders because his shoes were covered with dirt.[179] High crimes indeed! Hankin survived this but the refusal of the governor to allow him to give evidence to the committee or to provide it with the police force's financial statements led to some anxious moments.

That July was an uneasy time for Hankin for another reason. When giving evidence in the police court in reply to a question, he had stated that the Commercial Hotel, owned by a Mr. Turgoose, was a "particularly bad one and that prostitutes were in the habit of congregating there."[180] Mr. Turgoose sued Hankin for slander and demanded $5,000 in damages. Tyrwhitt-Drake's firm represented Hankin. The chief justice found in Hankin's favour and dismissed the case. Regardless of whether the words were slanderous, Hankin was protected, the court said, by a double privilege: that of a witness in court and that of a public officer doing his duty.

Soon, after much political strife and posturing, it was determined that the Colonies of Vancouver Island and British Columbia should be united. It did seem rather absurd, Hankin said, to have two separate colonies within a few miles of each other, with two governors and two sets of government officials. The British government pushed for the union as a way of reducing the animosities and strife between them. Seymour at first did not agree, but he soon acquiesced to the inevitable. When on an extended visit to England in 1865 and 1866 (where he was married), Seymour managed to extract promises that the mainland colony would be the dominant one, that the capital would be New Westminster and that he would be the governor of the combined colonies. The first two did not happen; the third did.

The two colonies merged. Seymour, as he had been promised, was appointed governor of the united colony, to be named British Columbia. Kennedy was recalled to England for another appointment. On May 25, 1868, after political negotiations and adroit maneuvering by Dr. Helmcken, Victoria was proclaimed the capital of the united colony. Together with a number of New Westminster officials, Seymour crossed the straits to live in Victoria. This migration of government officials inevitably caused disruption in the price of real estate in both capitals.

With the merging of the two colonies in November 1866 came the inevitable reduction in government employees. Obviously, there would have to be a reduction of government officials. Seymour gave many of the positions in the united colony to those he was familiar with from the mainland colony in New Westminster. He gave Hankin's job to the chief of police from the mainland. Those who were displaced received a letter from the governor, informing them their services would be dispensed within three months' time.

Rather than being angry or resentful, as were many of his colleagues, Hankin decided to make the best of it. Accepting the inevitable, he wrote a civil reply to the governor's letter, requesting that, instead of waiting three months, his services might be dispensed with at once. This request was granted. The government paid him three months' salary and paid for the passage back to England of Hankin and his wife. The *Daily British Colonist* wished him well and noted that he had proved an efficient and honest officer. Before leaving Victoria, Hankin asked Seymour for a letter of recommendation, which Seymour gave him, speaking favourably of him and expressing his regret at being obliged to dispense with his services. Seymour had not actually met Hankin and had relied on the opinions of others. Nevertheless, in view of what happened later, this letter is significant.

A week later Philip and Isabel started back to England. They went by way of the Isthmus of Panama. From Aspinwall they travelled to New York on the SS *Henry Chauncey*, arriving there on January 31, 1867.

When they reached London, they stayed at the Great Western Hotel. By now, Hankin had little money left. He began to wonder what on earth he should do, "as it was rather startling to find oneself in London with a wife and barely a £5 note in one's pocket." They stayed for a while with his father's second wife's sister and her husband, who were very hospitable to them. But, once again, Hankin had a pressing need for a job.

Admiral Denman now stepped in with a welcome letter of support. When the two colonies merged, he had written a letter to the British colonial secretary that for Hankin, looking for a job, would have been worth its weight in gold.

HMS *Sutlej*
San Francisco
December 29, 1866

My Lord,
I have had occasion frequently to avail myself of the services of Mr. Hankin, late superintendent of police at Victoria, V.I., and am anxious to bear my testimony to the great value of his experience and of the very important services he has rendered me on various occasions.

I wish especially to refer to October 1864, when he accompanied me on my flagship to Clayoquot Sound, where I proceeded in order to inquire into the destruction of a British vessel called the *Kingfisher* and the murder of her crew by the natives. He was one of my principal agents in the inquiries I instituted especially in investigating the facts and in the measures that followed ending in the inevitable punishment of the criminals. His intelligence, intrepidity and zeal were of the greatest assistance to me and he displayed a knowledge of the native character which informed me with the highest opinion of his value.

The loss of his appointment by the union of the Colonies of British Columbia and Vancouver Island has induced me to address you on the subject of Mr. Hankin's services which were performed under my own eyes and will, I trust, excuse me in offering my testimony in his favour which, under the circumstances, might perhaps be deemed irregular.

I have, etc, (Signed) Jos. Denman,
Rear Admiral and Commander-in-Chief.[181]

Hankin called on Arthur Kennedy—now Sir Arthur—who fortunately was in London at the time and about to leave for Sierra Leone, where, for the second time (the first being in 1852), he had been appointed governor. Kennedy asked Hankin to meet him at his club the following day. There he promised to take him to the Colonial Office and present him to the splendidly bearded Richard Temple-Nugent-Brydges-Chandos-Grenville, Duke of Buckingham and Chandos—let us call him "the duke"—who at that time was British secretary of state for the colonies in the government of Benjamin Disraeli.[182]

The duke received them both very kindly. Kennedy explained the situation, told the duke about Hankin's work and how he had served under him as Victoria's chief of police and governor of the jail, and had always done his work well and given great satisfaction. Kennedy then left the room. The duke and Hankin chatted for approximately ten minutes, both doubtless being aware that the duke was sizing Hankin up for a job. The duke asked him many questions about his experiences in the Royal Navy and as superintendent of police in Victoria. As Hankin was leaving, the duke told him he might be able to find him some employment. Leave it with him.

Colonial Secretary: British Honduras to British Columbia

1867–1868

Shortly after his meeting with the Duke of Buckingham, Hankin received a letter requesting him to return to the Colonial Office. Not wasting any time, he went and sent his card in to the duke's private secretary, who took him at once to the duke's office. The duke then offered him the position of colonial secretary of British Honduras at a salary of £600 a year. He asked if Hankin wanted the job and, if so, when he could be ready to start. He added that the late colonial secretary, G.C.B. Mathew—Hankin's generous friend from Barkerville—had died the previous June of yellow fever in Belize, the capital. His successor, whoever he might be, would be required to leave England as soon as possible. Hankin wrote in his memoirs:

> In the Navy I had been always accustomed to start everything at 4 o'clock in the morning, so I replied, "With many thanks to your Grace, I accept the appointment with much pleasure and can be ready to start at 4 o'clock tomorrow morning." The Duke smiled and said, "Oh, there will be no necessity to start at 4 o'clock in the morning. It will be soon enough if you go by the first steamer to Havana and from there, I believe, you will find some vessel going to Belize." At the present time [circa 1914] there is a regular communication between New Orleans and Belize, but 45 years ago it was rather a difficult place to get at. I was then very kindly invited

to dinner at Chandos House, the Duke's London residence, and His Grace added: "The Duchess will be very pleased if you would bring Mrs. Hankin with you."

The duke and his family—the duchess and their two daughters—were, Hankin wrote, "all most kind and charming in every way and made us feel quite at home at once." It appears that Isabel and the duchess—Caroline— became quite friendly. A little later, on May 13, 1867, his appointment was announced in the press.[183]

The Hankins set out on their long journey. The day before they arrived at Havana, Isabel came down with yellow fever, probably picked up in Saint Thomas, which they had visited en route. They went to a hotel, where it soon became clear she was dangerously ill. For three days, Hankin said, he thought she would not recover. He called on the British consul and told him of Isabel's illness. The consul recommended "a clever medical man, who has a great deal of experience in yellow fever cases." Hankin always believed he owed his wife's life to that recommendation. As soon as she was able to travel, the doctor advised them to go to a hotel on the other side of the island. Here the air was fresher, cooler and healthier. At length she did recover—although she had recurring problems arising out of it for the rest of her life.

After six weeks convalescing there, the Hankins went by rail to Batabano. There they embarked on the only available vessel, a small cat-tle steamer, going to Trujillo in Honduras. For this three-day voyage, they were the only passengers. They lived with the captain, who did his best, but as he could not speak a word of English and Hankin could not speak a word of Spanish, their passage was anything but lively. The ship, he said, was horribly dirty and full of insects. The food was filthy and everything was cooked in garlic and oil.

At Trujillo they found a small sailing schooner of thirteen tons, with a crew of four, about to leave for Belize. On this they crossed the Gulf of Honduras in rough weather, being battened down in a tiny cabin for much of the time. The smell and heat were, he recalled, appalling. It took them twenty-four hours but finally they reached their destination.

Hankin at once went to report to the governor, John Gardiner Austin, and explained how his wife's serious illness at Havana had delayed their arrival. Austin, who had already heard of his appointment from the Colonial Office, was very welcoming. He and his wife and two daughters were, Hankin said, a charming family and received the new arrivals most kindly. Mr. Graham, the colony's treasurer, and his wife were also hospitable and invited the Hankins to stay at their house for a few days until they could find a suitable home.

Hankin looked around Belize for somewhere to live:

The Duke of Buckingham and Chandos, the colonial secretary in Benjamin Disraeli's government. He became Hankin's patron. Wikimedia Commons.

We soon found a place which I rented for £6 a month, belonging to an old coloured lady. It was not very comfortable, but the only one I could get. I remember there was a kind of broad ladder to go up to the front door, about 30 steps. It was called a staircase, and one morning on entering the breakfast room, I found a large goat with its legs on the table eating the bread! There were no shutters or blinds to the house; and the sun used to stream in to the room in a very uncomfortable manner. The landlady, Miss Hume, said Shutters had been ordered from New Orleans. We used to hang up an old Curtain to keep the sun out. Sometimes we found a chicken or a big Turkey in the dining room, in addition to the Goat. However, this was only a slight inconvenience and we soon got accustomed to it.

He had to start work at nine o'clock every morning. He could walk to his office from his new home in ten minutes.

Hankin started his job as colonial secretary. His time working in the colonial secretary's office in far-away Victoria would undoubtedly have been helpful for him. He had the advantage of arriving in Belize knowing what the job entailed and what his duties were.

He found the climate of British Honduras hot and enervating. He wrote he always found it necessary to sleep under mosquito curtains but the greatest pests were the sandflies, "for these tiny little insects would creep through the mesh of the curtains, and their bite was as sharp as the prick of a pin, and would wake one out of a sound sleep. However, these discomforts had to be borne, and made the best of." Even though there were occasional epidemics of yellow fever and cholera, with his strong constitution he did not find the climate particularly unhealthy. However, it was a different story with Isabel. Her health suffered and the doctor recommended she return to England to recuperate. In her absence, Hankin began to feel he would be happy to obtain a post somewhere else.

British Honduras had been a colony since 1862. It was previously a Spanish possession, and the settlers there were originally loggers with a history of slavery. Although slavery was generally abolished in British possessions by the British Parliament in 1833, in British Honduras the slaves were freed only in 1838, after four years of apprenticeship. The settlers had been belligerent to the Spanish when they were in charge and were no less belligerent to the British when they took over. Austin's predecessor as governor in British Honduras had been Frederick Seymour, who at that time was, coincidentally, the governor of British Columbia.

So what did a colonial secretary actually do? To say he was the second most important official in a colony throughout the colonial empire shows his importance but not what his responsibilities actually were. The functions differed a little between colonies but basically he acted as the chief administrative officer, whereas the governor was the chief executive officer. He was also the primary adviser to the governor and was expected to meet with him daily. "His office—the Secretariat—is the office of the Colony," an experienced colonial official wrote, "the repository of its archives, and the centre of its correspondence. Into this office pours a steady stream of letters from every department and from every district in the Colony. In this office they are registered, studied, discussed and prepared for the necessary order. Through this channel alone all things that require the Governor's orders are submitted for his consideration."[184]

The colonial secretary wrote and issued public dispatches. He negotiated leases and grants on behalf of the government. He supervised the granting of licences. In some jurisdictions, he performed the role of what would now be described as home secretary or interior minister. Although he participated in political decisions, he was the one primarily charged with making sure that the political decisions were carried out. His fingers were on all the files. He was the one who got things done.

We can imagine Austin and Hankin sitting on a veranda after dinner, smoking cigars and sipping brandy, discussing the burning issues of the day, the demands of the planters, the correspondence, who was or was not good at his job and how to reduce expenditures or allocate funds. The sounds of the town and the cacophony of noises from the jungle, never far away, would have filled the balmy air.

On October 16, 1867, T.A. Woods, an American traveller, wrote to a New Orleans newspaper about his impression of British Honduras:

> Of the Colonial Government I can say nothing good of the General Assembly, and will let it alone; but of Governor Austin and the Colonial Secretary, the Hon. Philip J. Hankin, I can speak in the terms of highest praise. Were the General Assembly dissolved and the public affairs placed in their hands, their liberal policy and political ability would soon make this one of the richest colonies of Great Britain. Too much praise cannot be given either of them for the affability and courtesy with which they treat Southern gentlemen visiting here.[185]

Hankin wrote that Austin sold a large quantity of land in British Honduras to an American syndicate. The Colonial Office in London did not approve of this and fired off a telegram saying, "Land sales disallowed!" Austin was recalled but was then appointed as colonial secretary at Hong Kong. When Austin left Belize to return to England, Isabel went with him. James Longden was appointed governor in his place. For the short time between Austin's departure and Longden's arrival, Hankin was the administrator of the colony. In itself this was not significant but it did presage what would happen later in a larger colony. In any interregnum, Hankin knew well what his duty as colonial secretary was.

James Longden arrived and took back the reins of government. His wife, Hankin said, was a charming lady from Saint Kitts, who was a great addition to the local society and always did the honours of Government House most gracefully.

Not long after the new governor arrived, Hankin gave a formal dinner party. The guest of honour was the governor's wife. Hankin does not, though, mention whether or not her husband accompanied her. It was his first attempt at formal entertaining and he wasn't sure about his cook. He was nervous. This dinner, it has to be said, was a disaster. The first course was tinned soup and tinned salmon to allow the cook to concentrate her skills on the second, which was to be a large roast turkey. All went well until a long delay after the first course. No turkey appeared. Eventually Hankin went to find out what was causing the delay. To his horror, the cook "popped up from behind a screen and called out, 'I no go bodder wid de Tarkey. I trow him ober de warl.'" Mortified, Hankin did not know what to do. Fortunately, his guests saw the humour in the situation, laughed and said they weren't hungry. In any event, he found two large cans of salmon for his guests, together with some thinly sliced bread and butter. This, with more champagne, had to suffice. But Hankin was forever teased dreadfully about his first formal dinner party.

Hankin remained in British Honduras for almost a year and a half. He then received a letter from the duke informing him that Sir Arthur Kennedy, then the governor of Sierra Leone, had written to the Colonial Office, asking for Hankin to be appointed as his colonial secretary there. Susan Nagle, Isabel's sister, wrote in her diary that the duke had asked Isabel if Hankin wanted the job.[186] Knowing that her husband wanted to leave British Honduras, Isabel had accepted on his behalf. The duke

The Duke of Buckingham and Chandos's Stowe House, Buckinghamshire, where Hankin went to work as the duke's private secretary in 1872. Wikimedia Commons.

wrote to him and formally offered him the appointment at an annual salary of £700 a year. Hankin replied at once and accepted the offer. When his replacement arrived, he packed his bags to return to England to take up this new appointment.

He travelled with the chief justice of the colony on the SS *Trade Winds* to New Orleans, arriving in the second week of August 1868.[187] From there he booked a passage on a large, comfortable riverboat up the Mississippi River as far as Memphis. The journey took six days. The vessel was one of the immense sternwheelers that plied the Mississippi River in those days. Like the little *Maria* on the Fraser River, it always tied up to the riverbank at night. This, he said, was a most enjoyable way of travelling.

In his memoirs he does not describe conditions in the South, so recently defeated in the ruinous American Civil War, but he did make his voyage sound delightful. He had a comfortable cabin on board, which was described as a stateroom, and he enjoyed the dinners and dances. Seeing a pretty girl who danced well, he asked her for the next waltz. "When she looked at me from head to foot and replied, 'Well, Sir, you may dance the square dances right nice, but I guess you are getting pretty fleshy for the round one,' I couldn't help laughing. However, we had one or two dances together, when she said to me, 'Well, Captain, you are a real elegant dancer, and I've just had the tallest time with you aboard this boat that ever a Yankee girl had.'"

From Memphis he took the train to New York, and from there he went by ocean liner to Southampton. When he arrived in England, he found the duchess had taken Isabel under her wing and she was recuperating at Stowe, the duke's house in Buckinghamshire. Hankin went to Stowe, intending to stay for a week before leaving to take up his appointment as colonial secretary in Sierra Leone.

He had been at Stowe for only a few days when the duke told him that a vacancy had just become available in British Columbia. The experienced colonial secretary of the old Colony of Vancouver Island was William Young. At this time he was acting in the same capacity on a temporary basis for the united Colony of British Columbia. Young, Hankin would have recalled, was the official who had shown Lady Franklin, Miss Cracroft and himself round the government buildings in Victoria in 1861. Governor Seymour—the mainland man—thought Young too wedded to the Vancouver Island faction. Insecure, Seymour thought he posed a threat to his position. In June 1868, therefore, he had written to the duke saying that he no longer had confidence in Young and could the duke please appoint a new colonial secretary.[188] The duke, taking Seymour's letter at face value, told Hankin about Seymour's request. The duke, Hankin wrote, said, "The present man [Young] is only acting and if you like to go back there, I shall be very pleased to offer you the appointment at a Salary of £800 a year."

Was this not a happy coincidence? Hankin liked British Columbia and wanted to return. Dear Isabel's family lived there and she would be overjoyed to see them all again on a regular basis. Admiral Denman,

Captain Richards and Governor Kennedy had all given him glowing references. Hankin was now an experienced colonial secretary, who had done well in British Honduras. He was intelligent and vigorous and abounded with common sense. Moreover, he had experience with the Indigenous Peoples on the Pacific coast and spoke several of their languages. Furthermore, he was not tied to either of the troublesome factions that bedevilled the colony's politics and frustrated its efficient administration. He seemed ideal.

Would Hankin take the job? Yes, he would be delighted to accept. This was splendid and Hankin was grateful for the appointment. "It was of course a real joy to my dear wife," he wrote, "to have the chance of seeing her parents and family again, for she was greatly attached to them."

Hankin was not one to let grass grow beneath his feet. In less than a week, he and Isabel set off for New York. From there they took passage on the ss *Henry Chauncey* to the Isthmus of Panama, then continued on to San Francisco. At that time the journey generally took seven weeks. While they were travelling, a storm broke over their heads, one they knew nothing about. Until they reached San Francisco—unless warned by telegram—they would have remained in blissful ignorance.

The two colonies on the Pacific might have been united in law; the administrators and populations were not, however, acting harmoniously. The politics of the new Colony of British Columbia were fractious and bitter. There was deep animosity in Victoria between the officials from the old Colony of British Columbia on the mainland, the capital of which had been New Westminster, and those of the Colony of Vancouver Island. The officials on the island, many of whom had lost their jobs, felt they had been given the short end of the stick. Even though Governor Kennedy, with his attempts to cut expenditures, had not been popular, he was *their* governor and represented *their* interests. The new governor was, as they thought, someone who represented the interests of the mainland. For their part, officials from the mainland resented the fact that the capital of the new united colony was Victoria, which meant they had to sell their houses in New Westminster at deflated prices and move to the island.

When Seymour became the new governor of the united colony, he started losing his grip. He was not strong enough to quell the political infighting, which grew even more divisive. Furthermore, the economic depression reduced government revenues and put everyone in an even more fractious mood. Seymour became ill and erratic. It was rumoured he drank too much. He neglected his correspondence. He started to frustrate, then annoy, the authorities in London. The patience of the Colonial Office in London with Seymour may have been wearing thin.

In 1864, Seymour had recommended his private secretary, George Holmes, for the post of colonial secretary of British Honduras, where he was then governor. In making this recommendation, he had not mentioned that Holmes had a serious drinking problem. In Jamaica, on his way to take up his post, Holmes had an attack of delirium tremens—alcoholism—and his appointment had to be cancelled. In May 1865, Edward Cardwell, the colonial secretary in London, had administered to Seymour what can only be called a severe rebuke. "The regret with which I found at first that you had omitted to state facts which in recommending Captain Holmes you ought not to have kept back, has not been diminished by the tone of the letters which you have addressed to me in answer to my communications on this, to me, very painful subject."[189] Now, the authorities in London had accepted Seymour's request that the man most fit for the job of colonial secretary of British Columbia, Young, not be appointed.

The duke wrote to Seymour on October 8, informing him of Hankin's appointment. When the news arrived in Victoria in the third week of November, it hit the colony, it was said, like a thunderclap. Seymour was horrified. He immediately fired off a letter to the duke condemning the appointment, changing his mind entirely about Young and damning Hankin in intemperate and in many ways inaccurate terms. He intimated that Hankin would not be allowed to land without personal violence. The Fenians (a group of republican Irishmen active in the United States at the time) and Americans would undoubtedly riot. Was it too late to cancel the appointment? The duke, he said, must have misinterpreted his request that Young not be appointed. Seymour wrote in haste to London:

I received this morning with the greatest concern Your Grace's despatch No. 85 of the 6th October, informing me that you had appointed Mr. Philip Hankin R.N. to be Colonial Secretary of British Columbia. No mention is made of the present incumbent of the office, Mr. William A.G. Young.

I, on the 5th of June, requested Your Grace to defer the formal confirmation of Mr. Young until I had made some further communication on the subject. I have never made a complaint against him, nor have I had cause for being anything but fully satisfied with his zeal, integrity, temper, and knowledge. If I hesitated in recommending his final confirmation it was only because I was informed that he was too well acquainted with the place and had too many interests in it. There were statements of his having been indiscreet in his revelations to old friends but I do not believe in their truth. I was but little prepared for the interpretation put upon my letter by Your Grace. ... Possibly the matter may be reconsidered if Mr. Hankin shall not have left England. ...

How a man totally ignorant of what has passed in the Colony for the last few years can furnish the information which will be called for on every petty item of expenditure I am at a loss to know. Mr. Hankin, even if he were able to fill the place of Colonial Secretary, would come before the public with peculiarly bad grace. It is but last year that he received from the impoverished funds of the Colony £51.11.0 [51 pounds, 11 shillings] as compensation for loss of office and £165 for passages of wife and family to England. It is a little embarrassing to me to find that a man whose services I could not avail myself of in any of the offices of middling importance and with which therefore I had to dispense returns on my hands after due compensation for loss of office, to the highest post in the Colony. ...

Mr. Hankin, a Lieutenant in H.M.S. *Hecate*, resigned his commission for the purpose of proceeding to our Northern Mines to dig for gold. No one who does not know Cariboo can understand the strange associations and singular friendships which gold digging there entails, where muscle is nearly everything, the brain of little use. I should however say, he was accompanied by a brother. That brother has stuck to the diggings.[190] It is in no way discreditable to the Messrs. Hankin that they did not succeed in their labours. Mr. Philip Hankin returned "dead broke"—that is, without a farthing in his pocket. Worked his way down, on foot I believe, stopping necessarily at the... houses by the roadside.

On arrival in Victoria, after some delay he was appointed Junior Clerk in the Colonial Secretary's Office at a Salary of £200 a year, under Mr. Young, whom he is now to supplant. ...

I beg to refer Your Grace to Sir James Douglas's despatch No. 67 of the 25th of October 1861. He reports "I have been obliged to dismiss the Acting Harbour Master of the Port of Victoria, Mr. Jeremiah Nagle, in consequence of discovering irregularities in his accounts, and that he had been in the habit of charging and appropriating to his own use, fees for services rendered in his official capacity." Mr. Hankin married one of Mr. Nagle's daughters. The family is still in the Colony. Would this connexion be a desirable one for the highest officer in the Colony?...

The "dead broke" miner must have some curious friends. The Junior Clerk must have had associates of a class similar to his own. The Inspector of Police must be well acquainted with Public Houses and less reputable places. But he is not the man to lead the Legislative Council, more particularly if he comes back after having been paid in full for the abolition of his police appointment and in acquittal of any claim he might be thought to possess, previously, upon the Government of this Colony. ...

The news of Mr. Hankin's appointment reached Victoria this morning and I learn that great excitement prevails and that he would not now be allowed to land without personal violence. As to his managing the Legislative Council during the approaching Session I look upon that as impossible. Should he unfortunately have left England before my telegrams reach Your Grace, I do not know what circumstances may require, but the people are in no pleasant humour. Fenians, if not Americans, would probably join in any riot which may arise.

Your Grace will excuse me for speaking out thus plainly, but I know that you have but one object in view, that of promoting the peace, order and good Government of the Colony. All these I respectfully submit would be emperilled should I meet the Legislative Council with Mr. Hankin as President and Leader of it.[191]

Seymour's letter perplexed the officials in London. Seymour not only had requested Young be replaced but only two years before had given Hankin a warm letter of recommendation. What in heaven's name was he doing now in reversing his position so dramatically?

A departmental note on this letter reads:

I dare say that the appointment is an unfortunate one, but I also am under the impression that Mr. Seymour makes the worst of it—(It is rather his way to make the most of things)—and I think that he has brought it on himself. Mr. Seymour, having been Govr of B. Columbia since 1863, having been also Govr of V.C. Island since 1866 and having had the services of Mr. Young in the capacity of Colonial Secretary since July 1867, ought in June 1868 to have pretty well understood Mr. Y's merits & demerits.

But it has always appeared to me that Mr. Seymour & other persons connected with B. Columbia have shewn an adverse disposition towards Mr. Young—who has always been connected with the... interest of V.C. Island. ...

I do not see that anything now can be done. Mr. Hankin has by this time arrived—and it will have been seen whether he can or cannot maintain himself—between Mr. Seymour, Mr. Young and the Assembly, guided probably by Mr. Young's father in law, Sir James Douglas.

Another note on the letter reads:

Some private letters for H.G. [His Grace] from Mr. Seymour arrived by the same mail. I saw Mr. Hankin while he was in England, and thought his manner frank & prepossessing. He seemed a man of sense and self-reliance. He left England on the 4th of November and I suppose would arrive in B.C. towards the end of December.

Governor Seymour recognized he had perhaps been intemperate and wrote again a few days later, trying (but in no way succeeding) to provide a more balanced assessment. Perhaps he thought this would help, but it exasperated the officials in London even more. Writing on November 29, he said:

The steamer that brought Your Grace's despatch No. 85 of 6th October announcing the appointment of Mr. Philip Hankin to the office of Colonial Secretary only waited a few hours in port and consequently, being thus pressed for time, I fear that my despatch, Confidential, of 21st November, bears marks of the haste in which it was written. ... It is however my deliberate opinion that the appointment of Mr. Hankin is an unfortunate one. For many reasons: First; because in his mining pursuits and in his police employment he has been brought into immediate contact with the lowest classes of the community. ... The Office of Colonial Secretary is one of very great importance. We govern here by moral influence alone, and the social position of the principal public officers, as well as their official capabilities, is freely canvassed by all persons. I send Mr. O'Reilly to collect the Revenue at the Kootenay mines, 600 miles from Victoria, and to settle all disputes. He is respected and liked by everyone. How could I send the "dead broke" miner, Mr. Hankin, on such a duty? He would be simply made the laughing stock of the place. Yet the office of Colonial Secretary is higher than that of Gold Commissioner. ...

Mr. Hankin has not, as far as I am aware, shewn the slightest aptitude for business during the time he has been employed under the Colonial Government, and—not to make this despatch too long—he has married into a family with which it would not be pleasant for some ladies to associate.[192]

We may note that the duke and duchess did not find it unpleasant to associate with Isabel Hankin and perhaps would not have been impressed by Seymour's implication that she was someone they should not be sharing time and their home with.

The note on this letter shows that the authorities in the Colonial Office in England were exasperated by Seymour's change of mind. The minute by the anonymous civil servant in the duke's office reads:

I can only say that in my opinion any annoyance or difficulty that may fall to the lot of Governor Seymour as regards Mr. Young's removals from the Colonial Secretaryship he most fully deserves. ...

As to the appt of Lt. Hankin I can say nothing. I never heard his name till he was appointed, & never saw him but once which was two days before he started, on my return from my holyday. Officially, as far as I know, testimony is in his favor. ... Admiral Richards spoke in his favor whilst serving under him. ... And the testimonials sent in by Lt. Hankin... were so favorable that they apparently led to his appt as Col. Secy at Honduras (Mr. Kennedy, Admiral Denman, Judge Needham), Mr. Taylor remarking "if the testimonials are true Lt. Hankin is just the man for the place." As Governor Seymour now speaks so lightly of Lt. Hankin's antecedents & character I have thought right to state this much. ... I do not see why a man is the worse for having been what he somewhat unnecessarily calls a "dead broke" miner. It really shews little else but enterprise.

The appointment of Hankin was bound to be highly controversial. Less than five years before he had been a junior clerk in government service, serving under the same William Young, who now, unfairly, had been shunted aside. After that, Hankin had been the superintendent of police, with a staff of under a dozen, in which position, with his efficiency at enforcing the laws, he had made some enemies. Moreover, he was the protégé of the unpopular Governor Kennedy. Now here he was, appointed over everyone's head to the second most important office in the colony.

Jealousy and spluttering indignation were inevitable and, with hindsight, foreseeable. Many will have remembered his sense of fun, his high spirits and his fondness for pranks. They might well have thought he lacked the necessary gravitas for such an important position.

Governor Seymour was undoubtedly expressing the views of many in Victoria. The *Daily British Colonist*, noticeably anti-Hankin, railed against him and published editorials and letters bubbling with complaints. For example:

> The appointment of Mr. Philip Hankin to the position of Colonial Secretary of the Colony is another evidence of how little the feelings of the Colonies are taken into consideration by the Imperial Government. ... Against Mr. Hankin personally we have nothing to urge; but as the head of our police force, he proved certainly more ornamental than useful, and failed to inspire with confidence in his ability or efficiency. ... A more unsatisfactory appointment could hardly have been made.[193]

One correspondent, signing himself merely H., said, "No one, as far as I know, has the smallest confidence in Philip Hankin's ability, but all assert him to be an unfit man, to say the least."[194] On the other hand, a letter in the same edition by a correspondent calling himself Fair Play drew readers' attention to the fact that Hankin had served creditably as colonial secretary of British Honduras and had recommendations from many people of good judgment. Nevertheless, a petition was drawn up asking the governor not to confirm the appointment.[195]

Robert Louis Smith, writing in 1974 about Hankin's appointment and referring to Hankin, said, "His meteoric rise from the obscurity of minor officialdom was the result of his ability, industry and loyalty, which had won the influence of powerful men, and of the mismanagement of Governor Frederick Seymour."[196]

Meanwhile, Philip and Isabel Hankin were en route to their new responsibilities. In all likelihood, they were enjoying the scenery and innocently looking forward to their arrival in Victoria and to seeing family and old friends again. On arrival in San Francisco, however, they may have read in the *Daily Examiner* that "the appointment of Philip Hankin as Colonial Secretary over Mr. Young, the late incumbent, is sharply criticized."[197] So, trouble ahead.

They sailed north from San Francisco to Victoria on board the mail steamer *Active* at the end of December 1868.[198] On the last day of the year, a ferocious storm came up suddenly from the southeast and assaulted the southern coast of Vancouver Island. While Governor Seymour and his wife were being attentive to their guests at a brilliant New Year's Eve ball at Government House in Victoria, storm-battered ships fought for refuge in local harbours.[199] While attempting to reach Esquimalt Harbour, the American bark *Delaware* was driven onto the rocks and destroyed near Fisgard Lighthouse. The *Active*, unable to reach Victoria Harbour, did manage to reach Esquimalt safely. Susan Nagle, Isabel's sister, wrote that since all the conveyances were being used in taking guests to the governor's grand ball, the passengers had to walk as far as the first bridge before they found a conveyance.[200] The storm at sea presaged the storm Hankin would face on land.

Hankin's troubles started when Governor Seymour refused to swear him in as the new colonial secretary.

9

Governor Seymour and
Administrator Hankin

January–August 1869

W hen Hankin arrived in British Columbia on a stormy New Year's Eve, it did not take him long to realize that many people in Victoria were unhappy about his appointment. "We arrived safely at Victoria," he wrote, "but I very soon saw that my appointment was not a popular one in the Colony, but it was nothing but jealousy. Of course, the other officials did not like me to come back in a position above them all, so they always told all kinds of stories to Mr. Seymour and he had never seen me in his life, but was foolish enough to listen to mischief makers."

Over in New Westminster, the *British Columbian* reported that Seymour's reception of Hankin was frosty. Hankin, it said, presented himself to Government House the day after his arrival. He was informed that the Governor, in such good health at the Ball the night before, was ill and could not see him. It went on:

Returning to his hotel, [Hankin] addressed a letter to His Excellency of his arrival and solicited an early interview. The interview was granted. The Governor's manner was cold and embarrassed. Mr. Hankin drew from his pocket a letter from the Duke of Buckingham and handed it to the Governor, who, after reading it, asked to be allowed "three or four days for reflection." Mr. Hankin wished to know whether His Excellency wanted three days or four, and, in reply, the Governor said "four." The fresh appointee of Downing Street bowed himself out of the Vice-Regal presence.[201]

The newspaper reported that the press in Victoria was divided. The *Daily British Colonist* was violently anti-Hankin, calling him arrogant, tyrannical and incompetent, whereas the *Victoria News* was more circumspect. The view in the Cariboo was pro-Hankin solely because the appointment was so obnoxious to many in Victoria.[202]

The *Daily British Colonist* started to criticize him at once. "It would be an idle waste of words were we to reiterate our objections to the appointment of Mr. Hankin to the position of colonial secretary. ... He is not, consequently, in the opinion of nine-tenths of this community fitted to succeed so efficient and able an officer as Mr. Young has proved himself to be."[203]

Hankin was now in a difficult position. In his memoirs he gives the impression that he was philosophical, that he decided to carry on and do the best he could. "However, I had not asked for the appointment," he wrote. "But I thought I should be very foolish to refuse a good appointment because with some people it was not popular—so I said to myself, Do your best and live it down, which after a time, I succeeded in doing. Mr. Seymour was not very polite to me at first, but after a short time we began to get along very well."

In private he was more unsettled. His sister-in-law Susan Nagle wrote in her diary, "Philip is very much put out at the way he has been treated. It certainly is very hard after coming so far. We can't understand what it all means. P. tho', expects to have to leave."[204]

In January he had even gone so far as to think of applying to be sent to another colony. He asked Sir Arthur Kennedy, at the time in Cheltenham, for a reference. "My Dear Mr. Hankin," Kennedy wrote in February, "in any application you may make for Public Employment, you are quite at liberty to refer to me. I entertain a very high opinion of your zeal, efficiency and integrity. Your conduct of the important and responsible department of which you were the head, at Vancouver Island, was entirely successful and met with my full approval."[205]

A private letter Hankin wrote to Kennedy on March 5 suggests he was regretting having accepted the post. He wrote, "I cannot tell you how very pleased I was to receive by this mail (arrived today) your letter written from Accra & to find by it that you do not blame me for accepting this app't; although I can assure you I blame myself. Yet I could not have declined it without giving positive offense to the Duke. I most heartily wish I were the other end of the world. However, I suppose there is no help for it now, and I must make the best of a very bad bargain."[206]

In this March letter, Hankin wrote:

I have now been here nearly 3 months, and have not yet been permitted to assume my position as Col.Sec. I wrote to you by the last mail, and told you that Mr. Seymour had offered me the position of Chief Commissioner of Lands & Works, which I declined to accept. You can scarcely have any idea of what a difficult task I have to play here. The odds are so heavy against me that if I don't play my cards very carefully I shall lose the game. Mr. Seymour hates me and will move Heaven and Earth to get rid of me, simply because I am not a British Columbian [that is to say, from the mainland colony, where Seymour had been governor], and I am one of your men. I told him I sincerely hoped I might be removed as he didn't want me, but that if it was my lot to remain here he would always have my warmest support. But how I am to succeed with such a man as he is, I know not.

I don't mind telling you what I of course would never breathe here, viz, Mr. *Seymour drinks like a fish*, and a few days ago he was driving down Gov't Street in his trap, so tight that he could scarcely sit up! He is always so dreadfully ill & not long since was most dangerously ill. His nervous system is completely shattered and my own opinion is, he cannot live long. They say he eats nothing, but lives on cocktails. What a terrible thing for a man in his position to be in such a state! He only comes to the office about once a month, and Young told me that sometimes he will keep papers for three months & often loses them altogether. Is it not a bright prospect for me to serve with such a man?... I have written privately to the Duke, and have told him that I fear it will be an arduous task for me to succeed if I am thrust on Gov. Seymour against his will. Of course, I have carefully refrained from saying one word against him. I have simply stated my readiness to go to another Colony; but I much fear that I will be obliged to remain here.

Young and I get on very well together. Certainly he has been shamefully treated by Mr. Seymour. Young has many letters of a most flattering description from the Gov. & all the time Mr. Seymour was writing home against him. ...

I have made no ennemies [sic] since I have been here, on the contrary many friends, and Mr. Seymour's most unjust treatment of me has turned the popular feeling entirely in my favour. Not that I care a straw about popularity, if he would only give me a helping hand. I have taken an unfurnished house, and am living quite in the rough with 4 chairs and a table, as I do not care to go to any expense until I know whether, or no, I remain in the Colony. ... I have not seen Mr. Seymour for some time. He is dreadfully put out because I would not accept his offer of being Surveyor General, but really I could not give up a position which I hold from Her Majesty to accept an acting app't from the Governor of the Colony. Besides, I know nothing of the duties of Surveyor General. He might as well have asked me to be "Bishop." I wrote to him six weeks ago applying for my Salary, and I can get no reply to my letter, however, that I shall get it sooner or later.[207]

In writing about the Hankin appointment, Robert Louis Smith suggests that Seymour was exhausted, ill and baffled by the demands of governing the merged colonies. Colonial politics was exceedingly heated and Seymour seemed unable to cool it. Smith also suggests that Seymour objected to Hankin because he came from a modest social background. Sons of aristocrats, even illegitimate ones, were the people fit to govern, not jumped-up sons of insignificant country squires!

Susan Nagle recorded a joke going round Victoria at the time. Question: "Why was Mr. Hankin's return to this colony a Mistake? Answer: Because he came o'er young to see more of British Columbia."[208]

The Land Office—The Legislative The Colonial Office The Supreme The Treasury
Council Court Court

Victoria: the Land Office, the Legislative Council Court, the Colonial Office, the Supreme Court and the Treasury. These government buildings were known as the Birdcages. Image A-00934 courtesy of the Royal BC Museum and Archives

Clearly London was not happy with Seymour's prevarication. Granville George Leveson-Gower, Earl Granville, the colonial secretary in the new government in England, wrote to him, "The absence of any sufficient ground for the strong opinions which you have expressed as to Mr. Hankin's unfitness for office, joined to the evident animus which I regret to perceive in your Despatches lead me to doubt whether the disturbances you anticipate from Mr. Hankin's appointment are really much to be apprehended."[209] The colonial authorities in England, not impressed by Seymour's inflammatory letters and delays in swearing Hankin in, started to make moves to replace him. They wrote to Anthony Musgrave, the governor of Newfoundland, to see if he would be willing to take over from Seymour. He would. Musgrave had tried hard, but failed, to persuade Newfoundland to join Canada. He was to try again with British

The colonial secretary's office in Victoria, where Hankin's offices were located. Image A-00841 courtesy of the Royal BC Museum and Archives

Columbia with more success. In this he was encouraged and advised by Prime Minister John Macdonald.

Hankin might have thought he was building bridges, but Governor Seymour was still not prepared to accept Hankin as his colonial secretary. He did what he could to have the appointment rescinded. He kept Young on as acting colonial secretary, effectually ignoring Hankin. In this capacity, Young still presided over the executive council and toward the end of January presented the estimates—the budget—for the colony. Seymour offered Hankin lesser appointments in the colony. He wrote more letters. He stalled. It was no use. He perversely waited for three months after Hankin's arrival in the colony before he reluctantly swore him in.

On April 8, 1869, bowing to directives from London, Seymour did swear in Hankin as colonial secretary.[210] Poor William Young, who certainly deserved the appointment and probably would have made an excellent colonial secretary, went home to England. Hankin reported to London he had now been sworn in. Making a sly reference to those who forecast that disaster would immediately befall the colony, he wrote, "No disastrous consequences have arisen, neither do I apprehend the slightest problem of any arising."[211]

Hankin was now the second most senior official in the colony. The most senior, the governor, didn't like him. At a time when efficient, smooth government depended on a good working rapport between the two of them, all looked set for a rocky relationship between Seymour and his new colonial secretary.

That Hankin was not overly perturbed by the hostility among some in Victoria is shown by the fact that he gave public readings at Victoria's Mechanics' Institute. These were educational establishments originally set up in the United Kingdom to provide technical information for workers. Their scope had expanded to places of education and cultural entertainment for all. In January, soon after he arrived, Hankin stepped into the social circuit in Victoria by giving readings from Charles Dickens's novels. These, the *Daily British Colonist* said, were "capitally rendered and gave universal satisfaction. The gentleman's imitative powers are fine, and he threw all the life and spirit into the selection that the author appears to have intended it should possess."[212] At another soirée, in April, he presented a reading from Dickens's *Dombey and Son* and *The Schoolboy's Story* "with his wonderful facility and clearness of enunciation. The effect on the audience might be distinctly noted in the changing expression of the faces of the listeners and their wrapt [rapt] attention. Mr. Hankin was frequently applauded during the recital, and at the conclusion received the unanimous and loud expression of general appreciation."[213] He gave several more readings that year. In October he treated his audience of subscribers to readings from *David Copperfield*. In December, at a reading described by the *Colonist* as his most successful effort yet, he read the description of Dotheboys Hall in *Nicholas Nickleby* "with a richness that must have delighted the shade of Old Squeers himself."[214] The admission price was twenty-five cents each for women and children and fifty cents for a gentleman. This love for the novels of Dickens and his facility for public speaking would later serve him in good stead in, of all places, Florida.

Hankin started on his duties at once. His first official letter was on April 12, in which he gave approval for the expenditure of a hundred dollars on the clearing of a road or trail from Victoria to Cowichan. On April 16, he announced the appointment of three magistrates, one of whom, Andrew Charles Elliott, would later become premier of the province. On May 15, on behalf of the governor, he announced a public holiday for the Queen's birthday and the introduction of decimal currency in the colony.

He also made arrangements for the governor's official visit to the colony's northern coast to settle a few problems that had arisen there. While there, Seymour would also visit numerous coastal Indigenous communities. London seems to have been prodding Seymour to do more about some murders that had recently taken place at Metlakatla, near Fort Simpson. "I have had the honour," Seymour had written icily to London, "to receive Your Lordship's despatch... in reference to some Murders which the Indians in the neighbourhood of Metlakahtla had committed. Your Lordship does not, I regret to say, consider my explanation satisfactory. I have only therefore awaited the return of Spring to enable me to visit the North West Coast. I start in her Majesty's ship *Sparrowhawk* this afternoon for Metlakahtla."[215]

By June 2, Seymour was at Metlakatla, investigating the murders and presiding over a court at which Bill Stevens, skipper of the *Nanaimo Packet*, was found guilty of supplying Indigenous people with liquor. The court fined him $800 and confiscated his schooner. On June 4, Seymour inspected new workhouses, workshops and a soap factory and gave a feast for the Indigenous people. On June 10, when visiting Bella Coola, he suddenly fell sick and died.[216]

HMS *Sparrowhawk* returned to Esquimalt with Seymour's body in its stateroom, decorated with what the *Daily British Colonist* called the "sad emblems of grief."[217] After the body arrived, it was taken in a mahogany coffin to the naval hospital, where, in a ward hung with black cloth and white satin, it lay in state. On the coffin, around which were placed candelabras with beeswax candles, rested Seymour's cocked hat and sword.

The day after Seymour's body had arrived back in Victoria, Hankin, now the most senior official in the colony, went to the courthouse in James Bay and formally notified the legislative assembly that the governor had died. "I appear before you," he said, "to receive the oath of office as Administrator of the Colony of British Columbia." Chief Justice Joseph Needham then asked, perhaps hopefully, if there was a dormant commission in Seymour's desk appointing someone else to take over in the event of his death. On being assured there was not, he then, in a barely audible voice, administered the oath in terms that suggested he did so only because there was no legal way not to. "It is, then, my painful duty," he said, much affected, "to administer to you the usual oath which I am compelled to do in silence."[218]

The dismay and consternation that these events caused among those hostile to Hankin may be imagined. Until the new governor arrived, this thirty-three-year-old "dead broke" miner was now in charge of the colony.

This was not a reckless grab for power on his part. The *Daily British Colonist* informed its readers that, as the second most senior government official, Hankin had the clear duty of assuming the office. This comment comes with an implicit subtext of "like it or not, there's nothing you can do about it."

Of these events, Hankin wrote in his memoirs:

Then came a time when I am afraid I gave more offense, for as Senior Executive Officer, I was sworn in by the Chief Justice as Administrator of the Government, and assumed office, and drew a salary of £4,000 a year. This was, of course, a great lift, when only 3 years previously I had landed in the Colony with 25/- [25 shillings] in my pocket. However, I always used to think of the German proverb, "Armut ist Keine Schande" [Poverty is no shame], and I always did my best and tried to do my duty. How little it matters after all.

All these men who tried to do me harm, and were very unkind and angry, are now all dead.

Hankin made arrangements for the elaborate funeral with all the appropriate respect he could summon, now that death had removed this obstacle to his doing his job. Seymour's funeral cortège processed from the hospital on its last journey to the sound of seventeen naval guns—one every minute—from the ships in harbour. After the firing party and naval band came the corpse on the gun carriage, followed by contingents from the Victoria fire brigade, the Victoria police brigade and the Royal Navy. Then came the civilians, the city fathers and government officers, among them Hankin. The police escort followed at the rear. A firing party fired a volley of shots over the grave. All the great and good of the colony were there, paying their respects and supporting Mrs. Seymour. "I was very sorry for his widow," Hankin wrote, "who felt his death very much." Susan Nagle wrote, "Mrs. Seymour... walked from the church to the grave. Her friends all tried to persuade her not to do so, but she was determined to see him consigned to his last resting place. This is a sad, sad day for her, poor woman."[219]

Hankin reported these melancholy events to the Colonial Office in London. "His Excellency," he said, had been in a delicate state of health, suffering from extreme debility, but no danger was apprehended by his medical adviser. He had visited Nanaimo, Bella Coola, Bella Bella and the missionary stations on the Naas River and at Metlakatla, "when he was seized with an attack of diarrhea on the 8th instant and expired on the 10th instant on board Her Majesty's Ship *Sparrowhawk* at Bella Coola."[220] Hankin also reported that he had consequently taken the oaths of office and assumed the government of the colony.

The British Colonial Office, terse to the point of insensitivity, sent a telegram to Anthony Musgrave. "Governor of British Columbia is dead. You will succeed. Prepare to leave on receiving Commission by next mail."[221] Since at this time there was no easy way to cross the continent north of the United States border, it was going to be several months before Musgrave arrived in Victoria.

The caption with this photograph in the BC Archives states that these were "Members of first Legislature in front of Birdcages, Victoria after the union of the two colonies. From l. to r., on porch: W.A. Franklin, house messenger; Henry Holbrook; W.O. Hamley; E.G. Alston; P.J. Hankin; M.T.W. Drake; J.M. Trutch (sitting on porch at top of steps); T.L. Wood; H.M. Ball; E. Dewdney; A.T. Bushby; Charles Good (clerk, not shown). From l. to r., in foreground: Amor de Cosmos; H.P.P. Crease; D.B. King (seated on steps, with dog); T.B. Humphreys; John Robson." However, Hankin's position in the place of importance in the centre of the picture suggests that it might be from when he was colonial secretary between 1869 and 1871. Image C-06178 courtesy of the Royal BC Museum and Archives

Between June 14 and August 23, 1869, Philip Hankin, the penniless Barkerville prospector of a few years before, was the administrator of British Columbia. So how did he do? In both his jobs as colonial secretary and as administrator, he seems to have done well. He was honest and efficient. Even the initially hostile *Daily British Colonist* was grudgingly impressed. In wondering when Musgrave would arrive, it said, "We may look for Mr. Musgrave about—when? Meantime matters go on smoothly under Mr. Hankin, who, we honestly believe, is striving hard to make the most of very small financial means."[222] It seems Hankin, with his disarming charm, was winning hearts and minds.

Hankin administered a colony that was huge in size but small in population. A report to him in July 1870 noted that the non-Indigenous population of the colony was 10,496. Of these, 5,925 were males, 2,624 females and 1,947 Chinese. The estimate for the Indigenous population was between 30,000 and 50,000. The report noted sadly that these numbers had probably been reduced by the smallpox epidemic of 1862.

Hankin's correspondence shows a wide variety of responsibilities. Much of it was in the calm routine of administration. In July 1869, for example, he authorized a Captain Ball to spend $300 in exploring land for a new trail in the Kootenays. He confirmed the dismissal for drunkenness of one Mr. Haynes, who was a messenger in the Department of Lands and Works. He took steps to ensure that pensioners received pensions due to them from London. Working with the colony's treasurer, he also managed the colony's finances.

After the union of the two colonies, the value of real estate in New Westminster dropped. Property owners in the old capital, particularly officials who had been required to move to Victoria, pressed on Hankin their desire—nay, their right!—to compensation. This aroused the ire of the citizens of Victoria. Why should they have to pay for this? After all, many people (including Hankin) had lost their jobs as a result of the merger of the two colonies. Should not they all be compensated as well?

"We hope," the *Daily British Colonist* said, "that Mr. Hankin—notwithstanding two-thirds of his Executive are gentlemen who 'trusted not wisely but too well' in the permanent location of the Capital at New Westminster—if he do not by his vote and influence, stifle the compensation monster at its birth—will at least insist upon it being deferred until after the arrival of Governor Musgrave."[223] Hankin, who knew a political hot potato when he saw one, did postpone this matter for the new governor to deal with. In December of that year, on behalf of the new governor, he wrote that Musgrave, feeling "it is a most invidious duty cast upon him to decide a question arising out of circumstances long antecedent to his arrival in the Colony and with which he was not personally acquainted," could only discharge that duty in accordance with what he thought right.[224] Consequently he was not prepared to consider such compensation but he might be prepared to reconsider if the applicants wanted to resubmit their proposal.

After his swearing-in, Hankin's immediate concern was that the Fenian Brotherhood was threatening to invade the colony. This was an organization of republican Irishmen, founded in the United States in 1858, although it had roots going back to the previous century. At this time it was at the height of its activities against British North America. By raiding Canadian border posts and forts, its members hoped to persuade the British to leave Ireland. Between 1866 and 1870, Fenians raided Canada a number of times. They attempted to seize Campobello Island in April 1866 and Fort Erie later that year, which led to the Battle of Ridgeway. These clashes involved several thousand men, some of whom on both sides died in the fighting. In 1868, a man called Patrick Whelan, a Fenian, had been convicted and hanged for the assassination of Thomas D'Arcy McGee, a minister in the government of Prime Minister John Macdonald. The main consequence of Fenian activities was to give a powerful impetus for the movement toward the Confederation of British North America in 1867. This was especially true for the maritime colonies, which had been dithering about whether or not to join.

Governments in Canada kept a close eye on Fenian activities on both sides of the border. Gilbert McMicken, head of the Western Frontier Constabulary and, after Confederation, head of the Dominion Police, was Macdonald's spymaster. In addition to using his own spies, McMicken used the secret operatives of Pinkerton's National Detective Agency in both Canada and the United States to find out what mischief the Fenians were planning.[225]

Wherever there were Irish, there were Fenians, thirsting for the chance to strike at the British. On the west coast, San Francisco appears to have been the centre of Fenian fire breathing. The newspapers there were full of Fenian speeches, marches and parades. If their aim was to put pressure on the British, they clearly saw British Columbia as their nearest target. Much of the Fenian movement, though, was with their lips and not with their arms. There was a lot of bluster and braggadocio but, in the West anyway, little action. With the benefit of hindsight, it is easy to underestimate the Fenian threat, even ridicule it, but at the time the authorities had to take it seriously.

Enter George Francis Train. Boston born, Train was a wealthy businessman who had made a fortune with horse tramways and the Union Pacific Railroad. He also intended to be elected president of the United States in 1872. To support his bid, he espoused a number of popular causes, including female suffrage, temperance and the Fenian movement. Believing that Irish votes would be pivotal, he took up their cause with enthusiasm and eloquence. In 1868, he visited Ireland, where the authorities arrested him for having speeches (his own) supporting Irish independence in his possession. They released him on his promise not to promote the Fenian movement in Ireland or England. Train then embarked on a tour of the United States in which he planned to make more than three hundred speeches. In October 1869, Train wrote in a hotel register in LaSalle, Illinois, "George Francis Train, en route from Bloomington to Davenport to deliver his 269th successive lecture there tonight of his course of 600 since released from a British bastille, on his way to the White House in 1872."[226]

After Train addressed a rally in San Francisco in May 1869, the *Morning Chronicle* reported on one of his speeches, quoting him as saying, "The Irish are a power in California. Let them make that power felt by fitting out a Cuban expedition to capture Vancouver Island. ... All who are in favor of such an expedition say 'aye.'... Why don't you sink the British man-of-war with a Fenian torpedo?" The *Chronicle* noted he had arrived in the West "expecting to find an American State," he said. "It pains me to find an English colony instead. Hoping to see a grand American metropolis, I discover the English flag flying over an English city. ... I have sworn to free Ireland, and, so help me God, I will."[227]

A few days later he said that they had freed the Black slaves in America so why didn't they "do something about freeing the white slaves"—presumably the Irish in Ireland—"in England"?[228]

By all accounts he was a hugely entertaining speaker and he inflamed Irish audiences into fire-breathing frenzies. He certainly sounded like a buffoon, but was he actually dangerous?

At the beginning of June, a visitor from Victoria, while in San Francisco, thought he would go and meet the famous George Francis Train in his hotel. The *Daily British Colonist* wrote that after the Victorian was announced, he "started forward and found himself in the awful presence of Mr. Train, whom he found to be a portly gentleman of about 40 years of age, with a very agreeable expression of countenance and exceedingly affable manners." The Victorian introduced himself.

> G.F. [George Francis Train]: Ah, indeed!... I'm happy to make your acquaintance. You're the first gentleman I've met from your port; but you won't, I hope, be the last, as I expect to see a good deal of your people and your island within the next thirty days. What's your population?
>
> V. [Victorian]: About 10,000. ...
>
> G.F.: Any timber?
>
> V.: Yes, sir, lots.
>
> G.F.: Oh, then, I shan't have to take my pontoon bridges up with me. I'll get my material on the spot. I shall bridge the Straits of Fuca and cross my Fenian army upon them. I shall burn the bridges behind them. There'll be no retreat, Sir—no retreat. Fight's the word, sir, with me. The wrongs of Ireland must be avenged.
>
> V.: But, Mr. Train, what has Vancouver [Island] got to do with Ireland?
>
> G.F.: I shall create a diversion, sir. While the British lion is expecting an attack in Ireland, which is its head, I shall attack Vancouver Island, which is its tail. When it feels the fire in its rear it will

whip round to attack us in Vancouver. Ireland then becomes the tail, and the Fenians there will give it a prod, and so we shall keep on annoying the beast, until it will be worn out and fall an easy prey to us. Do you smoke, sir?

The Victorian left "by a private staircase feeling very much as though he had paid a visit to a private lunatic asylum in which there was a single inmate and no keeper."[229]

To such incendiary bombast, Train added real plots to raid British Columbia. He was overheard in an animated discussion with some Fenian friends about his plan for capturing Vancouver Island. Despite his comments that the straits of Juan de Fuca could be crossed on a pontoon bridge made from local timber, Train's plan was described as being remarkably practical and displaying a good knowledge of local conditions. In May 1869, an officer of the Fenian secret service told Train that his plot of making a raid on Vancouver Island had been betrayed. The San Francisco *Morning Chronicle* reported that it was well known that $45,000 had been deposited in a particular store in Victoria. Train's plan was that someone would report the discovery of new coal deposits somewhere on Vancouver Island. The reporting of such a find in Canadian and American newspapers would then cause a rush. Among the miners rushing to the colony would be 350 Fenians who would raid the store, steal the $45,000 and buy weapons to fund the raid. The men had been selected, it was alleged, and the seed money subscribed. One of the conspirators then got drunk and let the secret out. The secret agent feared that word of the plot might have reached the ears of the English consul in San Francisco. Indeed it had.

In late June, Lord Granville, in London, wrote to Hankin saying that the English consul in New York, informed by his colleague in San Francisco, had reported that the Fenians might be going to make trouble in the colony. "Though," he wrote, "I cannot regard it as very probable that a Fenian raid will be made on Vancouver Island, I have thought it right to place you in possession of this statement in order that you may exercise all necessary vigilance in this matter."[230] Hankin and his chief of police, Augustus Pemberton, consequently, were keeping an eye on Train and his associates.

The *Morning Chronicle* reported in June that, though the citizens of Victoria considered Train and his threat to be a joke, it being too ridiculous to claim serious attention, the authorities had brought HMS *Zealous* back to Esquimalt, along with the gunboat *Boxer*, and had alerted the Indigenous people along the coast to report the landing of any body of men. On being told this, Train said, "It was no joke whatever, and it might require a greater naval force than the *Zealous* and the *Boxer* to keep the Fenian boys on the United States territory."[231]

The *Daily British Colonist* was also watching Train, who seemed blithely unaware that everything he said in his speeches, so faithfully recorded in the San Francisco newspapers, was being read in Victoria. "That humbug and nuisance," the *Colonist* called him in January and reported that Train had said that before he left the coast, he would liberate Vancouver Island. "I will invade British Columbia," Train told a San Francisco audience, "seize as hostages ten leading Englishmen there, capture Vancouver Island and establish an Irish Republic, around which I will gather warm-hearted Fenians to drive the English aristocracy from the Continent." A man in the gallery rose excitedly and yelled at the top of his voice, "Will yees lade us?" Train replied, "I will: consider yourself enlisted." The *Colonist* continued, "Madmen have found followers and wrought terrible mischief ere now. We joke about Train's eccentricities; but for all that, it would be just and well if the Government were to keep a bright eye upon his movements.[232]

The people of Victoria may have seen him as a joke and realized, probably correctly, that he presented no threat. Hankin, though, could not take the risk. After all, Train had made his intentions clear. He had the money and a small army of Fenians breathing fire against the British. And had not the Fenians in the East mounted raids and assassinated a leading politician? Moreover, it could not be denied that a large number of people in the colony did want to join the United States. The potential for mischief was real.

Meanwhile, Train was on his way up to Victoria. On July 10, the *Colonist* wrote, "Angels and Ministers of Grace defend us! George Francis Train is on the *Hunt* and will be here early in the morning. ... Train is more of a talker than a fighter and we *should* like to hear one of his unique lectures."[233]

Hankin had been watching both Train and his fellow Fenians. At that time, British Columbia had a small police force under Pemberton, but no plainclothes detectives. Speculation, but no evidence, suggests that Hankin and Pemberton may have learned from McMicken, the head of Macdonald's secret police, that Pinkerton's were good people to use in San Francisco to keep an eye on the Fenians there.

When the *Wilson G. Hunt* arrived in Victoria, Inspector William Bowden, one of Pemberton's policemen, went on board and checked the passenger list. Yes, Train was on board,

George Francis Train, the blustering American who tried to stir up an invasion of British Columbia by the Fenians to advance his presidential ambitions. Wikimedia Commons.

but still sleeping. After Train appeared, Bowden discreetly followed him for the rest of the day, noting whom he met. "He walked to the American Hotel," Bowden duly reported, "kept by a man named Thomas Burnes, in Yates Street," and met a number of friends or confederates there.[234] Bowden was able to report that Train had behaved with all propriety and not broken any laws while in Victoria.

Train left Victoria later that evening without causing a revolution. He was affable to all he met. He talked a lot about himself but, in the way of such people, listened little. He annoyed many with his bombast. So much so that one Victoria merchant went on board his departing ship, picked a fight with him and knocked him down. After his visit to Victoria,

Train boasted that with fifty picked men from Portland he could have captured the city.

Hankin reported to Granville in London about Train's visit to Victoria:

Train had been for some weeks in San Francisco delivering lectures. He threatened to land in this colony with 20,000 men and take possession of the Colony. From San Francisco he visited Portland, and a few days before the Senior Naval Officer on this station, Captain Edye, of Her Majesty's Ship *Satellite*, received a telegram from the British Consul at San Francisco informing him that Train had left that place and might be expected in Victoria.

The day before he arrived, I received information through a Private Telegram that he would come here in a steamer called the *Wilson G. Hunt*, a regular trader between Victoria and the ports on Puget Sound. As the day on which Train was expected by the *W.G. Hunt* was not the regular day for that vessel to arrive, it created some uneasiness in my mind, and I made application to the Senior Naval Officer for the Gun Boat *Forward* to be sent round and anchored in Victoria Harbour, in order that we might be prepared to repel any acts of aggression on the part of Train or his followers; I thought it just possible he might endeavour to create some disturbance in the Town. However, he arrived quietly in the *Wilson G. Hunt* and left a few hours afterwards by the same vessel and I see no reason to apprehend any disturbance.[235]

Several badly organized Fenian raids on Canada in 1870 fell apart almost as soon as they were launched. After 1870, the Fenian threat dwindled to nothing, although there was a revival of threats in the 1890s.

In 1870, Train made a highly publicized trip around the world in eighty days, becoming, some have suggested, the inspiration for Jules Verne's *Around the World in Eighty Days*. A scandal in the Union Pacific finances destroyed even the faint chance Train had of becoming president. He moved away from the Fenian cause, and Fenians, probably realizing he was more hot air than action, moved away from him. As he aged, he grew more eccentric, even to one point when he was arrested and threatened with incarceration in an asylum. Train made another trip around the world, this one in sixty-seven days, a record at the time. He died in 1904.

As administrator, Hankin had the unpleasant duty of giving the order for sentences of execution to be carried out. For example, there was the case of the murderer of William Robinson, a Black settler on Saltspring Island. Robinson had been found in his cabin shot dead. The gun that hung over his mantelpiece was missing, as were his coat, vest, axe and auger. When the police found some of these items in the cabin of Ich-yst-a-tis (or Schuystasis), a Cowichan man also known as Tom, they arrested him. On this slender evidence, he was tried for murder, convicted and sentenced to death.[236] This was a decision ratified by the executive council, which summoned Chief Justice Needham to attend its meeting and confirm that he saw no reason why the sentence of death should not be carried out. On July 15, 1869, Hankin directed Andrew Elliott, now high sheriff of British Columbia, to proceed with the execution.[237] The hanging took place at the police barracks at Victoria's jail on July 25.

During Hankin's administration, the French and American flagships in the Pacific paid a visit to Vancouver Island, and both admirals called on him.[238] "Of course their visits were at once returned," Hankin wrote, "and I was received with a salute of 17 guns (or 13, I forget which), which inflamed the angry Passions of my friends in Victoria more than ever. Then I gave several entertainments on shore and dined with the French Admiral." Since Governor Seymour's widow was still living at Government House, Hankin entertained the admiral and his officers at his own home.

The French ship was the frigate *Astrée*, with Rear Admiral Georges Cloué on board. It arrived in Esquimalt Harbour on July 7, 1869. Hankin and his officials went on board for the formal welcome. The French ship fired a thirteen-gun salute, which HMS *Satellite* returned. "When I went on board the senior officer's ship at Esquimalt," Hankin wrote, "I was Saluted again—Oh dear! Oh dear! It was nothing but Salutes and everybody was very angry. They would not understand that it was not me they were Saluting but the office I held."

Offended susceptibilities aside, everyone seemed to enjoy the visit of the French warship. Captain Daniel Pender, Hankin's fellow lodger at Stone's lodgings in Portsmouth and the one who had steered Hankin toward Vancouver Island, invited the French officers to a picnic at Colwood, which Hankin and his wife attended.[239] The band played and the party had a singsong. On the following day, to the general delight of all, the ship's band returned the compliment and played at Foster's pier in Victoria.

The American ship, also a frigate, was the *Pensacola*, carrying Rear Admiral Thomas Turner. It visited Esquimalt on August 8 but stayed for only one day, seemingly having little time for such fripperies as picnics and band concerts. William Seward, the former United States secretary of state, was another American visitor to Victoria. He had been instrumental in the purchase of Alaska from Russia two years before. Despite his well-known expansionist views, he was given a warm welcome, with crowds gathering to greet him. Seward called on Hankin and they had a long chat. The welcoming banquet was deferred until his return, by which time Governor Musgrave should have arrived.

Hankin was not without critics but he also had defenders. In July, a letter in the *Daily British Colonist* from a correspondent who signed himself merely T.S. chastised an anonymous letter writer who had criticized Hankin:

It is not fair, Mr. Editor, for every disappointed man to attempt to bring those administering the Government into disrepute anonymously through your columns. ... Indeed, to those who thoughtfully look at matters, it is a cause for thankfulness that so much energy and willingness have been manifested by the present Administrator of the Government. Coming here in circumstances that rendered his appointment unpopular, he has commended himself to every sensible person. *More, for instance, has been done during the last four weeks for the efficient introduction of a good school system than in two years before.* [Author's italics.] Apart from this and other noticeable improvements, he has a right to expect that in his present peculiar and difficult position his hands will be strengthened by every person of intelligence and good feeling.[240]

Meanwhile, Anthony Musgrave was on his way from Newfoundland. Hankin did not know him. Musgrave had grown up in the West Indies, where he had deep family roots. In 1850, he had served as private secretary to the governor and possibly also to Frederick Seymour when he was a colonial administrator in the Leeward Islands (Antigua and Nevis). Seymour had certainly known him and had a high opinion of his intelligence and abilities. Musgrave had gone on to a promising career in government service. When he finally arrived and reviewed Hankin's tenure as administrator, would he be an Arthur Kennedy, affable and easy to get along with, or would he be a Frederick Seymour, insecure, suspicious and standing on his rights? Hankin must have awaited his arrival with some apprehension.

10

Governor Musgrave and

Joining Canada

August 1869–August 1871

A nthony Musgrave arrived in Victoria from San Francisco on the ss *Moses Taylor* on August 23, 1869.[241] A widower, he brought with him his two sisters and his son, also named Anthony, who was to act as his private secretary. Guns from HMS *Satellite* boomed a welcome. Hankin, together with the senior naval officers, Captains Edye and Mist, met them and welcomed them to Victoria. The party went first to Government House for breakfast and then on to the government buildings to meet the members of the executive council. That afternoon, Musgrave, escorted by Hankin, a band and a detachment from the Rifle Corps, went to the courthouse, where Chief Justice Needham swore him in as the new governor.[242]

Also arriving in Victoria on that day was Graham Hankin, Philip's younger brother. He had travelled from San Francisco on the ss *Rival.* (He would return to England the following week for health reasons and die soon after.) What with welcoming both the new governor and his own brother, Hankin had a busy day.

Any fears Hankin might have had about his new boss were soon put to rest. "When Anthony Musgrave was sent out to relieve me, I gave up the government to him, and returned to my old office as colonial secretary," he wrote in his memoirs. "About a year passed away, and I got on very well with Sir Anthony, who was an extremely pleasant man to serve under."

As soon as he arrived, Musgrave sent a telegram to the Colonial Office in London, saying, "Arrived and assumed Government. All well."[243] A few days later, he amplified his telegram by a letter. "Your Lordship," he wrote, "will be glad to learn that any fear of Fenian raids and such disturbances seems not to have had much real foundation. The information I gathered in San Francisco and since my arrival here seems to show that whatever may be their feeling on Irish Grievances the Irish in California had no desire to accept Mr. Train as a leader, nor did he seriously contemplate any mischievous attempt at disturbance of the peace."[244]

Hankin and Musgrave found they got on well together. "I like Mr. Musgrave immensely," Hankin wrote to the Duke of Buckingham. "I never wish to serve with a better man and I think he is as much liked as it is possible for British Columbians to like any governor."[245] One of Hankin's more attractive traits was his willingness to speak well of people. Hankin enjoyed many pleasant dinners and occasionally a small dance as Musgrave's guest at Government House. He took his part in the social life of the Musgraves, going out riding with them and playing croquet on the lawns at Government House. Musgrave went down to San Francisco to remarry and brought his bride back to Victoria. Jeanie Lucinda Musgrave wrote in her diary, "Sir James Douglas and Mrs. Douglas and Misses called for us at 10 and we rode till 1. They lunched here with Mr. Hankin and [we all] played croquet till 4."[246]

Hankin served as colonial secretary until British Columbia joined Canada in early July 1871. Then for a few weeks until the end of August 1871, when the lieutenant-governor for the new province arrived, he was again in charge of the government.

Governor Musgrave easily settled into his new position and became very popular. He arrived in a city that was changing fast. Its population was growing. Construction of houses, stores and all manner of other buildings proceeded apace. The search for gold was pulling prospectors into the distant corners of the colony. The missionaries expanded their calling to bring Christianity to Indigenous people and were settling in remote communities. Behind them came the government with gold commissioners and magistrates, and commerce with roadhouses and trail builders. The newspapers were filled with reports from mines in the Cariboo—Antler Creek, Cedar Creek, Keithley Creek and Grouse Creek, where Charles Hankin was mining. Prospectors were also pushing north into the Omineca Mountains and the Peace River. Almost as soon as he had settled in, Musgrave made a get-to-know-you tour of the colony to see for himself.

Thomas Hankin, one of Philip's younger brothers, had been employed by the Hudson's Bay Company at the Forks of the Skeena River for almost two years. By 1870, he was planning to establish his own store and transportation business at a new community there. The following year he would name it Hazelton. Thomas was in Victoria for two months at the end of 1870. With many others from the Forks, he presented a petition to the governor for the construction of a better trail from the Forks to the new goldfields in the Omineca Mountains. This small community of Hazelton became the central point for supplying prospectors and settlers who were opening the northern part of the colony and, after 1871, the province.

The telegraph had connected the province to the United States since 1866. It was only a couple of years since Frederick Seymour, when governor of the old Colony of British Columbia, had offered his own boat to carry the first telegraph cable across the river to New Westminster. Victoria was now in telegraphic communication with eastern Canada and London. Among the talk about British Columbia's joining Canada was the proposal that Canada should build a railway from the East to the Pacific coast. Prime Minister John Macdonald was planning to use this railway to bind British North America together from coast to coast as a way of preventing American territorial expansion.

One sign of the changing times attracting notice in Victoria was the appearance on the streets of bicycles, or velocipedes as they were called. (Some, with good reason, called them boneshakers!) "The velocipede mania is well under way," the Daily British Colonist reported in April 1869.[247] The two-wheeled vehicle was rather difficult to manage but two riders in the new park at Beacon Hill had been able to keep their equilibrium for quite a while. Dr. John Helmcken, the newspaper said, had imported one for his own use. The *Colonist* reported it had ordered half a dozen for its couriers. There was also a three-wheeled version for ladies on which they looked, the *Colonist* said patronizingly, very charming. Some people were complaining that these velocipedes should not be on the sidewalks, that they were damaging the wooden planking and running the risk of knocking pedestrians down. How the once quiet little village of Victoria was changing!

On November 2, 1869, Musgrave was mounting his horse near Government House when it reared and threw him.[248] His whole weight landed on his right leg, causing him to suffer a serious compound fracture, with a bone forcing its way completely through the leather of his riding boot. This injury, which rendered him bed bound for four months and intermittently thereafter, crippled him for the rest of his life. But it did not keep him from his paperwork. It was not until the first week of March 1870, though, that he was able to leave his room and descend to the ground floor of Government House.[249] By March 20, he was out riding in his barouche (an open four-wheeled carriage) with his daughter in his first excursion since the accident.[250] By mid-May, he was able to go to church and the theatre again.

During the months when Musgrave was unable to perform his official duties, Hankin deputized for him. The weight of responsibility thrown on Hankin's shoulders by this accident should not be underestimated. In his position as colonial secretary, he was the administrative cog around which the whole government revolved. It was his job to preside at meetings of the executive council. In this position he was in the thick of the crucial debates about the accession of British Columbia to Canada.

Hankin's duties as colonial secretary, as it had been when he was administrator, ranged from mundane routine administration—peace, order and good government—to existential issues of the greatest importance. In many of them, it is hard to know which were his decisions and which were those of Musgrave. When he wrote "His Excellency has

Anthony Musgrave. He came from Newfoundland to become governor of British Columbia after Governor Frederick Seymour died. He presided over the accession of British Columbia to Canada. Image I-46936 courtesy of the Royal BC Museum and Archives

commanded me to inform you..." he may have been expressing the governor's wishes, decisions he recommended to the governor or merely his own decisions framed in the formal language of the age. In the short periods when he had been the administrator of the colony, though, the buck necessarily had stopped on his desk.

Writing on behalf of the governor, he gave permission to government employees to take leaves of absence. He approved, for example, the application of Henry Pellew Crease for three weeks' leave in September 1869. Crease was later attorney general and sat on the supreme court bench of the province for twenty-six years. Hankin appointed notaries public and others to legal positions. In June 1870, he directed the acting colonial secretary, Charles Good, to prepare the papers to appoint a man named H.P. Walker to be in charge of all government prosecutions in the upper country. In July 1870, he reminded the governor that the salaries of schoolteachers were in arrears and that many of them were suffering hardship. Half of the arrears had already been paid. He asked for authorization for payment of the other half.

Hankin represented Musgrave at official events. When William Seward was on his way back from Alaska in August 1869, the government held a grand banquet in his honour. Hankin, representing Musgrave, who was too exhausted after a recent tour of the province to attend, sat next to Seward at dinner, replied to Seward's speech and, in a second speech, replied to a toast on behalf of the navy.[251] Seward was made much of in Victoria but in private circles he gave some offence. While in town he was reported as saying that "so long as British Columbia (including of course Vancouver Isld) remained a Crown Colony they (the Americans) would be content to let things go on as now—but that they would, in every possible way, oppose its union with the Canadian Confederation."[252]

At the end of April 1870, Hankin's old friends Lady Franklin and Miss Cracroft paid another visit to Victoria. An inveterate traveller, the lady and her niece were touring the world again. Lady Franklin was as famous and as formidable as ever. Before they arrived, Miss Cracroft wrote, "We hope also to find here our friend Hankin, a Lieut. in Captain Richards's ship when we visited here 9 years ago, who went with us up the Fraser river—then a harum-scarum fellow. He afterwards left the Service, and is now, I believe, the Colonial Secretary—an important post in which we can hardly fancy him."[253] When they arrived, they sent him a note, and he came to see them as soon as he could, "unaltered in most ways, but stouter," she wrote. "Mr. Hankin soon shewed us that he had not lost his fun."[254] While they were in Victoria, Hankin was assiduous in his attentions to them, showing them the changes in town since their first visit. He kept them both amused by recalling the good times they had had together on the Fraser River and some of his pranks. "And he recited an Address presented [by Rev. Crickmer] to my Aunt at Yale on the Fraser which (having an astonishing memory) he remembers word for word."[255]

Hankin took them and the younger Musgrave to pay a visit to Sir James and Lady Douglas at their house, which, Miss Cracroft wrote, was exactly as they had known it nine years before, with "the strait walk from the entrance gate on the road, between the roughest of lawns, bordered with detached bushes of roses and sweet briar."[256] Sir James was out but Lady Douglas received them all very cordially, which surprised everyone because she was known to be reclusive. Indeed, Musgrave had not even seen her yet.

They all attended the first dinner party Governor Musgrave gave since his accident. In addition to Lady Franklin, Miss Cracroft and Hankin, the sixteen guests included Chief Justice Matthew Baillie Begbie, Admiral Arthur Farquhar and Mr. and Mrs. Joseph Trutch. "It was a pleasant party," Miss Cracroft wrote, "and we had a talk about the Bill for giving women the Suffrage."[257] They also discussed the burning topic of the day: Should British Columbia join Canada? Miss Cracroft noted that British Columbia wanted three conditions to join Canada—a railway to New Westminster, a dock at Esquimalt and a hospital (and asylum) in Victoria. "If these conditions be accepted," she wrote, "we may still hope to keep this valuable Colony, instead of letting it fall into the hands of the Americans. I could write pages on this subject—it makes us so indignant that our Govern't can accept even as a *possibility* the loss of our only possession on this side of the Pacific with its enormous advantages."[258]

The debate about whether British Columbia should join Canada had raged in the colony ever since the Dominion had come into existence in 1867. Although this is not the place for a blow-by-blow account of the path the colony took to accession in 1871, a few comments may be in order.

From today's perspective, the union seems inevitable and obvious. At the time, though, it did not. There were three options: First, to remain an independent colony of Great Britain. This was not realistic because the colony was essentially bankrupt, thanks in part to the extensive road-building programs of Governor James Douglas. Furthermore, the British government did not seem interested in supporting the colony's independence for much longer. The second option was to join Canada on acceptable terms—but could they be obtained? And the third was to join the United States as a new territory or state, which many people in the colony did want. Indeed, a petition was prepared requesting annexation. This was delivered to General George Ihrie, a passenger on board the USS *New Berne*, to deliver personally to President Ulysses Grant.[259] This petition, signed largely by Americans and foreigners, was not significant in itself, but it did give encouragement to annexationist sentiment in the United States. The main effect, though, was to stiffen the resolve of many British Columbians to join Canada. Others merely wanted to postpone the decision.

The United States, newly emerged from its civil war, was in an expansionist mood. It was already disputing the ownership of San Juan Island in the Juan de Fuca Strait. In 1872, a decision of an arbitration commission appointed by Kaiser Wilhelm I awarded ownership of the island to the United States. Thanks largely to Seward, the United States had purchased Alaska in 1867. Why couldn't the United States annex British Columbia and connect the two pieces of American territory and have total control of the Pacific seaboard from Attu Island at the end of the Aleutians to the Mexican border? There was a fiery feeling among some Americans that the United States should actually annex all of British North America. This aggressiveness was stoked by the Fenians, always eager to poke Great Britain, as well as by the businessmen in Saint Paul, Minnesota, who wanted to reach mercantile fingers up into the Red River territory. There was also a desire to exact reparations from Britain for the damage done by the Confederate raider *Alabama*. The *Alabama* was a Confederate warship built in secrecy in Liverpool in 1862. Its capturing and burning of sixty-five Union ships caused great umbrage in the United States against Great Britain. Some members of Congress and their business supporters thought annexation of British North America was a grand idea. A bill for such an annexation was introduced into the United States Congress in July 1866.[260] This had been sent into committee for consideration but had quietly died there.

Popular opinion in British Columbia was split. The governing class in Victoria, mainly composed of British immigrants and the Hudson's Bay Company, supported the move to join Canada and maintain their British connections. American immigrants in Victoria and commercial interests with close contacts to San Francisco, as well as the large number of American prospectors seeking gold in the interior, wanted to join the United States. American influences were everywhere in the colony and offending many. In 1864, for example, Governor Seymour had complained to Edward Cardwell in London that the schools in British Columbia were using objectionable American books, which used American spelling! The sentiments of these school books were "violently republican," he wrote. "The United States are lauded at the expense of England and, finally, fables about alleged natural phenomena are gravely stated as truth."[261] He asked for some English school books to be sent out.

A few days before his accident, Musgrave wrote about the pro-American sentiments in the colony after his tour. It was not by any means clear, he wrote to the colonial secretary in London, that the majority of the community favoured union with Canada except on terms that probably would not be obtainable.[262] Prime Minister John Macdonald, carefully noting the threats from the United States and believing that a sea-to-sea British North America was essential, told Musgrave to prepare the proposal for accession but not to introduce it into the legislative council until he was sure it would be accepted. Canada had just finished negotiations for the acquisition of the North-West Territories. These were Hudson's Bay Company lands, which effectively included all land east of what is now the Ontario border. It was time, Macdonald thought, to extend Canada to the Pacific.

In the absence of Musgrave—still confined to his bed, Hankin presided over a meeting of the executive council on December 2, 1869. The purpose was to consider the latest dispatch from Ottawa on Confederation. This was also noteworthy because it was the first meeting that Dr. John Helmcken, Hankin's old acquaintance from as far back as 1857, attended after his appointment to the council. Although initially opposed to accession, Helmcken was a key figure in the negotiations with Ottawa in 1870.[263]

Working with the executive council, of which Hankin was the ranking member, Musgrave prepared a proposal that would be the basis of negotiations with Canada. On February 16, 1870, members of the legislative assembly gathered in the Birdcages to hear the governor's proposals. The governor himself, though, was absent because this was the day on which the doctors were removing the splints from his legs. They declared the union of his broken bones was successful.[264] (Perhaps this union was portentous!) It fell to Hankin to read the governor's message to the members and to handle the debate. This led to the resolution in March, after a three-day debate, to approve the opening of negotiations with the Government of Canada on the terms that Musgrave had proposed.

At times the political infighting irritated Hankin—as well it might—and he wrote about this to his now-out-of-office friend the Duke of Buckingham. In a private letter not intended to become public, he singled out Amor de Cosmos, the fiery, mercurial journalist and political activist. "We have a certain gentleman here, who has a good seat in the Legislative Council, by name 'Amor de Cosmos' (his real name is Smith). He is a thorough Democratic ruffian & has already given out that he will be Lieut't Governor. He is a great nuisance in the House & abuses the officials and the Government generally."[265]

Dr. Helmcken was one of the three-man team that went to Ottawa to conduct the negotiations. The other two were Dr. Robert Carrall, steady and reliable, and Joseph Trutch, representing commercial interests. Flexibility and calm responsibility were required in the delegates, and consequently the mercurial Amor de Cosmos was not included. The three delegates were surprised not only by the warmth of their reception but also by the generosity of the terms offered—among them, a completely representative assembly, the assumption of the colony's debts (which by then amounted to over $1 million), subsidies, maintenance of the naval station at Esquimalt and the promise that a railway to the coast would be completed within ten years. The terms were brought back to the colony and announced, under Hankin's name, in the *Daily British Colonist* on August 31, 1870.[266]

At this time, Hankin was living with his wife, Isabel, in a house on Dallas Road, not far from the legislative buildings. However, Isabel was not well. Hankin wrote to the duke in March 1870, "I am sorry to say Mrs. Hankin has been very delicate for some time. She never appears to have shaken off the effects of the Yellow Fever she caught in the West Indies, &, by the advice of her Medical Man, I am going to send her to California for a few months to stay with a married sister."[267] In October, Susan Nagle wrote in her diary, "Isabel left for England, accompanied by Charley Hankin, on September 24th. Philip has let the house to the Creases and gone to live with [friends]."[268]

At the end of December, Hankin sent a large amount of what was called his "superior furniture" to sale by auction.[269] The sale included mahogany bedsteads, bureaus, chairs, a sewing machine, bed linen, engravings, Brussels carpets and about two hundred books. The sale also included a side saddle. Why? Most likely, with his wife on her way to England, he no longer needed a house. He may also have been anticipating having to leave Victoria after the accession of British Columbia to Canada, which was appearing more and more likely every day.

In January 1871, Hankin was elected Speaker of the legislative assembly. This was the chamber of appointed and elected members, more of the former than the latter. It tends to show he had established himself and had been accepted.

The legislative council accepted the terms of Confederation that same January, and by April, after some haggling and compromises, the Dominion Parliament in Ottawa had also accepted. Joseph Trutch, an engineer and road builder of note in the colony and one of the team who had gone to Ottawa to negotiate the terms, then went to London to speed the approval of the union by the United Kingdom. On May 20, the imperial government in London issued an order-in-council that approved the accession of British Columbia to Canada. Prime Minister Macdonald chose Trutch to be the first lieutenant-governor of the new province, largely because he was widely liked and not too deeply entrenched in any of the factions. This was a popular choice at the time. In hindsight, it was an unfortunate decision. As lieutenant-governor and as commissioner of lands and works before that, Trutch reversed the more generous policies of James Douglas, took back land already given to Indigenous Peoples and denied the existence of Indigenous land rights. He has consequently become a deeply offensive figure in provincial history.

British Columbia officially joined Canada as a province on July 20, 1871. "Today," the Daily British Colonist said, "British Columbia passes peacefully and, let us add, gracefully into the confederated empire of Canada." There were no official formalities in Victoria to mark the event but this did not stop the citizens from celebrating. "At 12 o'clock," the *Colonist* reported, "there were manifestations of great rejoicing in the city. Bells were rung, guns fired, blue lights and Roman candles burned and crackers snapped. And people met on the streets and shook hands with and congratulated each other and cheered and cheered! Everybody seemed happy and jolly and the manifestations were kept up long into the small hours. They were celebrating the Birth of Liberty."[270]

For the short time between Governor Musgrave's departure from the new province on July 25 and the arrival of Trutch in August, Hankin was, in effect, if not in law, head of the provincial government. This does not appear to have been official. Although the *Daily British Colonist* noted on July 26 that on the previous day Hankin had been sworn in as administrator of the government, it reported the following day that he had declined to be sworn in because no one representing the Dominion government was present who had the authority to administer the oath.[271] Nevertheless, he kept the government ticking over during this short interregnum. It can loosely be said that Hankin was, de jure, the last colonial secretary of the Colony of British Columbia and, de facto, the first governing official of the new province of British Columbia.

What would the executive officers of the colony do now? It was decided that the attorney general, the chief commissioner of lands and works, the collector of customs and the colonial secretary were to be given either an appointment of equal pay to the one they were deprived of or a pension. But what was comparable to a colonial secretary?

In January 1871, Musgrave had conducted a performance review of the colonial officers and their potential for other and higher appointments. Like Captain Richards, he did have a reservation about Hankin's character. He wrote that Hankin was "thirty-three years of age and... an officer of much natural ability. He is loyal to his official superiors and renders willing service and assistance, though I would not perhaps repose implicit confidence in his tact or discretion. But under proper guidance, he is capable and useful."[272] The Royal Navy promoted Hankin to captain and offered him either command of a ship when he returned to England or retirement. He chose to retire.

The *Daily British Colonist*, Hankin's fiercest critic when he arrived—apart from Governor Seymour—was gracious when he departed. On August 16, it noted he was sailing for England that morning and was retiring "with the rank of Captain, R.N., on half pay with a pension from the Dominion Government of $533. He has been many years connected with the Colony in various capacities, during the last three years as Colonial Secretary, and has twice been called upon to administer the government. As a public officer he has been faithful and attentive, and as a citizen he has gained the good opinion of all."[273] Such words from a source initially so hostile were eloquent testimony to his ability and honesty.

Philip Hankin would never return to British Columbia in an official capacity.

In India with the Duke

1871–1880

O n their arrival in England, the Hankins went to Stowe House for a week's visit. Here, Hankin wrote in his memoirs, they were "received with the greatest kindness by the Duke and Duchess of Buckingham and their three charming daughters." Hankin wanted—or needed—a job, although if he accepted a government post his pension would be suspended. His sister-in-law, Susan Nagle, wrote in her diary that Hankin nevertheless was hoping for an appointment as lieutenant-governor for some island in the British possessions, but this never came to pass.[274] The duke by now was out of office and so had no patronage appointments to offer. So now what was Hankin to do?

There is a little evidence that Hankin may have invested in a business venture. He seems to have become a partner of John Henry Barber in the wine business of Barber & Hankin, with an establishment at No. 1, Gresham Building, Basinghall Street, in London. By mid-1874, he had decided to leave the partnership, perhaps because he had more interesting employment. This partnership was dissolved in August of that year and Barber continued the business on his own.[275]

In 1872, Hankin and his wife decided to see something of Europe. When visiting Menton, a resort town on the French-Italian border, he received a letter from the duke, who wrote that he had been looking for a gentleman to fill the office of his private secretary at Stowe for some time. If Hankin wanted it, the position was his. The duke offered him a comfortable salary and a "pretty little house 5 minutes' walk from Stowe," rent-free. About to leave for Naples and Malta, Hankin immediately changed his plans and returned to England. The day after their arrival back in England, Hankin and his wife went to Stowe so he could start his new job. He stayed there for two years.

News of the appointment found its way back to Victoria. The *Daily British Colonist* recorded a correspondent in England as saying, with more than a little sniff of jealousy, "Philip Hankin, the luckiest of the lucky, looks more self-complacent and comfortable than ever. ... You will probably shortly hear of his being in Parliament—oh! the luck of some people."[276]

For a while, all went well. The duke and duchess were gracious. The job suited him. As private secretary he handled the business of the duke's correspondence, much of it being routine work concerning the duke's estates and tenancies. On June 16, 1872, for example, he was writing on behalf of the duke about the supply of manure from the duke's estate to a contractor. On November 30, 1872, he was granting the duke's approval to the transfer of a tenancy.

Stowe was palatial and its gardens were among the finest in England with lakes, lawns and follies planned by Capability Brown, the famous landscape gardener. The Hankins were happy there, but it did not last. On February 23, 1874, after a lingering illness, the duchess died, "to the everlasting grief of her family and deeply regretted by all who knew her."[277]

Around this time, Benjamin Disraeli returned to power as prime minister. He offered the duke the governorship of Madras Presidency, which at that time comprised much of southern India and its east coast. Although it was almost a demotion for him, the duke accepted it as a public service and asked Hankin to accompany him as his private secretary.

Leaving Gravesend on the ss *Sultan* on October 15, 1875, they sailed to Madras, now known as Chennai. They passed through the Suez Canal, which had been opened only six years before. (On November 23, only a month after the duke and his party passed through the canal, Disraeli, on behalf of the British government, purchased a controlling interest in it.) The duke's three daughters accompanied their father. Going to India with them also was his sister, the redoubtable Lady Anna Gore Langton, together with her son and daughter.[278] Lady Anna was a formidable force in improving women's education. She was also a leader in the women's suffrage movement. Isabel Hankin joined her husband in Madras, coming from Vancouver Island, where she had been visiting her parents. On November 23, the duke assumed his new office in Madras.

Hankin spent five years with the duke in Madras. He and Isabel had rooms in Government House so that he would be readily available for the duke. Life would have been very pleasant. Here they were amid all the majesty and colour of the British Raj—the native servants (called peons), the strange foods and, somewhere not too far away, exotic animals such as tigers, elephants and cobras. There were glittering balls and receptions. Outside the tight little walls the British built around themselves in India, though, were the teeming masses, the poverty and the bewildering number of races, religions, castes and languages.

Madras was no glittering imperial capital. A traveller there in 1876, A.H. Wylie, called it "the dreariest city of the East."[279] Madras consisted of "a very straggling native town without any pretty European quarter to compensate for the native ugliness," he wrote. "There are one or two European shops, frightfully dear, near Government House. ... The evening drives up and down the beach, however, were charming and the sea breezes most welcome. Here the élite of Madras society, and the rest also, congregate every night. A band plays three times a week. Some of the avenue drives are beautiful, and offer a welcome shade—the trees are chiefly bamboos and palms, which wave about in the most graceful manner."[280]

Hankin had well-established connections to India. His brother Frederick was a colonel in the Madras Army. His brother Edward also had had an army career. When Hankin arrived in Madras, Edward was the joint magistrate at Ootacamund (Udhagamandalam), the summer capital of Madras Presidency in the Nilgiri hills.[281] Ootacamund was nicknamed Ooty or, by the irreverent, Snooty Ooty. In a year or so, Edward Hankin moved to Madras, where he became head of the civil pension service and later military secretary to the government. The newspapers in Madras suggested that his brother's being private secretary to the governor might have had something to do with his appointment.[282] Hankin's sister Constance, who had died in 1863, had married a major general of the Madras Army. Hankin's first cousins, George Crommelin Hankin and Mordaunt Hankin, were also serving officers in India. True, Hankin had not seen some of them since he had left home thirty years before, but still, they were family.

In the summer months, the Madras government moved to the summer capital at Ootacamund, much as the viceroy's government in the north moved to Simla. The governor's house there, the Cedars, was small and inconveniently perched at the top of a hill, which necessitated the carriage of water up to it every day. Since the duke's large family went with him and filled the Cedars, as well as another house close by, Hankin and his wife had to live in yet another house, as did the military secretary, Colonel George Bertie Hobart, and other members of staff.[283] But still, it was cool and lushly green.

Hankin became friends with Hobart, who was a distant relative of the duke. Despite this apparent nepotism, Hobart did have deep and legitimate roots in India, having served in the army since before the Sepoy Mutiny of 1857.

Without a wife who would normally do the honours, the duke's eldest daughter, Lady Mary, acted as hostess for formal functions at Government House. She and the duke, for example, were the hostess and host at a reception in 1876 to celebrate the Queen's birthday. Both the duke and Hankin attended in full court dress, which comprised "blue cloth coat, embroidered with gold lace, white breeches, white silk stockings, shoes with buckles, cocked hat with a fringe of ostrich feathers, and sword."[284] Indian and Burmese princes were present in their gorgeous reds and golds, turbans and jewels, bringing with them all the opulence, mystery and magic of the subcontinent. The band played "rather too severely classical pieces, and anything like dance music was carefully avoided, probably as being too tantalising. At eleven o'clock there was a general movement to witness the fire-works which had been carefully arranged on the opposite bank of the river Cooum, and were seen to advantage through the avenue of trees from the north end of the Hall."[285] Life in the Raj in Madras, with all its gold and glitter, pomp and power, was a long way from the muddy mines at Barkerville.

As private secretary to the duke, Hankin would have been at the centre of government and aware of all its decisions, corres-pondence and activities. He would have known everything that was going on and would also have been the duke's eyes and ears beyond official com-

Captain Philip Hankin at about the time he was private secretary to the Duke of Buckingham in India. Image A-01339 courtesy of the Royal BC Museum and Archives

munications. His experience as a colonial secretary in two jurisdictions would have been an excellent preparation for this.

In December 1875, Edward, Prince of Wales, paid his memorable visit to India and stayed at Government House in Madras for ten days. He arrived from Bombay and received a brilliant reception at the railway station. A huge crowd was waiting for him, including the duke, the chief justice and the commander-in-chief. On his way to Government House, a huge crowd of fourteen thousand people sang "God Save the Prince of Wales."[286] That night there was a splendid banquet at Government House, followed by fireworks.

The prince thoroughly enjoyed himself in Madras. A journalist accompanying the royal party wrote:

There was a certain unavoidable stiffness in the receptions and ceremonials at Bombay, but this has entirely worn off, and now, without the smallest sacrifice of dignity, the Prince is evidently deriving genuine enjoyment of his tour. The whole party gives preference to Madras as the pleasantest place they have yet visited. The society is charming, the racing and hunting excellent, and the Prince has repeatedly spoke of the Madras Club Ball as one of the pleasantest in his experience. He stopped there until 4 a.m. and danced frequently. ... The Prince is in excellent health. The change of climate, etc, evidently has done him good. He has decreased in weight, and is full of strength and activity.[287]

Hankin would have been in the thick of all this. He would have been the lubricating oil between the duke's staff and the prince's staff. His charm would have been useful in preventing misunderstandings and smoothing over the friction that such official visits have the potential to create. He had opportunities of seeing the prince frequently. It would have been, "Can you spare a few minutes for His Grace, Your Royal Highness?" and "Perhaps I could persuade you to look at the guest list for the ball tonight, Your Royal Highness?" Hankin wrote that the prince was most gracious and affable to everyone. "One day," he wrote, "he took me with him on board his ship, the *Serapis*, and shewed me his photographs, and anything he thought would interest me." The prince even gave him a signed photograph of himself. "He was one of the kindest and most charming of men," Hankin wrote, "and made one feel quite at ease immediately." The Hankin charm meets the royal charm!

"Shortly after this I was present at Delhi," Hankin wrote, "when Queen Victoria was proclaimed Empress of India and the Duke and his ladies and all his staff went to Delhi. Lord Lytton was then the Viceroy and it was a magnificent sight." All the great and good of the subcontinent attended this pre-eminent event in the history of the Raj, with all its pageantry and colour. Hankin's brother commanded one of the regiments in parade for the event.

As head of the government, the duke had to deal with a number of escalating crises. First came drought, then crop failure, then the Great Famine of 1876–1878. This famine affected over fifty million people in the Madras and Bombay presidencies, between six and ten million of whom

The Prince of Wales's voyage to India: quarterdeck of the *Serapis*. The prince is standing second from the right. He invited Hankin on board and showed him his photographs. *Illustrated London News*, November 12, 1875.

died. As with all such natural disasters, whether famine or pandemic, much more could have been done and, with the wisdom of hindsight, should have been done. The actions of British administrators, particularly those in the capital of Calcutta and the summer capital of Simla, in some ways worsened the famine by frustrating pragmatic efforts to alleviate it. The duke himself, though, was active and energetic in relieving the suffering. He organized food relief. He appealed for subscriptions in the main cities of the United Kingdom. In response to his appeal, London alone raised £475,000—approximately £50 million in today's money. He arranged for food to be imported. He deepened and extended the waterway known as the Buckingham Canal to facilitate the more rapid transport of food supplies around Madras. The government had to increase taxes to pay for the famine alleviation measures. This led to unrest, resulting in a rebellion of the Indian tribes in the northern part of the presidency.

A glimpse of Madras in the time of the duke was given by Edward Montagu, Viscount Hinchingbrooke, a member of Parliament in London and later eighth Earl of Sandwich, in his book about his travels, *Diary in Ceylon & India, 1878–9*. Montagu arrived in Madras on December 1, 1878, and stayed for a week. After a mix-up in the mail about the date of his arrival, a hastily dispatched aide-de-camp rescued him from having no hotel to go to (they were all full) and nothing to eat. He stayed with the duke at Government House, where, he wrote, the servants anticipated his every want. After lunch with the duke and his family and Hankin, they all went out to "the verandah, and fed the kites," he wrote. "It is wonderful how tame the birds are in India; crows and other birds come hopping about the verandahs and rooms. ... In the evening we drove in a *char-à-banc* and four, with outriders, to the Fort Church and afterwards along the sea-shore."[288]

The next day Montagu went with the duke and his staff on the annual official visit in state to the Prince of Arcot. "Salutes were fired when the Duke started from Government House, and on his arrival, and guards were drawn up in the compound of the Prince's palace. They received us at the entrance. The Duke walked up arm-in-arm with the Prince. I followed with his brother in like manner. We were received in durbar, and the circle was full of relatives and dependents who live upon the prince. ... The Rajah of Pittapur sat next to me, but at these interviews it is not etiquette for anybody to speak except the host and principal visitor; so we listened."[289]

Forty people sat down for dinner at Government House that night, which was followed by an evening party. "The governor's first-rate private band," Montagu wrote, "played during dinner—food excellent. The Duke has a French cook and an Italian. Magnificent gold services of plate. The peons, fine dark fellows, are dressed in white, with red and gold belts and bands, turbans, ditto; their feet are always bare, so the waiting is delightfully noiseless. Dinner never exceeds an hour. Last night the insects were so innumerable that we had covers to all our glasses to keep them out, and the tablecloth was black with them but they were much fewer tonight. Candles are always covered with glass on account of the punkahs [ceiling fans]. I took in Lady Mary, who does the honours very well, and is very civil to all the guests."[290]

After breakfast one morning a troupe of the best jugglers in Madras came to the entrance hall of Government House and entertained them all with their tricks, including, Montagu wrote, "the basket trick, making the mango grow from a seed to a plant in a few minutes, mixing a variety of sands in a basin of water—bringing them out separate and dry, snake-charming, and all manner of acrobatic feats. ... There can be no gammon or deception here, as you can go amongst the men while they are performing."[291]

The duke was a solicitous host and ensured that his guest saw the sights. Montagu visited the old Arsenal and went to the barracks for a parade of the Fifteenth Regiment of Madras Native Infantry. He also visited the Mount, where Saint Thomas the Apostle had allegedly preached and suffered martyrdom in AD 72. Hankin took him to the Madras museum, where the director received them and showed the collections—specimens of all the various woods, antiquities, stuffed animals and the skeleton of a fifty-foot-long whale found on the Malabar Coast. On an excursion out to the Red Hills, Montagu noted the large camp where thousands had lived and been fed by government relief during the famine. At the time, only twenty-five people were still living there.

Montagu commented on the famous surf at Madras. While he was there, the surf was so rough that the only boats that could manage them were the massulah boats, constructed of planks without ribs or nails, fastened together with coconut twine so that they bent in the pounding waves. Smaller two-man versions of these were called catamarans. The surf was so high that passengers on board the ships in harbour were unable to land, including numerous young ladies who had arrived for their marriages and who were waving from the decks of the ships to their fiancés, who in turn were gathered on the shore and waving back.

Hankin took his guest to make a courtesy call on the Rajah of Pittapur. "He received us at the entrance," Montagu wrote, "and led me to a gorgeous chair in the centre of the room. Some of his relatives were present and lots of servants stood about the room. He spoke in English, and pretty freely, as none of the natives could understand, and he told me he had lost caste, having been brought up under English tutelage. His grandmother especially seemed to give him great annoyance in this respect. Our conversation was frequently interrupted by his showing off his tame birds, which he made perform tricks and fly about the room." Montagu remembered Hankin as being rather informal with their host and as saying, "Now then, Rajah, show us some of your things worth seeing."[292] The rajah, though, appeared happy to show them round his gardens. Afterwards some dancing girls and musicians decorously entertained them.

Another visitor to Madras, less exalted than Montagu, was Sir Robert Nicholas Fowler. When the duke heard Sir Robert was staying at the Elphinstone Hotel in town, he invited him to stay at Government House instead, where he "was treated with unbounded hospitality by himself, his daughters and his staff," Fowler wrote.[293] He described Government House as being "situated about a mile and a half inland. It is a large building in Indian style, standing in a pretty park. The walls are adorned with portraits of governors and native princes connected with the history of the Presidency. Dinner-parties are given in a large hall, with its sides open to the air, which makes it very pleasant in this climate." When Sir Robert set out for his tour of the provinces, Hankin gave him a number of introductions, including one to his brother Colonel Hankin, with whom Sir Robert had dinner on his travels.

In 1880 the duke's term as governor expired. Hankin now left the duke's employment. Tantalizingly, Hankin gives no explanation for this. Perhaps the duke felt he no longer needed a private secretary. More likely, Isabel felt the need to care for her ailing parents and it was to British Columbia they headed. The Hankins arrived in Victoria on June 30, 1881.[294] Her father, Jeremiah, died in January the following year. At the time, Isabel's mother was described as being feeble and bedridden.

So here Hankin now was, forty-five years old, retired with a pension, with years ahead of him. How would he fill his time?

12

The Years of Travel

1880–1923

After 1880, Hankin had no other job for the rest of his life. His annual pension would have seemed more than adequate at the time. He appears to have done little but wander from place to place. The records, such as they are, are a blur of arrivals and departures from foreign ports—New York, Honolulu, Buenos Aires, Sydney, Hong Kong. Although there is no evidence for it, it is possible that Hankin felt constrained by the need to attend to Isabel's increasing ill health. But he was someone who needed a discipline such as a job to challenge him. Without one, he seemed to drift, restless and bored. Unable to settle, he and his wife travelled widely but he does not provide us with many details. Indeed, at times, his memory lets him down on dates and the sequence of events. His recollections of the next forty years cover only a few pages in his memoirs.

He and his wife travelled for some time in Europe, visiting Paris, Turin, Venice, Rome and Naples. He spent nearly two years in Paris to perfect his knowledge of the French language. He may also have lived for some time in Germany because he became fluent in German as well as French. These would have been magical years for an Englishman with an independent income to be travelling in Europe: Rome, with its carnival and ancient ruins; Venice, with its canals, gondoliers, Saint Mark's Basilica and glittering mystery of the East; and Paris, with its newly created boulevards, Impressionist paintings and all the colour and frivolity of La Belle Époque—of these Hankin writes nothing.

In the summer of 1884 the Hankins were living in a house on the South Parade at Abergele on the north coast of Wales. But not for long. Soon they moved south to the Isle of Wight.[295] They then went back to Vancouver Island so Isabel could visit her widowed mother, who, sometime in her last years, moved to be with her other daughter in Oakland, California. The Canadian Pacific Railway would not open for passenger traffic until the summer of 1886, so they would have crossed the continent by rail south of the Canadian border. Hankin may have recalled his crossings of

Philip Hankin, perhaps in the mid-1880s. Image G-07582 courtesy of the Royal BC Museum and Archives

the Isthmus of Panama in mosquito-infested trains. How long ago it must have seemed to him! Isabel's mother died in 1886. After a stay in Victoria, they returned to England. With or without Isabel—the record is not clear—Hankin visited the United States again in 1887, arriving in New York in November on the SS *Germanic*. With his friend Colonel George Bertie Hobart, who had been with him in India, he visited Hawaii and stayed there over Christmas before returning to San Francisco in early 1888.[296]

We know little of what the Hankins were doing in the 1890s. There is one reference in a newspaper article to their having lived in a waterside cottage in James Bay, in Victoria, for six or seven years. That is possible but there is no readily discoverable evidence to support it.[297] It is also possible they spent some years in France or Germany.

In his travels, Hankin had heard much talk about orange growing in Florida. This was said to offer a pleasant and lucrative employment. So he thought he would try his luck at that. He went to a place called Fruitland

Park, originally named Gardenia, which was a small town in Lake County, Florida, not far from Orlando.

His first impression was that, despite the name, there was in fact a great scarcity of fruit of any kind there. Fruitland was a small place started by an Englishman who had persuaded a number of other young Englishmen to go out there, buy land and start to grow oranges. They bought land, spent all their money and planted tiny orange trees, about four inches high. Then they had to sit down and watch these trees for seven years, at which time they would have a fine crop. They could then sell the oranges easily in New York, Hankin was assured, for a rich profit. In the winter there could, however, be a sharp frost, and all the trees could easily die. Hankin said he was "nearly eaten up by mosquitoes and insects of various kinds, to say nothing of snakes," so he decided to give up on orange growing. (Did Fruitland perhaps remind him of the swampy mirage of Eden in Dickens's *Martin Chuzzlewit*?)

He had spent too much money on this venture in Florida. In order to recoup his expenses, he decided to travel through the southern United States and give public readings from the novels of Charles Dickens, knowing him to be an author the Americans much admired. He paid one of his orange-growing friends ten dollars a week and expenses to accompany him, knowing he could leave his orange trees for a few weeks. Hankin always sent his friend ahead of him a day in advance to advertise his readings and to stick posters everywhere, "announcing in large letters that Commander Hankin of the British Navy would arrive on such and such a date and would give some public readings from Dickens." This proved to be a good idea, for he managed to make about a hundred dollars a week, clear of all expenses. He always was a good reader, with clear and distinct enunciation, and, as his readings in Victoria showed, he was a great lover of the novels of Dickens and had an appealing ability for effective caricature.

Hankin recalled stopping at a small town near Key West and calling on the mayor in order to solicit his patronage for a proposed reading in his community. He was greatly discouraged when the mayor said, "Well sir, I don't believe your Show will pay expenses, our people here 'aint gone on public readings but if you was to come along with a barrel organ and a monkey, you'd make a pile of dollars!" He decided not to give any readings in that particular town, it being evident they would not be appreciated. However, he moved on to other towns where he did very well. After about six weeks of readings, he returned to New York and then back to England, having made enough to pay all the expenses of his trip.

He and Isabel now settled down in Ryde on the Isle of Wight for nearly two years. The 1901 census records them boarding at No. 28, the Strand, in Ryde, a few yards from the wide sandy beach. "We were very comfortable there, but in the winter," he said, "it was deadly dull." Ryde became like a deserted city. He got to know a few people there, and occasionally the pleasure of his company was requested to tea. But he grew tired of these teas; besides, he found it was impossible to eat his dinner afterwards.

Sometime in 1901, wanderlust came over him again and he decided they should go to Tasmania. He had heard Tasmania spoken of as a most delightful place with a glorious climate and as a cheap place to live. (Was inflation starting to squeeze his pension?) Isabel said she could be ready in a fortnight. They travelled in a small vessel of two thousand tons, in which the accommodation, he said, was wretched. The ship did touch at Cape Town, but this was the time the Boer War was starting so the passengers were not allowed to land. Soon after leaving the Cape, the weather became cold. The little ship pitched terribly but, considering the heavy seas they encountered, proved itself a good sea boat. It was, however, six weeks before they reached Melbourne, from where they managed to catch another ship to Hobart, the capital of Tasmania.

He was disappointed with Hobart. The climate about which he had heard so much was not good. "The thermometer at 11:30 a.m. would be 98 degrees Fahrenheit and at 4:30 p.m. down to 40 degrees," he wrote, and they "had to sit over a large fire." He did relate that Tasmania was a wonderful country for apples and greengages and there was excellent trout fishing to be had. There was only one good hotel in town, which charged eight pounds a week for two people. He thought that anything but cheap. And, he said, he "never saw in any country so many house flies, tarantulas and venomous snakes." He wrote he killed two or three snakes in the garden.

They stayed a couple of months in Hobart and then took the train to Launceston, which was, he recalled, though smaller, a much nicer and prettier town than Hobart. Here they stayed for ten days before crossing in a small and uncomfortable vessel to Melbourne. And then on to Sydney.

The Hankins left Sydney on the RMS *Aorangi* on May 19, 1902. They reached Hawaii on June 5. Some passengers were going on to England for the coronation of King Edward VII. If they made all their connections, they could arrive a day before the coronation.[298] Hawaii was now a territory of the United States. If Hankin could have arranged it in the time available, he might have been able to find friends he had known in the old days, forty years before. But he and Isabel stayed only a day before taking passage by way of the Fiji islands to Vancouver Island.

They reached Victoria safely on June 11, 1902, and once more Hankin found himself in familiar territory. He found the city much grown and improved and he met many old friends and acquaintances. They stayed in rooms for a month and then built a "pretty little house close to Beacon Hill," with lovely views of the sea and snow-capped mountains. He wrote that Victoria was "the most charming residential spot" he had ever seen."[299] They settled down there to enjoy their remaining years.

Then Isabel fell seriously ill and announced she wanted to return to England. Hankin managed to sell their house on Battery Street together with all its contents at an auction on April 1, 1903. The auction list included his signed photograph of the Prince of Wales, the newly crowned King Edward VII, and several signed photographs of the king and queen of the Sandwich Islands. They set out for England on what was probably a sad, difficult journey. Isabel's health deteriorated. On September 17, 1903, in Hamilton, Ontario, she died.

After Isabel's death, Hankin settled into a middle-age ennui that only deepened as the years passed. Now sixty-four years old, he returned to London soon after the funeral, a lonely and unhappy man. After staying a few days at a hotel by himself, he took rooms where, he said, he was comfortable but still lonely.

Over the next twenty years Hankin travelled widely. It was as if he was trying to fill a void inside him by being continually on the move. The hustle and bustle of travel would have pushed loneliness away. He liked being at sea better than anything, for he generally met pleasant people. Chatting with them made him forget his troubles. Furthermore, it would not have escaped him that by travelling on board a comfortable ship with meals provided, he was avoiding the business of living by himself— the meals, finding and renting accommodation and hiring, firing and managing servants.

His troubles with servants vexed him. He, who had administered a colony and stood at the elbow of an imperial proconsul in India, could not manage servants at all. He grumbled about them and at them. Invariably they all came to him with excellent references. He once summoned up the courage to ask a newly hired cook for some jelly to eat. "Well, Sir," she replied, "Jelly is rather 'igh class cooking, isn't it? I've never made a jelly myself, but I've lived in families where they's 'ad 'em made. I know you puts it before a fire and covers it with a cloth for twelve hours." She left in a huff when he tried to correct her. Another, a most respectable elderly woman, had vague medical problems which required treatment with a glass of beer at every meal. She left before dawn one morning (before she could be fired) after having come back drunk in the middle of the previous night. Another, a smart young man, was caught having stolen one of Hankin's diamond rings. He too departed under a cloud. Yet another, a cook, stole from his larder so that he was always short of food, though the cook's son was not. And then there was an elderly German man, whose wife had no teeth left. He had pale-green, short-cropped hair. He seldom shaved and wore a shabby tailcoat to his ankles. He and his wife had the habit of eating at midnight and leaving the gas on in the kitchen, increasing Hankin's gas bills. Finally, Hankin shut up house and went travelling in Europe.

Restless, he returned to Canada and visited his wife's grave in Hamilton. That, he said, only made matters worse.

Back in Europe, he visited Hamburg. From there he sailed on a German vessel to Hong Kong. On January 10, 1906, after a month in Hong Kong, he sailed on the *Empress of China* for Japan and Vancouver. After

Philip J. Hankin. Image G-07582 courtesy of the Royal BC Museum and Archives

a rough crossing of the Pacific, he arrived in Vancouver on February 2.[300]

The *Vancouver Daily World* sent a couple of reporters to interview him. Under the headline "One of the Oldest of the Old-Timers," the journalists wrote that Hankin told them he spent his life travelling. They persuaded him to talk of his early days in the colony. Of English Bay, where they were interviewing him, he said, "I remember anchoring in this bay when there was not a single tree cut anywhere around. That was after I left the *Plumper* and was on the *Hecate* with Captain Richards. We were surveying. I sailed 12 times around Vancouver Island. We used to shoot ducks on what is now Vancouver Harbour."[301] In a later conversation, he said he had once been offered Deadman's Island, near Stanley Park, for one dollar but had turned it down because he was not in the real estate business.[302] The reporters wrote that he looked hale and vigorous, with a jauntiness in his air and carriage that was surprising for one his age.

In June he placed an advertisement in the *Vancouver Daily World* that read, "Captain Hankin, R.N., who has resided ten years in France and ten in Germany, is prepared to receive a few pupils, either children or adults, at his residence, 1300 Ninth Avenue, Fairview, for the study of French or German."[303] (One wonders whether, as with Mrs. Micawber's Boarding Establishment for Young Ladies in *David Copperfield*, he had any pupils.) This raises the question, though, When did he spend ten years in France and ten in Germany? Or was he adding up a number of lengthy visits and sojourns and generously rounding upward?

In February 1907, he left Vancouver and returned to England. He went westward, by way of China and Japan. In noting his departure, the newspapers reported that "Captain Hankin passed the winter in Vancouver, and leaves behind a huge circle of friends, who regret his departure and look for his early return."[304] Back in London, he took a small flat and looked up a few old friends. Still lonely, he noted sadly that "after all, they can't do much for you."

In 1909, on his travels again, he went to the Cape of Good Hope, where he found only one of his old friends still living. Bonny Cloete, one of his favourite dancing partners from the old days, was still there and they reminisced about the heady days in Government House with Lady Smith over fifty years before. How the world had changed! He stayed in Cape Town for three weeks, then went to Durban and Delagoa Bay. Then—back to England on the *Dover Castle*. On this trip he was travelling with Mary Jane, the widow of his brother Charles, who had died in 1876, and his niece Ida May Hankin. For a while he lived with them at their home at No. 14, Elms Hill Road, in Muswell Hill, which is where he was at the time of the 1911 census.

He said he found London tiring and expensive so he took a small house in Southsea. Here he stayed. He improved his German and French. He read many books. He said his only amusement was to ride about on top of the tramcars or walk about in Palmerston Road and look at the shops. He paid some calls and was invariably asked to tea. He grew sick and tired of tea parties and cake. He grew old.

The First World War came and went. At Southsea, in Portsmouth, he would have been able to observe the warships scurrying about the harbour and going out to deal with the kaiser's fleet. But being now all iron and modern, the Royal Navy was vastly different from the navy of wooden ships under canvas in which he had served. Commodore Wyvill, his first captain, he might have recalled, had joined the Royal Navy in 1805, the year of Trafalgar.

In about 1914, he sat down to write an account of his life to interest and amuse, as he said, some of his old friends. After writing of his time in British Columbia, though, he seemed to lose interest, or energy, and his account grows thin.

After the war, he visited Victoria again to see old friends. Only two remained from the old days. One was Dr. John Helmcken, born in 1824, who had come to the Colony of Vancouver Island in 1850 and married Sir James Douglas's daughter. He and Hankin doubtless reached back through the mists of time to recall the late 1850s when Victoria was still called Fort Victoria and when the Hudson's Bay Company fort and warehouses were still within the stockade. They may have reminisced happily about the dances that the young naval officers held for the local belles on board the *Plumper* in Esquimalt.

Back in England, Hankin could not stay still. In 1922, at the age of eighty-five, he had one last journey to make. Always happiest at sea, he took passage on the SS *Ballarat* on its maiden voyage to and from Australia. When he returned to England, he settled in Aldrington, in Sussex. There, on November 23, 1923, he died of heart failure and what was then called senile decay. His body, he had written, would never be found, for he had left strict instructions that after his death he was to be cremated and his ashes "blown to the four winds of Heaven." Notwithstanding his wishes, he was buried in the cemetery of Saint Philip's Church in Aldrington.

Philip Hankin's life had been long, full of twists and turns: a dead-broke failed prospector one moment, chief of police the next. He had hunted slavers with the Royal Navy under canvas. He had governed a colony and walked with monarchs. His travels as a rolling stone were extensive and, in truth, as he wrote in his memoirs, he had indeed gathered some moss.

Key Dates in the Life
of Philip Hankin

Chapter 1: A Victorian Childhood, 1836–1849

1836, February 18: Philip Hankin is born in Stanstead Abbotts, Hertfordshire.

1849, May 12: He joins the British navy and is appointed to HMS *Castor*.

Chapter 2: Hunting Slavers on HMS *Castor*, 1849–1852

1849, August 30: HMS *Castor* arrives in Cape Town.

1850, April 29: HMS *Castor* visits Zanzibar.

1850, June 8: HMS *Castor* attacks slave centre at Keonga.

1852, February 26: HMS *Birkenhead* sinks.

1852, June 15: Hankin arrives back in England.

Chapter 3: To Vancouver Island on HMS *Plumper*, 1852–1857

1852, summer and autumn: Hankin works as a brewer's clerk in London.

1852, December: He is appointed to HMS *Sidon*.

1853, February: His mother dies.

1853, August 1: He is appointed to HMS *Plumper*.

1856, November 30: He arrives back in Portsmouth, England.

1857, March 14: He passes his examinations for lieutenant.

1857, March 16: He is reappointed to HMS *Plumper* and sails to the Colony of Vancouver Island.

1857, October 16: HMS *Plumper* arrives in Honolulu.

Chapter 4: From Vancouver Island to the Mediterranean and Then Back, 1857–1861

1857, November 10: HMS *Plumper* arrives in Esquimalt.

1858, April 25: The *Commodore* arrives in Victoria and the Fraser River Gold Rush starts.

1858, June 5: Hankin's promotion to lieutenant is confirmed and he is ordered back to England.

1859, May 11: He is appointed to HMS *Cadmus*.

1860: He is transferred to HMS *Orion*.

1860, May 17: He arrives back in England on HMS *Orion*.

1860, May 19: He is appointed to HMS *Hecate*.

1860, December 23: HMS *Hecate* arrives in Esquimalt.

Chapter 5: HMS *Hecate*, Lady Franklin and Hankin's Crossing of Vancouver Island, 1861–1864

1861, February: Lady Franklin and Miss Cracroft visit the colony and Hankin is asked to be their escort.

1862, May–June: Hankin makes an early crossing of Vancouver Island, from Kyuquot Sound.

1862, December 22: HMS *Hecate* leaves Esquimalt to return to England.

1863, June 26: HMS *Hecate* arrives in Sydney, Australia.

1864, January: HMS *Hecate* arrives back in England and Hankin leaves the navy.

Chapter 6: Looking for Gold in Barkerville, 1864

1864, March 31: Hankin returns to the Colony of Vancouver Island.

1864, spring: He prospects for gold in the Cariboo.

Chapter 7: Hankin Becomes Chief of Police for the Colony of Vancouver Island, 1864–1866

1864: Hankin works for a law firm in Victoria and then is offered a job as a clerk in the civil service.

1864, October: He assists Admiral Joseph Denman during the *Kingfisher* affair.

1864, December 23: He is appointed superintendent of police for the Colony of Vancouver Island.

1865, August 3: He marries Isabel Nagle.

1866, July: Inquiry into the police in the colony.

1866, November: The Colonies of Vancouver Island and British Columbia unite and Hankin loses his job as chief of police.

1867, February: Hankin and his wife arrive back in England.

Chapter 8: Colonial Secretary: British Honduras to British Columbia, 1867–1868

1867, May 13: Hankin is appointed colonial secretary of British Honduras.

1868, October: He is appointed colonial secretary of British Columbia.

1868, November 4: The Hankins leave England to return to British Columbia.

Chapter 9: Governor Seymour and Administrator Hankin, January–August 1869

1868, December 31: The Hankins arrive in British Columbia.

1869, April 8: Hankin is sworn in as colonial secretary of British Columbia.

1869, June 10: Governor Frederick Seymour dies suddenly.

1869, June 14–August 23: Hankin serves as administrator of the Colony of British Columbia.

1869, July 11: The Fenian leader George Francis Train visits Victoria.

Chapter 10: Governor Musgrave and Joining Canada, August 1869–August 1871

1869, August 23: Governor Anthony Musgrave arrives in Victoria and Hankin resumes his position as colonial secretary.

1869, November 2: Governor Musgrave is seriously injured.

1870, April: Lady Franklin and Miss Cracroft return to the colony for a visit.

1871, January: Hankin is elected Speaker of the legislative assembly.

1871, July 20: British Columbia joins Canada and Hankin loses his job.

1871, August 16: The Hankins leave British Columbia and return to England.

Chapter 11: In India with the Duke, 1871–1880

1872–1880: Hankin serves as personal secretary to the Duke of Buckingham and Chandos.

1875–1880: The duke serves as governor of the Madras Presidency and Hankin is his personal secretary.

Chapter 12: The Years of Travel, 1880–1923

1899, June 29: Hankin and his wife, Isabel, arrive in Ryde, on the Isle of Wight.

1902, June 11: The Hankins arrive back in Victoria and build a house.

1903, September 17: Isabel dies in Ontario on their way back to England from Victoria.

1906, January: Hankin visits British Columbia again and stays a year.

1912, approximately: He settles in Southsea.

1914/1915: Aged seventy-nine, Hankin writes his memoirs.

1922, January 26: He sails from England for Australia on the ss *Ballarat*.

1923, November 23: Philip Hankin dies in Sussex.

Philip Hankin's Journey across Vancouver Island, 1862

To His Excellency Gov. Douglas, C.B.
H.M. Surveying Ship *Hecate*,
Nanaimo, V.I. 20th June, 1862

Sir:—I have the honour to enclose you a sketch map of the interior of Vancouver Island, from Kuyuquot Inlet, on the Western Coast, in latitude 50°.00 N. to the Nimpkish river, which empties itself on the eastern side on to Johnstone Straits, about 15 miles below Fort Rupert; as also Copies of reports from Lieut. Hankin and Dr. Wood, of this ship, who performed the journey between the two places in May and June of this year.

It has been my desire, and practice, whenever the more immediate duties of the Maritime Survey would permit, to gather as much information as possible of the interior of this island, as well as the adjacent Continent, and with this view, parties have from time to time been equipped and despatched from the *Plumper* and *Hecate*. I am quite aware that the limited time I have been able to devote to these objects—the physical difficulties of the country, and above all, the obstructions always incident to first explorations, will deprive such attempts of much of the value which at first sight might seem to attach to them, and that the results can scarcely be considered commensurate with the labour and risk frequently attendant on their accomplishment; yet, I believe such preliminary explorations will serve materially to aid future research, and as I know your Excellency's views on the subject are not dissimilar to my own, I have never been discouraged from attempting them—however problematical or remote the advantages to be derived may appear to be. And I should not be doing justice to the efforts of the officers employed on such service were I not to say that I have always found them ready and anxious to carry out my views to the utmost.

It may not be out of place here to inform Your Excellency that the survey of the greater part of the Western Coast has been completed, and several new harbours and anchorages discovered, which when published for general information will I trust prevent a recurrence, or lessen the frequency of disasters which have annually befallen vessels navigating in this boisterous neighbourhood.

I have the honour to be Your Excellency's most obd't servant,

Geo. Henry Richards, Captain

Copy of Lieut. Hankin's Report to Capt. Richards of a Journey Across Vancouver Island.
H.M. Surveying Ship *Hecate*,
Nanaimo, June 17th

Sir—In obedience to your instructions to endeavour to cross the Island from the head of the Kayuket Inlet, on the Western Coast, to the Nimpkish river, on the Eastern, with a view of making some exploration of the interior of the country, I have the honour to inform you that, accompanied by Dr. Wood, I left the ship on the 25th of last month at Queen's Cove, Esperanza Inlet, in a Canoe with 4 Indians for Kayuket, where I trusted we should obtain a sufficient number of men to carry our provisions, instruments, etc.

We arrived at Kayuket Island the following day at Noon, where I found a very large Indian settlement, called by the natives "Actiss." There are between 700 and 800 people living here, and they are a finer looking race than any other Natives I have seen on Vancouver Island. The Chief of the tribe is quite a young man, apparently not more than 22 or 23 years of age;

his name is Kai-ni-nitt. He appeared to possess more influence with his tribe than any other Chief I have hitherto met.

We found the Natives here most civil and obliging. They helped us to pitch our tent and carry our traps out of the canoe. I had afterwards occasion to remain with these people several days, & although they had both temptation and opportunity, it is worthy of remark that not the smallest trifle was stolen from us. On one occasion, I lost a meerschaum pipe, which was afterwards found and returned to me.

With the exception of occasional visits from trading schooners, they had seen but little of the Whites; but two of them had visited Victoria and they had returned with such wonderful accounts, that many others were eager to go, & their anxiety to see the *Hecate* was intense.

I found my Knowledge of the Barclay Sound language most useful to me. In fact, without it, we should have been quite unable to proceed, for they were totally ignorant of Chinook. The Kayuket language differs from that spoken at O-hi-at (Barclay Sound), principally in the expressions, very many of the words being similar. I cannot but consider the latter language to be the most useful one spoken on the West Coast for with a competent Knowledge of it, one may be understood from Nitinat to Port Brookes.

Having explained to the Natives the object of my visit and told them of my anxiety to start as soon as possible, and of my wish to obtain 8 or 10 Indians to accompany me, I succeeded, after some trouble, in securing the services of 7, who promised to start early on the morrow for the payment of 3 Blankets and a Shirt each.

I was up at daylight the following morning, & having packed everything as snugly as possible (for I foresaw that 7 Indians would have almost more than they could carry with our blankets, provisions, instruments & collecting material of Dr. Wood's, in addition to baskets of dried halibut for their own use), I commenced to get my men together, which, after no little difficulty, I succeeded in doing, for they could not see with me, the necessity for such an early start & as yet were scarcely awake; however, after a couple of hours, I had them all collected on the beach, with their canoe, ready for a start to the Tarshish River, some 14 miles up the Kayuket Arm, from whence the trail commences.

By 8 a.m., we were fairly on our way, & after 6 hours paddling arrived at the Tarshish River, where we camped for the night. I saw here the remains of a considerable Indian village, which is inhabited during the Salmon season by the Kayuket Indians, who all report this as being an extremely good fishing ground.

The following day (the 28th) was unfortunately wet, but I could not to afford to remain the whole day at Tarshish, so we quickly packed up, & made the best of our way in the Canoe; but we had scarcely ascended the river a mile when both rain and wind beat heavily in our faces, and we found it extremely difficult to make any progress. The Indians now began to object to proceed, so I was reluctantly obliged to camp for the day which I did on the west bank of the river.

The Tarshish River has an average width of not more than 40 yards, and is very rapid, only navigable for canoes for about 4 miles.

The next day, to my disappointment, it was still raining, and the river being much swollen, the Indians began not to like the state of affairs, and talked about returning to Actiss.

I think they were intimidated by the rapid rise of the river, and they said it was much too deep, and swift, to attempt a crossing with any degree of safety; and in the afternoon, to my regret, they told me they had made up their minds to return; so, shortly, all our traps were in the Canoe, and we were on our way back to Kayuket, where we arrived early the following day. We were received by the Natives as before, with every kindness; & pitching our little tent, took up our old quarters.

I now feared that the whole expedition would entirely fail; & it was my intention to remain at Kayuket until the arrival of the ship, which was expected in a few days.

During my stay here, my time was principally occupied in improving my Knowledge of the language, and adding considerably to my already extensive vocabulary.

In the evening, I would get up games among the Indians, leaping, jumping, racing etc. by which they appeared much amused. They also had one or two games of their own, which they showed us. One especially, a trial of strength, appeared to be a favourite. 50 or 60 of them, with their naked bodies, & faces daubed with red and black paint, would seize a long pole, and then, using it as a battering ram, looking more like demons than men, would, with tremendous yells and shouts, charge against some 150 others, who with their united strength would endeavour to rout the Invaders. Another, more quiet one, was sticking a feather in the ground, when an Indian standing on one foot would stoop down &, without touching the ground with his hands, extract the feather with his teeth. This feat I tried several times, and generally tumbled, when a hearty laugh was raised at my expense.

During the day, an intelligent Indian would draw for me on the sand the trail across the Island to Nimpkish, putting in the lakes and rivers, and telling us their native names. Several would volunteer their services for this office, and it was amusing to see their disputes about the differences of the distances they had marked.

On the 3rd day of our stay here, it struck me that it would still be possible to cross the Island in time to meet the ship at Fort Rupert by the 15th, according to my instructions, if I could but get Indians to accompany me.

We had a long talk with the Chief on the subject, who promised to do his best in assisting us to obtain men, but he seemed to think the payment not sufficiently remunerative for this time of year. I was, therefore, obliged to increase each man's reward by 2 blankets, or give up entirely the idea of going, and, feeling that the latter course, for the sake of saving the expense of half a dozen blankets would be absurd, I held out the reward of 5 blankets and a shirt to each Indian, and before evening 6 volunteers, stimulated no doubt by the additional bribe, offered their services, which were immediately accepted. Two of them had started with me on the former occasion, and they were only enlisted a second time on conditions, that surmounting all difficulties, we were to push boldly forward, never once looking back. They promised all I could wish, and early next morning we were once more off for Tarshish.

I endeavoured to discover if these Indians had any religious ceremonies or impressions, or if they held one day more sacred than another; and they appear to be perfect heathens, worshipping neither sun, moon, nor stars, nor having any idea of a Supreme Being.

They are clothed principally in the blanket & cape, made from the bark of the Yellow Cypress, from which most invaluable tree they also manufacture canoes, paddles, fishing-nets, mats, twine and hats, and the Chief had a quantity of very strong stout rope, which they use for whale-fishing, made from the fibre of the same tree.

On account of our inability to obtain more than 6 Indians, Dr. Wood was reluctantly obliged to leave behind all his collecting gear, & in a great measure give up the idea with which he had accompanied me; for our provisions were getting short, and our time being necessarily limited, we were unable to make a couple of days stay in any peculiarly interesting spot, as we had intended, in order to examine more minutely the features of the country; but, diverging neither to the right nor left, were obliged to push on, making the best of our way to Nimpkish.

It was a beautiful clear morning, & with a fresh breeze from the S.W., we rapidly arrived at Tarshish, and by 5 o'clock the same evening, camped some four miles up the river, on the north bank. Here, the Indians hid their Canoe in the bush, being unable to proceed further by water on account of rapids and falls. We had some difficulty in proceeding even thus far by canoe, and in one place had to make a portage of about 200 yards. On examining our stock of food, we discovered that we had barely enough to last us across, even with the strictest economy, having but 15 lbs of flour, a few beans, and a small quantity of preserved meat. After our first disappointment at having to retrace our steps, we had been too lavish of provisions, not thinking to make a 2nd start, and I had given both flour and meat to Kai-ni-nitt the Chief, at Kayuket, but having my gun with me, and plenty of powder and shot, we anticipated Venison Steaks in abundance, but in this, were disappointed.

On the following morning, June 3rd, we started at 8 a.m., & commenced our first attempt at packing, when, having at last succeeded in arranging everything to the satisfaction of the Indians, we followed the trail along the bank of the river to the Eastward, but very shortly, leaving the water, we struck off into the bush and followed a zig-zag course to the North-eastward, catching occasional glimpses of the river, which wound in the same direction.

The Indians assured me that Elk, about this part of the country, were very numerous. We certainly saw plenty of tracks, although we did not meet the animals themselves, but, considering so large a party cracking through the bush, one could hardly expect it. The land on either bank of the river was very thickly wooded, rocky with small hills of from 100 to 250 feet.

After the walk of about 2½ miles, we again came to the bank of the river, where we wished to cross. There was a fall a little below us of 25 or 30 feet, and the river was rushing furiously by, tearing over the Cataract with a deafening noise. Here the natives were quite afraid to attempt a crossing, and sat down on the bank to think about it. They told me that the year previously an Indian had been drowned while attempting to cross. He had lost his footing, and been swept over by the rush of water. They even hinted at returning, but that we wouldn't listen to; and told them that if it could not be managed here, we must try higher up the river, when after waiting nearly two hours, we managed to get them to start again. Now diverging from the regular trail, we struck off into the bush when after a march of about 3 miles we again came on the river, where we hoped to be able to effect a crossing.

Here we camped for the night, & strolled about a little to look at the country, which was perfectly flat & level for about 3 or 4 miles, not bad soil, little or no brushwood, but thickly timbered with many of the most beautiful spars I ever saw, averaging from 170 to 180 feet in length.

The whole of the following day, it rained in torrents, & the Indians would not proceed in consequence, and it was not until the morning of the 6th that we were enabled to cross the river. It was rather a difficult undertaking and attended with no small amount of risk. The river here was about 40 yards wide, nearly breast deep, & fearfully rapid. We accomplished the crossing in safety by all holding to a long pole, and wading into the water at the same time; thus, by our united efforts resisting the strength of the current.

On arriving at the other side, we found a very excellent trail, which we followed in a N. Easterly direction for about 2 miles, crossing the river repeatedly, when, instead of continuing to follow the circuitous bend of the stream, we struck off to the Westward, and after a walk of some 5 or 6 miles, over a hilly and thickly wooded country, again met the river, close on the border of Lake Atluck, from which it flows. Crossing it, a walk of ½ a mile, now brought us to the Lake itself, and I must say I was most agreeably surprised, and pleased, by the magnificent scenery which presented itself to view.

The Lake is a beautiful sheet of water, running in a N'ly direction, some 3½ miles in length and 1½ wide. Lofty mountains rise on either side, where numbers of black bear find a safe & undisturbed retreat. On its Eastern side, towering high above the rest, a very peculiar pinnacle shaped mount, whose summit, some 3,000 feet high, was covered with snow, to the North-eastward of which were several almost needle-pointed mountains of sharp, barren rock towering their blackened summits in fantastic forms above the waters of the Lake. We found no Canoe here, but we quickly felled a few light spars, and having lashed them together with strips of cedar-bark, packed our traps on them, and started early the following morning for the opposite shore. A fresh breeze, springing up from the N.E., greatly retarded our progress, but we crossed in safety by 5 p.m., and camped for the night.

I carried a sounding line with me, and found as much as 30 fathoms of water 25 yards off the shore. I was unable to sound in the centre of the Lake (where I was told it was much deeper) owing to the wind, which freshened so considerably as to render it imprudent to venture far from the shore.

The following day was Sunday, but we could not afford to make it a day of rest, for our provisions were getting very short. So, soon after 5 a.m., we broke up our camp and started on foot, following the trail to Lake Hoostan which is situate about 4 miles to the N.W. of Atluck.

It was a splendid Summer morning, and the Lake, whose waters yesterday were so turbulent, was today calm, and unruffled.

I wounded a Beaver last night at Lake Atluck, but he managed to escape. The Natives informed me that they were numerous at the other lakes.

There is no good land between the two Lakes. It is all hilly, rocky and very thickly-wooded, although for the greater portion of the way there is an excellent trail.

We arrived at Lake Hoostan by eight o'clock, and commenced constructing a raft, as before. We heard the drumming of grouse about here, in fact they appear to be very plentiful everywhere. We killed one on the banks of the Lake.

I found the latitude here to be 50°14'47" N. By 3 p.m. we had landed on the opposite shore and commenced our walk to Lake Anutz, where we arrived at ½ past five. There was an extremely good trail nearly the whole way, and we passed over a mile or so of very fair land, with fine timber on it. We saw no perfectly clear land anywhere.

Lake Anutz runs in a N.N.W. direction, is about 2 miles long and 1 broad. I was told it was very deep, but had no opportunity of sounding. It is connected with Lake Hoostan by the Tarshish River.

We started at daylight the following morning for Lake Karmutsen, following for a mile a general NW'ly direction, when we came to the river connecting Lake Anutz with Lake Hoostan which I named Famine River; here we crossed, and found the water nearly breast deep, and extremely rapid. On the opposite bank, we halted for about ½ an hour, and had our morning meal of tea, and damper; the Indians eating roots and ferns for their stock of provisions was by this time completely exhausted.

Starting again, we followed a Northerly course until we sighted Lake Anutz and then followed on the brow of a hill, along its western shore until we came to Lake Karmutsen. Immediately after leaving Famine River, I observed some 300 acres of very good, quite park-like land, not very thickly wooded, and covered with fern. This was the first & only piece of good land available for agricultural purposes I saw.

The Eastern shore of Lake Anutz is densely wooded; its western moderately so. Willows and Larch prevail. Shortly after Noon, we arrived at Lake Karmutsen which proved a magnificent sheet of water 16 or 17 miles in length, with an average width of ½ mile. It runs in a NW'ly direction into the Nimpkish river, thus completing an entire chain of lakes throughout the Island; it is extremely deep. I tried for soundings with 50 fathoms. Mr. Moffat afterwards informed me that he had done the same with 80, but could obtain no bottom.

I saw several fishing weirs lying on the banks of the Lakes, & the Natives informed me that Salmon were very numerous here, and during the Salmon season many Nimpkish Indians collect here for the purpose of fishing.

We were disappointed at not finding a canoe of any description here, but we observed a large log lying on the beach, which after some trouble we succeeded in launching, and having packed our traps on it, commenced to paddle across the Lake, but we had scarcely left the shore when we found our most extraordinary craft to roll so heavily as to keep us in momentary expectation of its completely capsizing.

We found it impossible to proceed in this way, so we paddled to the bank as quickly as possible, and obtained a smaller spar, to act as an outrigger, which we lashed to the Big one with strips of Cedar bark, and then with a blanket for a sail, began to make satisfactory progress. We continued proceeding in this manner until 11 p.m. when the wind began to freshen considerably, and a disagreeable sea getting up, rendered ours anything but an enviable position, so I persuaded the Indians to paddle in shore, and tie up to a tree for the night. We now contrived to snatch a couple of hours sleep, and were off again at 3 a.m. the following morning; and by 9 o'clock had arrived at the Nimpkish river. We found the stream far too rapid to attempt to venture down it unless in a good Canoe; so we here discarded our log and took to the trail following a general Northerly Course. The land on both banks of Lake Karmutsen is densely wooded, with mountains on either side varying from 1,800 to 2,000 feet in height.

About 3 miles from Lake Karmutsen we came to a very large uninhabited Indian village, situate on the west bank of the Nimpkish river. There were 15 houses here, and many Nimpkish Indians reside here during the Salmon season. We camped that night on the banks of the river, and after a couple of hours walk the following morning were pleased to see the distant mountains of British Columbia opening to view, and very shortly afterwards the Nimpkish village at the entrance of the river appeared in sight. We found but one canoe here, which we immediately hired, and arrived the same evening at Fort Rupert, where we were most hospitably entertained by Mr. Moffat until the arrival of the ship.

I have the honour to be, Sir, your most obt' and humble servant,
Philip Jas. Hankin
Lieut. R.N.

Acknowledgements

I am grateful for the unrivalled support and skill of my wife, Alice, who carefully read the drafts of this book with a fine pencil and made many valuable suggestions, and to Stephen Mynett, Annika Reinhardt and Peter Mynett for their unstinting support and encouragement. I also want to thank Vici Johnstone, Sarah Corsie and Malaika Aleba of the team at Caitlin Press for their continued support and for publishing my books. Again, I thank Meg Yamamoto for her always sharp and incisive editing. Morgan Hite of Hesperus Arts in Smithers has again supplied a map that illustrates the text. I also want to thank the staff at BC Archives for their assistance.

Notes

Unless otherwise noted below, all the quotations in this book are taken from *Philip Hankin's Memoirs*, Old Manuscript Collection, E/B/H19, BC Archives. The newspaper references are from Newspapers.com, except for those in the *British Colonist*, the University of Victoria's online edition, 1858–1980.

Preface

1   The age at which Philip Hankin joined the Royal Navy was not unusual. Before there was such a thing as a teenager, boys were considered to be young adults after puberty and were expected to work. Only a few had the advantage of continuing their education. Many thirteen-year-olds were sent into the navy, including Captain George Henry Richards and Admiral Joseph Denman.

2   The Colony of Vancouver Island was established in 1849. The Colony of British Columbia, on the mainland, was established in 1858, largely to maintain British control and to legitimate the enforcement of British law on miners during the Fraser River Gold Rush. In 1853, the Queen Charlotte Islands were established as a colony, largely to prevent any adventurous American from settling there to mine and claiming it for the United States. No separate administration was set up and the only officer was James Douglas. This colony was rolled into British Columbia when it was set up in 1858. The Colonies of British Columbia and Vancouver Island were united in 1866 as the Colony of British Columbia. This colony joined the Dominion of Canada as a province in July 1871.

1: A Victorian Childhood

3   The main claim to fame of Stanstead Abbotts—often shortened to Stanstead—is that it is the location of Rye House, the site of the 1685 famous Rye House Plot. The plotters planned to assassinate King Charles II and his brother the Duke of York, later King James II.

4   In addition to Philip (1836–1923), Daniel Hankin and his wife, Elizabeth Potter, had numerous other children. Frederick (born 1830) became a colonel in the Madras Army. Edward Lewis (born 1831) became a lieutenant colonel in the Madras Army and military adviser to the government. Daniel Bell (born 1834) became a clergyman. Harry (born 1839) and Henry (born 1840) both died young. Robert (1842–1861) died at sea. Charles (1838–1876) and Graham (1846–1870) came to the Colony of Vancouver Island in 1858 and were partners with Billy Barker. Thomas Hankin (1843–1885) came to British Columbia at much the same time, perhaps with his brothers. In 1871, Thomas was one of the founders of the small town of Hazelton on the Skeena River in northern British Columbia. Philip's sister Constance (born 1833) married a major general in the Madras Army. Philip had other sisters, some of whom died as children.

5   The quote comes from Alfred Tennyson, "Lady Clara Vere de Vere," *Poems* (London: Edward Moxon, 1842), 155.

6   Sir Henry Ward (1797–1860) was a politician, diplomat and colonial administrator. He was first secretary of the Admiralty, a civilian appointment from the House of Commons, 1846–1849. Many years later he was appointed governor of Madras (now named Chennai) but he caught yellow fever a few weeks after his arrival and died.

7   *Hampshire Telegraph and Sussex Chronicle* (Portsmouth), May 5, 1849, 5. HMS *Castor* was a fully rigged, thirty-six-gun, fifth-rate frigate. It had been launched in 1832 and had cost £38,292 to build. With a complement of 275 men, it served in the Mediterranean and China Station. From 1860 to 1902, when it was broken up, it served as a training ship.

8   Philip Hankin joined the navy in May 1849, when he was thirteen years old. Based on naval records in the United Kingdom's National Archives, Hankin's ships and dates of service were:

	Admitted	Discharged
HMS *Castor*	1849	1852
HMS *Sidon*	1853	
HMS *Plumper*	October 9, 1855	December 9, 1856
HMS *Plumper*	March 14, 1857	May 14, 1858
HMS *Cadmus*	May 10, 1859	February 20, 1860
HMS *Orion*	February 21, 1860	May 20, 1860
HMS *Hecate*	May 21, 1860	January 18, 1864

9   *Hampshire Telegraph and Sussex Chronicle*, May 12, 1849, 5.

2: Hunting Slavers on HMS *Castor*

10   *Hampshire Telegraph and Sussex Chronicle* (Portsmouth), May 5, 1849, 5.

11   *Hampshire Telegraph and Sussex Chronicle*, May 12, 1849, 5.

12   *Hampshire Telegraph and Sussex Chronicle*, June 30, 1849, 5.

13   George Sulivan, *Dhow Chasing in Zanzibar Waters and on the Eastern Coast of Africa* (London: Sampson Low, Marston, Low and Searle, 1873), 12. Admiral George Lydiard Sulivan (1832–1904) came from a naval family and had a distinguished naval career. He was active in suppressing the slave trade, not only on the *Castor* but also later, when he was based at Zanzibar. He was promoted to full admiral on the retired list in 1897.

14   *Hampshire Telegraph and Sussex Chronicle*, November 3, 1849, 4.

15   Sir Harry Smith (1787–1860) was a distinguished soldier. He had seen service in the Peninsular War and in the United States, where he was present at the burning of the White House. After the humanity and respect for the French population he had witnessed when the Duke of Wellington's armies invaded southwest France before Napoleon's collapse, the burning of the White House horrified him. Wellington, still alive in 1850, approved of his conduct of the Xhosa War. The British government, though, did not and replaced him.

16   The convict ship *Neptune* left England in April 1849, with 289 convicts on board (their names are listed in the records), and arrived in Van Diemen's Land, as Tasmania was then called, in April 1850.

17   *Hampshire Advertiser* (Southampton), September 22, 1849, 6.

18   *Hampshire Advertiser*, November 24, 1849, 2.

19   *Hampshire Telegraph and Sussex Chronicle*, September 15, 1849, 4.

20   The escape of the convict John Oakley from a prison ship (not the *Neptune*) in South Africa was the subject of a novel by Francis Brett Young, *They Seek a Country* (London: William Heinemann, 1937). The fictional Oakley was transported for poaching in Worcestershire when starving and found freedom when he went with the Boers on the Great Trek.

21   *Hampshire Telegraph and Sussex Chronicle*, April 27, 1850, 4.

22   James (Jan) Morris, *Heaven's Command: An Imperial Progress* (London: Folio Society, 1992), 21. Originally published by Faber and Faber in 1973.

23   Morris, *Heaven's Command*, 21.

24   *Report from the Select Committee on Slave Trade Treaties*, ordered printed by the House of Commons, August 12, 1853, iii, para. 3.

25   The number of British sailors who died in the naval campaigns to end slavery ranges from 2,000 to 20,000 and is the subject of disagreement. Those who advocate the lower number tend to use shorter reference years and record only the deaths on the West Africa Station. Those advocating the higher number tend to refer to a longer period and include deaths in the South Atlantic and Indian Ocean. Christopher Lloyd in his *The Navy and the Slave Trade: The Suppression of the African Slave Trade in the Nineteenth Century* (London: Frank Cass, 1968) includes an appendix that sets out the mortality rates among sailors on the West Africa Station between 1825 and 1845. The average annual mortality rate in West Africa was 54.4 deaths for every 1,000 men. This compares with 9.3 in the Mediterranean. The annual numbers varied. In 1829, 204 men of the

792 men in service died. In 1839, the number was 60 out of 790. There are too many variables to be confident of any exact number. Perhaps "many thousands" is the closest we will get, or need to get, to the actual number. Books and articles record the number of slaves liberated by the Royal Navy as approximately 150,000. I have not found the primary source for this number.

26 Peter Collister, *The Sulivans and the Slave Trade* (London: Rex Collings, 1980), 99–100, 128. See also Anthony Sullivan, *Britain's War against the Slave Trade: The Operations of the Royal Navy's West Africa Squadron, 1807–1867* (Yorkshire: Pen and Sword Books, 2020), 43, 246; Siân Rees, *Sweet Water and Bitter: The Ships That Stopped the Slave Trade* (London: Chatto and Windus, 2010), 81.

27 *Hampshire Telegraph and Sussex Chronicle*, November 23, 1850, 5.

28 Collister, *Sulivans*, 99–100, 128.

29 Sulivan, *Dhow Chasing*, 54.

30 Morris, *Heaven's Command*, 22–26.

31 *Hampshire Telegraph and Sussex Chronicle*, November 23, 1850, 5.

32 *British and Foreign State Papers*, vol. 40, *1850–1851* (London: James Ridgeway and Sons, 1863), 279–81.

33 *British and Foreign State Papers*, 40:278.

34 *British and Foreign State Papers*, 40:516–17.

35 Sulivan, *Dhow Chasing*, 19.

36 Sulivan, *Dhow Chasing*, 75.

37 *Hampshire Telegraph and Sussex Chronicle*, April 5, 1851, 4.

38 John Kincaid, *Random Shots from a Rifleman* (London: T. and W. Boone, 1847), 292–96, quoted in Sir Harry Smith, *The Autobiography of Lieutenant-General Sir Harry Smith*, ed. G.C. Moore Smith (London: John Murray, 1902), 1:63.

39 Smith, *Autobiography*, 1:69.

40 Smith, *Autobiography*, 1:72.

41 Hankin reportedly made the statement in a letter in 1910, *Daily Colonist* (Victoria), March 26, 1961, 16. I have not been able to find independent corroboration of this.

42 Rudyard Kipling, "Soldier An' Sailor Too," in *Pearson's Magazine*, vol. 1, *January to June 1896* (London: Pearson, 1896), 386.

43 Corporal William Butler, quoted in A.C. Addison and W.H. Matthews, *A Deathless Story, or, The "Birkenhead" and Its Heroes* (London: Hutchison, 1906), 246.

44 *Hampshire Telegraph and Sussex Chronicle*, April 10, 1852, 6.

45 *Hampshire Advertiser*, June 19, 1852, 8.

3: To Vancouver Island on HMS *Plumper*

46 Alfred Barnard, *The Noted Breweries of Great Britain and Ireland* (London: Sir Joseph Causton and Sons, 1889), 2:293–309.

47 Spithead is an area in the Solent, between the Isle of Wight and Portsmouth. It was a protected anchorage for the Royal Navy.

48 *Morning Post* (London), December 11, 1852, 6.

49 *Daily News* (London), February 16, 1853, 8.

50 *Hampshire Telegraph and Sussex Chronicle* (Portsmouth), January 15, 1853, 4.

51 *Morning Post*, August 2, 1853, 5.

52 *Morning Post*, August 18, 1853, 8.

53 *Hampshire Telegraph and Sussex Chronicle*, September 17, 1853, 4.

54 James (Jan) Morris, *Heaven's Command: An Imperial Progress* (London: Folio Society, 1992), 28.

55 Sir William Winniett (1793–1850). See Phyllis R. Blakeley, "Winniett, Sir William Robert Wolseley," in *Dictionary of Canadian Biography*, vol. 7, University of Toronto/ Université Laval, 2003–, http://www.biographi.ca/en/bio/winniett_william_robert_wolseley_7E.html.

56 *Hampshire Telegraph and Sussex Chronicle*, April 7, 1855, 5.

57 The Krumen or Kroomen were people from the Kru or Kroo tribe in what is now Liberia on the West African coast, including Sierra Leone. The navy employed many of them to assist in the suppression of the slave trade. Many of them were ex-slaves themselves.

58 William Garden Blaikie, *The Personal Life of David Livingstone: Chiefly from His Unpublished Journals and Correspondence in the Possession of His Family* (New York: Harper and Brothers, 1881), 165.

59 *Standard* (London), February 12, 1856, 2.

60 *Times* (London), December 3, 1856, 10.

61 Daniel Pender (1832–1891) was a shipmate of Hankin on the *Hecate* and surveyed the coast of Vancouver Island and British Columbia under Captain George Henry Richards. He replaced Captain Richards on the *Plumper* and afterwards was appointed captain of the *Beaver*, on which he surveyed and named many places on the coast (1857–1870).

62 Sir George Henry Richards (1820–1896) was commander of HMS *Plumper* and HMS *Hecate* from 1857 to 1864. He surveyed the coasts around Vancouver Island and named many landmarks, including False Creek, Brockton Point and Mount Garibaldi. Appointed hydrographer of the Royal Navy in 1863, he was knighted in 1877 and appointed an admiral in 1884.

63 *Hampshire Advertiser* (Southampton), March 14, 1857, 8.

64 *Daily News*, March 16, 1857, 3. The London *Times*, though, did spell his name correctly.

65 *Daily News*, March 17, 1857, 6.

66 Philip Hankin has a number of features in British Columbia named after him, including Mount Hankin near Alberni Inlet, Hankin Cove near Kyuquot, Hankin Rock in Clayoquot Sound, Hankin Point in Quatsino Sound and the Hankin Range between Bonanza and Nimpkish Lakes.

67 R.C. Mayne, *Four Years in British Columbia and Vancouver Island* (London: John Murray, 1862). Rear Admiral Richard Mayne (1835–1892) was a naval officer, explorer and later a Conservative politician in England. He served on Vancouver Island and in British Columbia on the *Plumper* and *Hecate* and also with Colonel Richard Clement Moody in New Westminster. Mayne Island is named after him.

68 *Hampshire Advertiser*, November 21, 1857, 8.

69 *Polynesian* (Honolulu), October 24, 1857, 8.

70 King Kamehameha IV (1834–1863) reigned from 1855 to 1863. When he came to the throne, his first action was to end the negotiations his father had been having for the annexation of Hawaii by the United States.

71 Mayne, *Four Years*, 15.

72 This is an early reference to the tango, which is generally thought to have originated in the 1880s. When Hankin wrote his memoirs, the tango was well known in Europe and considered scandalous—the vertical expression of a horizontal desire, as it has been described.

73 Mayne, *Four Years*, 19.

4: From Vancouver Island to the Mediterranean and Then Back

74 R.C. Mayne, *Four Years in British Columbia and Vancouver Island* (London: John Murray, 1862), 25.

75 Mayne, *Four Years*, 27.

76 Mayne, *Four Years*, 31.

77 Edward Cridge (1817–1913) was one of the first clergymen on Vancouver Island, having been appointed chaplain to the Hudson's Bay Company there in 1855. He tended toward the Low Church and so had doctrinal and personal differences with the Anglican bishop George Hills, which led to a split. He was the first Reformed bishop of British Columbia. He officiated at the marriage of Philip Hankin and Isabel Nagle on August 3, 1865.

78 John Wark, or Work (1792–1861), established one of the founding families of Victoria. He was a factor in the Hudson's Bay Company. He went to Fort Simpson in 1834. His journals, from 1823 to 1835, are among the earliest first-hand accounts of the Pacific Northwest.

79 Mayne, *Four Years*, 33.

80 *Daily British Colonist* (Victoria), December 22, 1862, 2.

81 *Royal Cornwall Gazette, Falmouth Packet and General Advertiser* (Truro, Cornwall), May 7, 1858, 7.

82 The main obstruction in Seymour Narrows was Ripple Rock. The top of this rock was blown off in a huge explosion in 1958.

83 Daniel Marshall, *Claiming the Land: British Columbia and the Making of a New El Dorado* (Vancouver: Ronsdale Press, 2018), 63. A more recent—and excellent—book about the 1858 Fraser River Gold Rush is: Alexander Globe, *Gold, Grit, Guns: Miners on BC's Fraser River in 1858* (Vancouver: Ronsdale Press, 2022).

84 Browne, J. Ross, "A Peep at Washoe," *Harper's New Monthly Magazine* 22, no. 127 (December 1860): 3.

85 Margaret Ormsby, *British Columbia: A History* (Vancouver: MacMillans in Canada, 1958), 139.

86 Ormsby, *British Columbia*, 140.

87 Ormsby, *British Columbia*, 139.

88 Captain James Prevost to Governor James Douglas, June 28, 1858, GR-0332, B16916, vol. 3, pp. 300–302, BC Archives.

89 *Hampshire Telegraph and Sussex Chronicle* (Portsmouth), June 5, 1858, 5.

90 Aspinwall (Colón) was named after William Henry Aspinwall (1807–1875), who had founded the Pacific Mail Steamship Company in 1848 to provide a service to California.

He then promoted the railway across to Panama. The railway was begun in 1850 and was completed in 1855.

91 John Emmerson, *British Columbia and Vancouver Island: Voyages, Travels and Adventures* (Durham, England: W. Ainsley, 1865), 17.

92 *Standard* (London), May 11, 1859, 6.

93 *Hampshire Telegraph and Sussex Chronicle*, June 25, 1859, 4.

94 *Hampshire Telegraph and Sussex Chronicle*, April 7, 1860, 4.

95 *Hampshire Telegraph and Sussex Chronicle*, May 19, 1860, 4.

96 *Hampshire Telegraph and Sussex Chronicle*, June 30, 1860, 4.

97 *Polynesian* (Honolulu), December 1, 1860, 2; *Hampshire Telegraph and Sussex Chronicle*, February 2, 1861 (calling him Hawkin).

98 Thomas Gowlland, quoted in George Henry Richards, *The Private Journal of Captain G.H. Richards: The Vancouver Island Survey (1860-1862)*, ed. Linda Dorricott and Deirdre Cullon (Vancouver: Ronsdale Press, 2012), 104. John Thomas Gowlland was the second master on the *Plumper* and *Hecate*. He was responsible for much of the surveying work. He drowned in Sydney Harbour, Australia, in 1874, aged thirty-six.

5: HMS *Hecate*, Lady Franklin and Hankin's Crossing of Vancouver Island

99 Jane, Lady Franklin (1791–1875), was the second wife of the Arctic explorer Sir John Franklin. Sarah Cracroft, her husband's niece, was her long-time companion and secretary.

100 Thomas Gowlland, quoted in George Henry Richards, *The Private Journal of Captain G.H. Richards: The Vancouver Island Survey (1860-1862)*, ed. Linda Dorricott and Deirdre Cullon (Vancouver: Ronsdale Press, 2012), 108.

101 Sophia Cracroft, *Lady Franklin Visits the Pacific Northwest: Being Extracts from the Letters of Miss Sophia Cracroft, Sir John Franklin's Niece, February to April 1861 and April to July 1870*, ed. Dorothy Blakey Smith (Victoria: Provincial Archives of British Columbia, 1974), 5. See also reel A00280, MS-0245, BC Archives (BCA).

102 Cracroft, *Lady Franklin*, 5.

103 *Daily British Colonist* (Victoria), September 23, 1862, 3.

104 Cracroft, *Lady Franklin*, 31.

105 Cracroft, *Lady Franklin*, 18.

106 Cracroft, *Lady Franklin*, 46.

107 Cracroft, *Lady Franklin*, 47.

108 Cracroft, *Lady Franklin*, 49.

109 Cracroft, *Lady Franklin*, 54.

110 Cracroft, *Lady Franklin*, 55.

111 *British Columbian* (New Westminster), March 14, 1861, 3.

112 Rev. William Crickmer (1830–1905) was appointed to be the first missionary chaplain for the goldfields. He arrived in Victoria on HMS *Plumper* on Christmas Day, 1858. He moved to Yale, built a church there and returned to England in 1863. *Vancouver Historical Journal*, 1959, published by the Archives Society of Vancouver, 77–85, 97–98.

113 *Daily British Whig* (Kingston, ON), September 27, 1912, 7.

114 *British Columbian*, March 14, 1861, 3.

115 Cracroft, *Lady Franklin*, 67.

116 Cracroft, *Lady Franklin*, 71.

117 Gowlland, quoted in Richards, *Private Journal*, 128.

118 George Henry Richards to Governor James Douglas, June 20, 1862; enclosed with that letter was Philip Hankin's report to Richards, June 17, 1862, GR-1372.98.1215, Colonial Correspondence, HMS *Hecate*, BCA. This was reprinted in the *Daily British Colonist*, December 13, 1862. The story of this crossing is recounted in detail in Michael Layland's *A Perfect Eden: Encounters by Early Explorers of Vancouver Island* (Victoria: TouchWood Editions, 2016), chapter 14. See also George Nicholson, *Vancouver Island's West Coast, 1762–1962* (Victoria: George Nicholson, 1965), 110–15. Richard Mayne crossed from the Alberni Inlet to Nanaimo in May 1861.

119 Hankin to Richards, report, June 17, 1862.

120 Dr. Charles Wood to George Henry Richards, report, June 14, 1862, GR-1372.98.1215, Colonial Correspondence, HMS *Hecate*, BCA.

121 Richards, *Private Journal*, 180.

122 Hankin to Richards, report, June 17, 1862.

123 Hankin to Richards, report, June 17, 1862.

124 Hankin to Richards, report, June 17, 1862.

125 Wood to Richards, report, June 14, 1862.

126 Hankin to Richards, report, June 17, 1862.

127 Wood to Richards, report, June 14, 1862.

128 Hankin to Richards, report, June 17, 1862.

129 Richards, *Private Journal*, 211.

130 Richards, *Private Journal*, 197.

131 *Daily British Colonist*, December 22, 1862, 3.

132 *Daily British Colonist*, December 22, 1862, 3.

133 Gowlland, quoted in Richards, *Private Journal*, 231.

134 *Polynesian* (Honolulu), March 28, 1863, 3.

135 *Sydney Morning Herald*, December 14, 1863, 5.

136 *Morning Post* (London), December 23, 1863, 6.

137 *Morning Post*, September 21, 1863, 5; *Times* (London), September 23, 1863, 25.

138 *Morning Post*, January 5, 1864, 7.

139 Naval records, United Kingdom National Archives.

6: Looking for Gold in Barkerville

140 John Emmerson, *British Columbia and Vancouver Island: Voyages, Travels and Adventures* (Durham, England: W. Ainsley, 1865), 27.

141 *Daily British Colonist* (Victoria), April 1, 1864, 3.

142 Damper was an unleavened bread or cake made of flour and water and baked in hot ashes. The name is Australian and applies to the iconic food that stockmen took with them when making long journeys in the bush. It may have become slang in the British navy.

143 Archdeacon Rev. Henry Press Wright (1814–1892) was the first archdeacon of New Westminster. He had been senior chaplain to Lord Raglan's army in the Crimean War. He served the church in British Columbia from 1861 to 1865.

144 Emmerson, *British Columbia and Vancouver Island*, 69.

7: Hankin Becomes Chief of Police for the Colony of Vancouver Island

145 The colonial secretary was William Young (1827–1885), a man Hankin would later supersede. Young was a naval captain with an honourable service in the Crimean War. He had been in Victoria since 1857 and put down roots in the Colony of Vancouver Island, marrying one of Governor James Douglas's daughters. He was appointed colonial secretary in March 1859 and later acting colonial secretary of the united colonies. But Governor Frederick Seymour did not trust him, thinking he was too deeply a Vancouver Island man. He was undoubtedly the better candidate to be the colonial secretary and did not deserve to be shunted aside. After Hankin was appointed to his job, he left the colony and went on to be financial secretary of Jamaica and then governor of the Gold Coast in Africa, where he died in 1885.

146 *Daily British Colonist* (Victoria), August 30, 1864, 3.

147 This was probably E.J. Nesbitt, chief clerk in the colonial secretary's office.

148 Sir Arthur Kennedy (1809–1883). After the two colonies merged, Kennedy was appointed governor of the West African Settlements (1867–1872). He was then knighted and went on to be governor of Hong Kong (1872–1877) and then Queensland (1877–1883).

149 Frederick Seymour to Henry Pelham-Clinton, Duke of Newcastle, September 14, 1863, Colonial Despatches of Vancouver Island and British Columbia 1846–1871, edition 2.4, ed. James Hendrickson and the Colonial Despatches project, University of Victoria, https://bcgenesis.uvic.ca/index.html.

150 Rear Admiral Joseph Denman (1810–1874) was the son of a chief justice of England. He was a passionate abolitionist and was very active in suppressing slavery on the West Africa Station. He was rear admiral in charge of the Pacific Station, 1864–1866.

151 To a greater or lesser extent, slavery was part of the culture of Indigenous communities in the Pacific Northwest, notably the Haida and Tlingit peoples. "Every traditional Northwest Coast community contained at least a few slaves," wrote anthropologist Leland Donald in *Aboriginal Slavery on the Northwest Coast of North America* (Berkeley: University of California Press, 1997), 33. The Canadian Museum of History states that the Haida people went to war primarily to acquire slaves. Some were prisoners of war and some were captured for buying and selling. In chapter 9 of his book, Donald attempts to estimate how extensive slavery was. He shows that the assessments of percentage of slaves in the region vary widely. George Simpson, the governor of the Hudson's Bay Company, wrote that in the 1840s one out of every three people in the coastal region was a slave. Other estimates are lower. I have not done any independent research but it sounds to me that one in three is far too high. By the 1860s, though, the practice was in decline, being illegal and under pressure from the missionaries. Many non-Indigenous people at the

time were of the opinion that slavery existed on the coast and, with Victorian abolitionist sentiment, were horrified by it.

152 Barry M. Gough, *Gunboat Frontier: British Maritime Authority and Northwest Coast Indians, 1846–1890* (Vancouver: University of British Columbia Press, 1984), 80. This account is perhaps the best and the most detailed account of the *Kingfisher* affair of 1864.

153 Gough, *Gunboat Frontier*, 116.

154 *Daily British Colonist*, October 17, 1864, 3.

155 *Daily British Colonist*, December 3, 1866, 3; November 26, 1961, 5; and April 20, 1962, 5; item B-06641, BC Archives (BCA).

156 *Daily British Colonist*, October 15, 1864, 3.

157 *Illustrated London News* 45, no. 1295 (December 31, 1864): 664; *Frank Leslie's Illustrated Newspaper* 23, no. 580 (November 10, 1866): 125.

158 Gough, *Gunboat Frontier*, 121, cited in entry on the *Kingfisher*, Colonial Despatches.

159 *Daily British Colonist*, October 12, 1864, 3.

160 Arthur Kennedy to Edward Cardwell, October 14, 1864, Colonial Despatches.

161 Kennedy to Cardwell, July 7, 1864, Colonial Despatches.

162 *Daily British Colonist*, November 5, 1864, 3.

163 Kennedy to Cardwell, December 3, 1864, Colonial Despatches.

164 *Government Gazette, Vancouver Island* 1, no. 38 (December 27, 1862): 1.

165 Robert Louis Smith, "The Hankin Appointment," *BC Studies*, no. 22 (Summer 1974): 29.

166 Arthur McBride became the first warden of the province of British Columbia's prisons. His son Richard was premier of the province from 1903 to 1915 and considered the founder of the Conservative Party of British Columbia. He instituted party politics in the province. In recent years, his reputation has become controversial.

167 *Victoria Daily Chronicle*, February 24, 1865, 3.

168 Philip Hankin to the colonial secretary, July 5, 1865, GR-1372.112.1396a, Police Department (Victoria), July 1865, BCA.

169 Hankin to colonial secretary, July 5, 1865.

170 *Victoria Daily Chronicle*, February 6, 1866, 3.

171 *Daily British Colonist*, August 4, 1865, 3.

172 Susan Abercrombie Nagle, diary entry, August 7, 1865, MS-2576, BCA.

173 *Victoria Daily Chronicle*, March 6, 1866, 3.

174 *Daily British Colonist*, October 23, 1865, 3.

175 William Govett Romaine to Philip Hankin, February 7, 1865, Colonial Despatches.

176 Kennedy to Cardwell, April 12, 1865, Colonial Despatches.

177 Kennedy to Cardwell, February 13, 1866, Colonial Despatches.

178 *Evening Telegraph* (Victoria), July 6, 1866, 3.

179 *Daily British Colonist*, July 6, 1866, 3.

180 *Daily British Colonist*, July 12, 1866, 3.

181 Admiral Joseph Denman to Richard Grenville, Duke of Buckingham and Chandos, December 29, 1866, MG-26-A, box 343, Library and Archives Canada.

182 Richard Temple-Nugent-Brydges-Chandos-Grenville, third Duke of Buckingham and Chandos (1823–1889), was a good friend and patron of Philip Hankin. He assisted Hankin materially at turning points in his career by choosing him to go to British Honduras and then to British Columbia as colonial secretary. He then employed him as

his private secretary, taking him to India for five years. His sister, Anna, was a prominent women's rights campaigner, working with the Women's Printing Society to improve education for women. She also went with them to Madras. After a career in the army and politics, the duke served as secretary of state for the colonies in Benjamin Disraeli's government from March 8, 1867, to December 1, 1868. He left office when Disraeli's ministry resigned. He was succeeded by Granville George Leveson-Gower, second Earl Granville (1815–1891) (George Granville). This can be confusing: Richard *Grenville* is Hankin's patron, the duke, and George *Granville* was the colonial secretary in William Gladstone's government. Consequently it was with Granville that Colonial Secretary Hankin had most of his official dealings. When Disraeli returned to power, he appointed the duke to be governor of Madras (Chennai), where he served for five years (1875–1880). Philip Hankin was his private secretary and would have been at the centre of government.

8: Colonial Secretary: British Honduras to British Columbia

183 *Standard* (London), May 13, 1867, 3.
184 Sir Anton Bertram, *The Colonial Service* (Cambridge: Cambridge University Press, 1930), 34.
185 *Times-Picayune* (New Orleans), November 17, 1867, 8.
186 Susan Abercrombie Nagle, diary entry, May 8, 1868, MS-2576, BC Archives.
187 *New Orleans Crescent*, August 11, 1868, 1.
188 Frederick Seymour to Richard Grenville, Duke of Buckingham and Chandos, June 5, 1868, Colonial Despatches of Vancouver Island and British Columbia 1846–1871, edition 2.4, ed. James Hendrickson and the Colonial Despatches project, University of Victoria, https://bcgenesis.uvic.ca/index.html.
189 Edward Cardwell to Frederick Seymour, May 30, 1865, Colonial Despatches.
190 Seymour implies that when Hankin was at Barkerville he was in the company of one of his brothers, probably Charles. If true, this casts a different light on Hankin's time there and raises a doubt about his story.
191 Seymour to Grenville, November 21, 1868, Colonial Despatches.
192 Seymour to Grenville, November 29, 1868, Colonial Despatches.
193 *Daily British Colonist* (Victoria), November 23, 1868, 2.
194 *Daily British Colonist*, November 24, 1868, 3.
195 *Daily British Colonist*, November 28, 1868, 3.
196 Robert Louis Smith, "The Hankin Appointment," BC Studies, no. 22 (Summer 1974): 26.
197 *Daily Examiner* (San Francisco), December 12, 1868, 3.
198 *Daily British Colonist*, January 1, 1869, 3.
199 *Daily British Colonist*, January 1, 1869, 3.
200 Nagle, diary entry, January 1, 1869.

9: Governor Seymour and Administrator Hankin

201 *British Columbian* (New Westminster), January 16, 1869, 3.

202 *British Columbian*, January 9, 1869, 3.

203 *Daily British Colonist* (Victoria), January 5, 1869, 2.

204 Susan Abercrombie Nagle, diary entry, January 2, 1869, MS-2576, BC Archives (BCA).

205 Arthur Kennedy to Philip Hankin, February 17, 1969, MG26-A, box 343, Library and Archives Canada.

206 Hankin to Kennedy, March 5, 1869, Stowe Papers, 1175–1919, STG 107, folder 53, Huntington Library, California.

207 Hankin to Kennedy, March 5, 1869.

208 Nagle, diary entry, January 10, 1871. (A dreadful pun—over Young to Seymour of British Columbia.)

209 Granville George Leveson-Gower, Earl Granville, to Frederick Seymour, April 19, 1869, Colonial Despatches of Vancouver Island and British Columbia 1846–1871, edition 2.4, ed. James Hendrickson and the Colonial Despatches project, University of Victoria, https://bcgenesis.uvic.ca/index.html. This letter was actually written before Granville knew that Hankin had been sworn in. It took some time for letters to be delivered.

210 *Daily British Colonist*, April 7, 1869, 3.

211 Hankin to Leveson-Gower, June 18, 1869, Colonial Despatches.

212 *Daily British Colonist*, January 22, 1869, 3.

213 *Daily British Colonist*, April 22, 1869, 3.

214 *Daily British Colonist*, December 9, 1869, 3.

215 Seymour to Leveson-Gower, May 17, 1869, Colonial Despatches.

216 *Daily British Colonist*, June 15, 1869, 2; Hankin to Leveson-Gower, June 14, 1869, Colonial Despatches. Frederick Seymour's life was insured for £30,000, which was paid to his brother, an equerry to the Prince of Wales, *Daily British Colonist*, March 6, 1870.

217 *Daily British Colonist*, June 16, 1869, 3.

218 *Daily British Columbian* (Victoria), June 15, 1869, 3. As chief justice, Needham's position was anomalous. When the two colonies merged, Matthew Baillie Begbie remained chief justice for the mainland and Needham remained chief justice for Vancouver Island. It was Joseph Needham, therefore, who swore Hankin in as administrator of the colony. In 1869, an ordinance was passed to provide that when there was a vacancy the two offices would be combined. Needham did resign in 1870 and he moved to become chief justice of Trinidad.

219 Nagle, diary entry, June 16, 1869.

220 Hankin to Leveson-Gower, June 14, 1869, Colonial Despatches.

221 Leveson-Gower to Anthony Musgrave, undated, Colonial Despatches.

222 *Daily British Colonist*, July 13, 1869, 3.

223 *Daily British Colonist*, July 15, 1869, 2.

224 Hankin to Richard Grenville, Duke of Buckingham and Chandos, December 1, 1869, GR-1372.38.336(2), Colonial Secretary, BC, 1869, BCA.

225 David Ricardo Williams, *Call in Pinkerton's: American Detectives at Work for Canada* (Toronto: Dundurn Press, 1998), 44–47.

226 *Missouri Republican* (Saint Louis), October 17, 1869, 3.

227 *Morning Chronicle* (San Francisco), May 23, 1869, 1. George Francis Train (1829–1904) reminds me, as he perhaps reminded Hankin, of that great American patriot Jefferson Brick in Dickens's novel *Martin Chuzzlewit*. Like Train, Brick was not an Irishman, but he was a similar blowhard of dubious honesty.

228 *Morning Chronicle,* May 29, 1869, 3.

229 *Daily British Colonist,* June 8, 1869, 3.

230 Leveson-Gower to Hankin, June 26, 1869, Colonial Despatches.

231 *Morning Chronicle,* June 8, 1869, 3.

232 *Daily British Colonist,* June 26, 1869, 3.

233 *Daily British Colonist,* July 10, 1869, 3.

234 William Bowden to Augustus Pemberton, July 11, 1869, GR-1372.113.1406, Police Department (Victoria), 1869, BCA.

235 Hankin to Leveson-Gower, July 12, 1869, Colonial Despatches.

236 *Daily British Colonist,* June 3, 4 and 26, 1869, 3.

237 Hankin to A.C. Elliott, July 15, 1869, GR-1372.38.336(1), Colonial Secretary, UC, 1869–1871, BCA.

238 *Daily British Colonist,* July 9, 1869, 3; Hankin to Leveson-Gower, July 12, 1869, and August 11, 1869, Colonial Despatches.

239 *Daily British Colonist,* July 10, 1869, 3.

240 *Daily British Colonist,* July 16, 1869, 2.

10: Governor Musgrave and Joining Canada

241 Anthony Musgrave (1828–1888), born in Antigua, was studying law in London in 1854 when the Duke of Newcastle, secretary of state for the colonies, appointed him to be the colonial secretary of Antigua; then in 1862 he appointed him lieutenant-governor on Saint Vincent. In 1864 Musgrave was appointed governor of Newfoundland, where he took one look at its problems and determined that the only way to solve them was for Newfoundland to join Canada. In his efforts to accomplish this he was unsuccessful. After he left the Colony of British Columbia, where he served as governor from 1869 to 1871, he went on to be governor of Natal (1872–1873), South Australia (1873–1877), Jamaica (1877–1883) and Queensland (1885–1888).

242 *Daily British Colonist* (Victoria), August 27, 1869, 3.

243 Anthony Musgrave to Granville George Leveson-Gower, Earl Granville, August 23, 1869, Colonial Despatches of Vancouver Island and British Columbia 1846–1871, edition 2.4, ed. James Hendrickson and the Colonial Despatches project, University of Victoria, https://bcgenesis.uvic.ca/index.html.

244 Musgrave to Leveson-Gower, August 25, 1869, Colonial Despatches.

245 Philip Hankin to Richard Grenville, Duke of Buckingham and Chandos, March 11, 1870, *British Columbia Historical Quarterly*, vol. 13 (Victoria: Provincial Archives of British Columbia, 1949), 37.

246 Jeanie Lucinda Musgrave, diary entry, August 8, 1870, PR-0518, BC Archives (BCA).

247 *Daily British Colonist* April 29, 1869, 3.

248 *Daily British Colonist,* November 3, 1869, 3.

249 *Daily British Colonist*, March 9, 1870, 3.

250 *Daily British Colonist*, March 20, 1870, 2.

251 *Daily British Colonist*, August 28, 1869, 3. William Henry Seward (1801–1872) had been the United States secretary of state, governor of New York and a senator in Washington. He had helped negotiate the purchase of Alaska from the Russians in 1867.

252 Sophia Cracroft, *Lady Franklin Visits the Pacific Northwest: Being Extracts from the Letters of Miss Sophia Cracroft, Sir John Franklin's Niece, February to April 1861 and April to July 1870*, ed. Dorothy Blakey Smith (Victoria: Provincial Archives of British Columbia, 1974), 126.

253 Cracroft, *Lady Franklin*, 113.

254 Cracroft, *Lady Franklin*, 114.

255 Cracroft, *Lady Franklin*, 118.

256 Cracroft, *Lady Franklin*, 118.

257 Cracroft, *Lady Franklin*, 119.

258 Cracroft, *Lady Franklin*, 116.

259 *Daily British Colonist*, November 13, 1869, 3.

260 *Daily British Colonist*, February 9, 1870, 3.

261 Frederick Seymour to Edward Cardwell, November 28, 1864, Colonial Despatches.

262 Musgrave to Leveson-Gower, October 30, 1869, Colonial Despatches.

263 *Daily British Colonist*, December 2, 1869, 3. John Helmcken (1824–1920) was one of the earliest pioneers in the colony, having arrived in 1850. He was first elected to the legislative assembly in 1850. He left politics at the time of Confederation but lived until 1920. Philip Hankin visited him when he came back to Victoria in 1919.

264 *Daily British Colonist*, February 17, 1870, 3.

265 Hankin to Grenville, March 11, 1870, *British Columbia Historical Quarterly*, 13:37; *Daily British Colonist*, September 21, 1919, 22. De Cosmos went on to become the second premier of the province (December 1872–February 1874). John Foster McCreight was the first premier (November 1871–December 1872).

266 *Daily British Colonist*, August 31, 1870, 3.

267 Hankin to Grenville, March 11, 1870, *British Columbia Historical Quarterly*, 13:37.

268 Susan Abercrombie Nagle, diary entry, October 5, 1870, MS-2576, BCA.

269 *Victoria Daily Standard*, December 28, 1871, 2.

270 *Daily British Colonist*, July 20, 1871, 2.

271 *Daily British Colonist*, July 26 and 27, 1871, 3.

272 Musgrave to John Wodehouse, January 18, 1871, Colonial Despatches.

273 *Daily British Colonist*, August 16, 1871, 3.

11: In India with the Duke

274 Susan Abercrombie Nagle, diary entry, January 30, 1871, MS-2576, BC Archives.

275 *Western Daily Press* (Bristol), April 4, 1873, 4; *London Gazette*, August 25, 1874, 4181.

276 *Daily British Colonist* (Victoria), April 13, 1872, 3.

277 *Pall Mall Gazette* (London), May 18, 1875, 10. The *Gazette*, noting that the duke was accepting a position less than his position in the government should have entitled him to,

said, "In undertaking the duties of Governor of Madras, the Duke of Buckingham shows that he is willing to render useful rather than splendid service." The *Friend of India*, a little less charitably, commented in its edition of January 29, 1876, "We are not aware that the Duke of Buckingham is gifted with superior genius, but thorough conscientiousness will go far to supply the deficiency."

278 *Observer* (London), October 17, 1875, 5.
279 A.H. Wylie, *Chatty Letters from the East and West* (London: Sampson Low, Marston, Searle and Rivington, 1879), 25.
280 Wylie, *Chatty Letters*, 29.
281 *Friend of India* (Serampore, West Bengal), July 17, 1875, 668.
282 *Friend of India*, October 7, 1876, 24.
283 *Friend of India*, June 17, 1876, 552.
284 *Friend of India*, February 12, 1876, 140.
285 *Friend of India*, February 12, 1876, 140.
286 *Hampshire Telegraph and Sussex Chronicle* (Portsmouth), December 15, 1875, 4.
287 *Derby Mercury*, December 29, 1875, 6.
288 Edward Montagu, Viscount Hinchingbrooke, *Diary in Ceylon & India, 1878-9* (London: W.S. Johnson, 1879), 21.
289 Montagu, *Diary*, 21.
290 Montagu, *Diary*, 22.
291 Montagu, *Diary*, 24.
292 Montagu, *Diary*, 27.
293 Robert Nicholas Fowler, *A Visit to Japan, China and India* (London: Sampson Low, Marston, Searle and Rivington, 1877), 137.
294 *Daily British Colonist*, July 1, 1881, 3.

12: The Years of Travel

295 *Isle of Wight Observer* (Ryde), November 15, 1884, 5. The Hankins sent a mirror as a wedding present when the Duke of Buckingham's daughter, Lady Mary Grenville, was married.
296 *Pacific Commercial Advertiser* (Honolulu), January 9, 1888, 3; *Hawaiian Gazette* (Honolulu), January 10, 1888, 8.
297 *Daily Colonist* (Victoria), March 26, 1961, 16.
298 *Pacific Commercial Advertiser*, June 5, 1902, 10.
299 *Victoria Daily Times*, June 12, 1902, 5.
300 *Vancouver Daily World*, February 2, 1906, 7.
301 *Vancouver Daily World*, February 5, 1906, 6.
302 *Vancouver Daily World*, August 1, 1906, 1.
303 *Vancouver Daily World*, June 13, 1906, 9.
304 *Vancouver Daily World*, February 16, 1907, 2.

Index

About the Author

Geoff Mynett was born in Shropshire, England, and qualified there as a barrister. Coming to British Columbia, he requalified and practised law in Vancouver until his retirement. A believer in the importance of knowing our histories, he is also an amateur artist. He and his wife, Alice, live in Vancouver.

In 2019, Ronsdale Press published his biography of a pioneer doctor in Hazelton in northern British Columbia in the period 1900–1936: *Service on the Skeena: Horace Wrinch, Frontier Physician.* In 2021

Stephen Mynett photo

it won the Jeanne Clarke Local History Award and the George Ryga Award for Social Awareness in Literature. Caitlin Press published his book *Pinkerton's and the Hunt for Simon Gunanoot*, in 2021; *Murders on the Skeena: True Crime in the Old Canadian West, 1884–1914*, in 2021; and *River of Mists: People of the Upper Skeena, 1821–1930*, in 2022.